CHARLOTTE
MEW
AND HER FRIENDS

Penelope Fitzgerald

D1348679

COLLINS
8 Grafton Street, London W1
1984

by the same author

EDWARD BURNE-JONES
THE KNOX BROTHERS
THE GOLDEN CHILD
THE BOOKSHOP
OFFSHORE
HUMAN VOICES
AT FREDDIE'S

I should like to thank the owners and photographers who have
kindly supplied, or permitted me to reproduce, the illustrations:
The Lord Louis Library, Isle of Wight County Council, p. 11;
The Greater London Council Photograph Library, p. 15, p. 42, p. 89;
Duckworth & Co. Ltd, p. 19; Trustees of the British Library, p. 29, p. 65;
Camden Local History Library, p. 38; The National Portrait Gallery, London,
frontispiece and jacket, p. 167, p. 190; Trustees of the Tate Gallery, p. 69;
Trustees of the Thomas Hardy Memorial Collection, Dorset County Museum,
Dorchester, p. 173; The Zoological Society of London, p. 183;
Dr T. S. Boll, p. 115, p. 121; Mrs Marjorie Watts, p. 107, p. 114, p. 135;
Mark Pepper, p. 207; John Lake and Maria Fitzgerald, p. 214.

William Collins Sons & Co. Ltd
London · Glasgow · Sydney · Auckland
Toronto · Johannesburg

BRITISH LIBRARY CATALOGUING IN PUBLICATION DATA

Fitzgerald, Penelope
Charlotte Mew and her friends.
1. Mew, Charlotte
I. Title
821'.912   PR6025.E8Z/

First published 1984
© Penelope Fitzgerald, 1984

ISBN 0-00-217008-6

Photoset in Linotron Baskerville by
Rowland Phototypesetting Ltd
Bury St Edmunds, Suffolk
Made and printed in Great Britain
by Robert Hartnoll Ltd, Bodmin

In memory of
THE POETRY BOOKSHOP

Acknowledgements

I should like first of all to thank Mrs Marjorie Watts, daughter of Mrs Dawson Scott, the founder of International PEN. Mrs Watts has been most generous in giving me her own reminiscences of Charlotte Mew, in letting me see Charlotte's letters to her mother, and in lending me photographs

No-one could undertake to write a life of Charlotte Mew without being indebted to the unpublished doctoral thesis by Mary C. Davidow (Brown University, 1960.) Mary Davidow made her researches while relations and old friends of the Mew family were still alive, and she was able to interview some of them. She also printed for the first time letters from the F. B. Adams Collection, five unpublished poems and *The Minnow Fishers*.

In 1982 Virago Press, in association with Carcanet, published *Charlotte Mew: Collected Poems and Prose*, edited and introduced by Val Warner. I owe a very great deal to this book, and have given page references to it in my notes whenever I have quoted from Charlotte Mew's work.

The following have kindly given me permission to see or use copyright material: Frederick B. Adams (F. B. Adams Collection); New York Public Library (Henry W. and Albert A. Berg Collection); The State University of New York at Buffalo (The Poetry/Rare Books Collection of the University Libraries); University of California, Los Angeles (William Andrews Clark Memorial Library); Lloyd's Bank Ltd Trust Division (Florence Hardy estate); The University of Texas at Austin (Humanities Research Center); The Librarian and Governing Body of Somerville College, Oxford; Wilfrid Blunt (S. C. Cockerell's literary executor); Mrs Marjorie Watts.

I am most grateful to the following people who have helped me in so many different ways: Percy Birtchnell, secretary of the Berkhamsted Local History Society, Dr T. M. Boll, Patric Dickinson, Dr Robert Gittings, Joy Grant, Jim Hepburn, Michael Holroyd, Mary Knox, Katherine Lyon Mix, Terry Pepper (National Portrait Gallery Archive), Bob Pocock, Ruth Tomalin, Pamela Travers (who gave me Charlotte Mew's candlesticks), Val Warner, Professor Stanley Weintraub, J. Howard Woolmer, bookseller – and to the staff of the Camden Local History Department, the GLC Record Office, the Isle of Wight Record Office, the Isle of Wight County Reference Library, Kensington and Chelsea Public Library, Marylebone Public Library, the R.I.B.A. Library, Southwark Public Libraries and the Library of the Zoological Society of London.

I may add that I could never have finished this book without the help of John Lake and Maria Fitzgerald, Tina and Terence Dooley and my patient and understanding book editor, Richard Ollard.

P.M.F.

Contents

CHAPTER 1

The Day of Eyes

THE MEWS came from the Isle of Wight. It was a common name all over the island and still is, but by 1832 when Fred Mew, Charlotte's father, was born, his own branch of the family had settled near Newport. Some of them were carpenters and labourers, some were known to have bettered themselves. This was certainly true of Fred's grandfather, Benjamin Mew, the brewer – who was a member of the corporation and a prime mover of the Carisbrooke Water Company, which brought Newport its first public water supply in the 1820s. One of Benjamin's sons, Richard, farmed at Newfairlee, a mile or so to the north-east of Newport, while another one, Henry, kept the Bugle Inn in the High Street. Henry imported wine and spirits, with premises in both Newport and Cowes; the farm at Newfairlee supplied milk and vegetables for the guests at the Bugle and grazing for their carriage horses in summer. These profitable arrangements brought the two families very close. Fred was the seventh and youngest of Henry's children, and for all of them 'Theirn' and 'Ourn' – the farm and the inn – were both home. Fred grew up largely at Theirn, over at Newfairlee.

Henry Mew, however, was determined not to put his sons into the licensed trade, but to send them to London to make their fortunes. George and James went first, and were set up in a small business. Fred was to be an architect, or rather something between an architect and a speculative builder. Evidently there was money in that. In the Island itself, Seaview Villas were going up all round the coast in response to the new holiday trade, and new Gothic churches were ready for them, including St Paul's, Barton, where the Mew family worshipped on Sundays. Royal Osborne, five miles north of Newport, was begun in

9

1845 (when Fred was thirteen), and went forward in the charge of the great builder Thomas Cubitt (Queen Victoria's 'our Mr Cubitt') over the next three years. It might have been thought, then, that a bright boy could be apprenticed and have good prospects without leaving the Island. But one of Fred's uncles was already a partner in a London architect's firm, Manning and Mew, at 2 Great James Street, Bedford Row. The firm seems not to have been particularly successful, but it had the great virtue of being 'in the family'. Fred was despatched, and arrived at the age of fourteen straight from the sea breezes and cow pastures and the old-fashioned Bugle Inn to London's East End. His elder brothers had a house off the Old Kent Road, and he was to be lodged there.

To begin with they sent him for a little further education to Mr Walton's Albany House Academy, also in the Old Kent Road. Walton's place was not quite as grand as it sounded, being a commercial school which gave a grounding in business correspondence, practical arithmetic and some Latin. After a year Fred's father took him and paid the premium for his articles with Manning and Mew, where he was to learn architectural drawing, 'improving', and surveying, and to make himself useful on the sites.

The only building by which (if at all) Manning and Mew is remembered is the New School of Design at Sheffield (commissioned in 1856). The drawing for it, the only one which the firm ever exhibited at the Royal Academy, is by Fred. But in the following year he found himself a more hopeful position, transferring as architectural assistant to H. E. Kendall, Junior, of Spring Gardens, Trafalgar Square. Henry Edward Kendall called himself Junior, or H.E.K., out of respect for and to distinguish himself from his grand old father. This father, the son of a Yorkshire banker, had been a pupil of Thomas Leverton and a friend of Pugin. In the Gothic manner he had designed churches, prisons, workhouses and castles, helped to develop the fashionable Kemp Town district of Brighton, and later designed Mr Kemp's own mansion in Belgrave Square. He was responsible, 'wholly or in part', to quote his obituary in *The Builder*, 'for the houses of the Earls of Bristol, Egremont and

The Bugle Inn, Newport High Street,
where Charlotte Mew's father was born in 1832.

Henry Mew's trade card.

Hardwicke'. Everything was done with spirit. Kendall was tall, distinguished and generous, loved dogs and guns, and continued to shoot even after he had blasted off his left hand in an accident. At a time when Thomas Hardy, it seems, had to sit through a sermon in Stinsford church against 'the presumption shown by one of Hardy's class in seeking to rise, through architecture, to the ranks of professional men', and these professional men themselves weren't always clearly distinguished from jobbing builders, Kendall was, without question, 'gentlemanly'. One example was his conduct in the affair of Kensal Green Cemetery; in an open competition for the chapel he was awarded first prize for his Gothic design, and second for his 'Italianate'. There seemed not much room for manoeuvre here, but the chairman, Sir John Paul, ignored the decision and ruled that his own design, which had won no prize of any kind, must be accepted and that Kendall should carry it out, which, with what was thought 'very proper spirit', he refused to do. By the 1850s he already had thirteen grandchildren and several great-grandchildren, and in his grey-haired dignity was known as 'the Nestor of architects'.

H. E. Kendall, articled to his father, loved him. He had more imagination than the old man, but was less confident, and partly suppressed it. They worked well together, and were both active in the 'formation of an institute to uphold the character and improve the attainment of Architects' which met, at first, at the Thatched House Tavern and Evans' Cave of Harmony. These were the very early days of the R.I.B.A.

H.E.K. specialized in private houses, from a villa to a mansion, Board Schools, and lunatic asylums. In 1857, when he took Fred Mew, the country boy, into his office, he was also district surveyor for Hampstead, and a very busy man. The pages of his publication *Kendall's Modern Architecture*, with its handsome illustrations, showed the clients exactly what to expect. Gothic was always in stock, but as tastes changed you could have Greek, Italian Renaissance, Early English (or Tudor), Jacobean, Queen Anne, or a combination of two or more. Several of the office's pupils had distinguished themselves – for example, J. T. Wood, who discovered the remains of the Temple of Diana at Ephesus – but what was needed, with the 1860s in sight, was a hard-working young man who for a salary of fifteen shillings a week would make the working drawings and collect the details and 'appropriate ornament' which were the hackwork of the conscientious Victorian architect. Professional examinations were not compulsory until 1863, and Fred Mew never took any. He settled down to the assistant's work in Spring Gardens. Although he was not without temperament – in fact he was given to occasional black depressions – he dedicated himself whole-heartedly to Kendall's service. He left his lodging in his brother's house, and took a room in Lincoln's Inn Fields. This gave him only three miles to walk to work in the morning, a great improvement. Then, in 1859, Kendall nominated him as associate of the R.I.B.A.; old Kendall, in very shaky handwriting, supported the nomination. In 1860 Fred was made a junior partner.

Fred, in the old phrase, 'filled a place'. H.E.K. had a son of his own, Edward Herne, who had been articled to him in the accepted family manner but, for reasons which were not talked about, had never finished his training. A nephew, Thomas Marden, had also been articled, but never practised. After these two failures, Fred became what he could never have expected to be, a confidant. When Kendall drew up his will he made Fred not a beneficiary, but a joint executor. In 1860 he offered him a junior partnership. Fred, on the strength of it, took the lease of a house, No. 30 Doughty Street, which was close to (though much less expensive than) Brunswick Square, where the Kendall family lived. The house, though modest, was too large for a single man, and it can hardly have surprised anyone when, early in 1862, he asked Kendall for the hand of his daughter.

Anna Maria Marden Kendall may perhaps have been in love with her father's tall, countrified assistant, or she may have felt that, at twenty-six, she oughtn't to let this chance slip. What is certain is that she was a tiny, pretty, silly young woman who grew, in time, to be a very silly old one. But she had the great strength of silliness, smallness and prettiness in combination, in that it never occurred to her that she would not be protected and looked after, and she always was.

The wedding took place at St George's, Bloomsbury on December 19th 1863, and the witnesses were Henry Kendall, his sister Mrs Lewis Cubitt, and Sophia Webb, wife of the proprietor of the Fountain Inn, West Cowes. But Fred was not allowed to put down his own father's profession as 'inn-keeper'. It was given as 'Esquire'.

The intention is clear enough. As Anna Maria's husband, Fred was of course bound to keep her in the style to which she was accustomed, and to do this he had, in the first place, to set about making himself into a gentleman. The architect's profession, even though since the 1830s it had been organizing itself as something distinct from the building trade, was not, as has been said, able to do this quite on its own. Fred, it was recognized, was not likely to be anything up to his father-in-law. H.E.K. was on easy terms with his titled clients and with Bishop Wilberforce, to whom he had dedicated his *Designs for Schools and Schoolhouses, Parochial and National*. Mrs Lewis Cubitt, Anna Maria's aunt, was married to the youngest brother in the famous firm, and though the Cubitts had been the sons of a Norfolk carpenter, look at what, through hard work and royal patronage, they had become! But Fred could at least see to it that he did not fall too far short. This pressure on him, as might be expected, came from the women. To Henry Kendall he was simply a young friend and assistant whom he liked, and could trust completely.

Fred took his bride to 30 Doughty Street, which he also used as a drawing-office. The house was narrow and steep between the basement kitchen and the attic nursery, but well placed at the end of the street, overlooking the airy plane trees of Mecklenburgh Square. Brunswick Square, with its far superior society and a mother always ready to listen to Anna Maria's complaints, was only just round the corner, and Mrs Kendall took steps from the beginning to make sure that her daughter would hold the balance of power. From her own household she selected Elizabeth Goodman, a tall upstanding north-country-woman, a 'treasure', with all the value and inconvenience of treasures, an old-fashioned servant who asked for nothing beyond service and due reward, but whose prejudices could

Mecklenburgh Square and Doughty Street, W.C.1.
No. 30, where Charlotte Mew was born, is on the extreme right.

never be shifted, not by an inch. 'She herself', according to Charlotte, 'came of very humble stock', and had no book-learning, but somewhere she had learned perfect manners, 'and, in speaking, an unusual purity of accent' – 'purer', very likely, than Fred's. Proud of her skill, proud even of her servant's caps and aprons, which she made herself, she knew absolutely her moral and social role at 30 Doughty Street. She was to make life tolerable for her young mistress, who had married beneath her. Doughty Street was a comedown, but there are ways of managing everything. This did not, of course, mean any insubordination towards the master, quite the contrary; only there was a constant 'making do' and contrivancing of the boot-patching, collar-turning and left-over cold meat variety, which had never been necessary in Brunswick Square, and of which Fred cannot have been left unaware. When her wages were paid it was Elizabeth Goodman's habit to buy a small present for everyone in the house 'except the too exalted head', that is to say, Fred, in his drawing-office on the second floor. No one in the house could in fact be too exalted for Elizabeth, who was in charge of everything, but in treating Fred as beyond the range of her little presents we may be sure that she kept him in his place. Through a ceaseless round of cooking, nursing and laundrywork she remained a stern ally of Anna Maria, and, by implication, a silent reproach to the man she had chosen to marry.

And Fred continued to work perseveringly, but without 'rising'. His idea of an evening out was a smoking concert, or Jolly, at the R.I.B.A. All his friends were architects – in fact, nearly all the houses in Doughty Street were occupied by architects, except for Solomon Fisher and Samuel Lazarus, who were solicitors. Sometimes he crossed the street to the Foundlings' Home in Coram's Fields to talk to the orphans, and see them eat their dinners. Either Fred did not know how to better himself, or he would not.

Over the years seven children were born to the Mews, and in the matter of the christenings battle was joined between Fred and Anna Maria. She was determined that all her sons should be named as Kendalls. Fred – though he knew his obligations – couldn't see anything wrong with his own family. Henry Herne (b. 1865) was named for Anna Maria's father, and for one of her aunts, Mrs Caroline Herne. Frederick George Webb (b. 1867) had the Mew Christian names, with an added compliment to Mrs Webb, of the Fountain Inn. Charlotte Mary (b. 1869) was the first daughter, followed by Richard Cobham (b. 1871) – a kind of truce, this, Richard Mew being the farming uncle at Newfairlee, while the Cobhams were the well-to-do family of Anna Maria's mother. Caroline Frances Anne was born in 1872, and then came Daniel Kendall (b. 1875) who was actually renamed, a few months later, as Christopher Barnes; the Barnes were relations of Fred's by marriage. The last child, who was born in 1879, and who would then have been called 'an afterthought', was a third girl. She was christened Freda Kendall.

In the background of these sad disagreements was death, the remorselessly punctual infant mortality of the Victorian nursery. Frederick George Webb died on an outing to Broadstairs, aged two months. In one terrible year, 1876, the Mews lost two more of their children. Christopher Barnes, shortly after receiving his new name, died in March of convulsions, which were then thought to be the result of 'anger and grief' in the nursing mother. Richard Cobham, five years old, died of scarlet fever.

> Oh! King who hast the key
> Of that dark room,
> The last which prisons us but held not thee,
> Thou know'st its gloom.
> Dost thou a little love this one
> Shut in to-night,
> Young and so piteously alone,
> Cold – out of sight?
> Thou know'st how hard and bare
> The pillow of that new-made narrow bed,
> Then leave not there
> So dear a head!

This verse, *Exspecto Resurrectionem*, is Charlotte Mew's, written thirty years later. So, too, was *To A Child in Death*, with its wretched question from the suddenly left alone – 'What shall we do with this strange summer, meant for you?' Charlotte, at seven years old, was certainly brought in, as elder sisters were in the 1870s, to see her little brother 'in death'. Richard had been the nearest to her in age, the one she loved to order about. Neither of her poems describes the stupor, or the acute ulcerated throat, of scarlet fever. They are not exact recollections so much as the first experience of grief, locked unchanged in her memory. She never suggested that writing the poems made the grief any less.

What would be surprising, if we didn't know that the life of children is conducted on a totally different system from that of adults, is that Charlotte Mew always spoke of her childhood as a time of intense, but lost, happiness. She was known then as Lotti, and her nursery, high up in London's clouds, contained among its heap of solid toys one which was most particularly hers and her sisters', a doll's house, designed and made by Fred Mew himself. Evidently it was a pleasure for him to have daughters. The doll's house had fashionable Queen Anne bow windows, although the straight up-and-down Doughty Street had none. This was their mansion, but the attic rooms themselves were a self-contained kingdom, where Elizabeth Goodman reigned, even if the tiny Lotti, curly, brilliant, irresistible and defiant, proved to be a difficult subject. 'To us as children she was as fixed a part of the universe as the bath (cruelly cold in winter) into which she plunged us every morning, and the stars to which she pointed through the high window, naming some of them, in the evening sky.' Under authority they were all safe, even when they had to be whipped for wildness.

Everything that pleased children in the 1870s pleased Lotti extravagantly. She was carried away by the 'sheer excitement' of colour in a box of chalks or the maddening sound of her penny trumpet, or the strange transformation of sugar which, heated in a saucepan over the nursery fire, turned to dark crimson 'pig's blood'. At Christmas she was 'half-mad'. She declared, in later life, that she 'never outgrew the snowflakes'. Elizabeth Goodman, who in the ordinary way read only the Bible and a popular comic, *Ally Sloper's Weekly*, at Christmas time 'flung into the festooned disorder of the nursery a pile of Christmas numbers, and thence forward walked with us, for a week or two, in a world of pure romance. Red lights gleamed from Manor House windows: ostlers bandied jests in the courtyards of lonely inns: the crack of whips and the hoofs of post-horses drowned the wheels of the crawling cab and the bell of the Muffin-man ting-tinging down our long, dull street; while we glided down broad oak staircases and swore in the halls of holly-decked mansions, where above, ghosts stalked through the corridors, and below there was always dancing, or lost ourselves on the great white road outside where the snow was always falling, in a whirl of highwaymen and elopements.'

Henry, as the eldest by four years, and a boy, a Victorian boy, was admired, but separate from the others. He was quick at drawing, and would be apprenticed to his father at Kendall and Mew as soon as he turned sixteen. A kind word from an elder brother of this sort goes a long way. The three girls, when they were taken out to the square or to music lessons, had to remember that they were ladies. They must not be flushed,

Charlotte Mew and her nurse Elizabeth Goodman.
'To us as children she was as fixed a part of the
universe as the bath . . .'

their hair must not be tossed, they must go out looking neat and return in the same condition, with clean handkerchiefs.

Few visitors ascended the creaking top flight of stairs to the nursery. For this reason the queer little sewing-woman, who came twice a week, made a disproportionate impression. In an essay of 1901 Charlotte calls her 'Miss Bolt', recalling her minutely as she sat mending, making and darning in the nursery chair, biting off the thread with her two protruding front teeth, because it saved the expense of grinding scissors. To her ready listeners Miss Bolt droned on about her own relatives in Lambeth. In speaking of the dead her voice assumed 'a dirge-like tone'; out of the living she made her own mythology. Scraping and denying herself for the sake of her no-good brother's family, she tottered away with Fred Mew's cast-off suits and anything else she could scrounge, even the candle-ends and scraps, all to be sold on her relatives' behalf. 'Ain't there something to be done to your ma's mackintosh?' she would enquire irrelevantly. 'I fancy she mentioned it. What serviceable articles they are!' She got the mackintosh at last, but never wore it. It was pawned at once. The little Mews collected their own possessions into a parcel to give to her, but this was absolutely forbidden. Miss Bolt, disappointed, repeated the ambiguous rhyme:

> Give a thing, and take a thing
> Is a dirty man's plaything.

What truly impressed Lotti in her child's-eye scrutiny was the recklessness of this dowdy woman in her endless self-sacrifice, and her pride. Pride was as important as survival. Miss Bolt would use low shifts, but would never condescend to be found out. Asked to come for an extra day's work, she would sometimes pretend to be 'previously engaged'. It was a crushed but unrepentant courage, the product of the London streets. Lotti saw through it immediately, and respected it.

Miss Bolt called for the last time, looking even shabbier than usual, in the autumn of 1876. On this occasion Charlotte, aged seven, was sitting with three-year-old Anne (who must have been almost as tall as she was) clasped on her lap. Miss Bolt asked where Richard was, and it was Lotti's responsibility, apparently, to tell her that he was dead. Miss Bolt, in return, confided that her niece, young Fanny, for whom she had done everything, had gone to the bad. She then withdrew downstairs to the kitchen, where the supper was, 'leaving me, like the childhood in which I knew her, mysteriously and without farewell'.

Though Lotti clearly can't have understood that Fanny had gone on the streets, she responded to the hushed tone of voice. Her fascination with the prostitute's story seemed the first hint of an end to childhood. In Charlotte Mew's original draft for her article there was a good deal more about Fanny: 'Even at fourteen, she must have borne the indelible marks appointing her to be slain. I wonder sometimes if I have ever met her; if I and the unhappy girl, who was once such a real and well-known person to me, have since passed each other with a cold unmeaning stare.' In this first draft, too, another of Miss Bolt's odd connections appears – a female impersonator, for whom her sister-in-law made drag costumes which 'suited 'im identical to the female shape . . . . 'e nearly took me off my feet, when 'e put up 'is train hover 'is arm and offered to see me 'ome.'

The point of Miss Bolt's visits, however, was to help in the process of mending and making do. The Mews were reasonably well off during the 1870s, though not within reach, of course, of the grandeur of Brunswick Square. Fred could confidently expect, in the course of time, to become head of the firm. There was Henry, too, to come after him, but then there were three daughters for him to support until marriage. Elizabeth Goodman's stern economies were an investment for the household's future. But they were also thé product of that wondrously strong Nonconformist ethic which put thrift as high as charity. Waste was not only an ingratitude to the Creator and an injury in a world where so many went hungry, but an insult to the nature of substance itself – shirts were turned because 'there was still plenty of life in them', and the skin of boiled milk must not be thrown away because 'it was perfectly good milk'. Furthermore, the squandered despised object itself might spring up and confront you in reproach. You might – and in the nursery's cautionary tales you did – face total disaster one day, just for want of a few drops of that same boiled milk.

At 30 Doughty Street Anna Maria was protected from worry. It was agreed that she had suffered enough. But Lotti, a 'noticing' child, had a clear glimpse of the nether depths which Miss Bolt so narrowly avoided, and into which Fanny had disappeared.

To a family so closed in, the seaside holiday was a release, and almost unmanageably exciting. In late May or June every year the Mew children went to the Isle of Wight. This represented a very considerable victory for Fred, particularly since the Kendalls had a seaside house in Brighton (No. 6 Codrington Place). During the development of Kemp Town, in fact, they had become a Brighton family of distinction, and Mrs Kendall, with her unmarried daughter Mary Leonora, spent every summer there. Anna Maria, it seems, preferred to join them at Codrington Place. But the children went on by the Mid-Sussex Railway to catch the boat at Southampton for the Island, in the care of Elizabeth Goodman.

At Newport they were met by their aunt from the farm, with a wagonette for the luggage and a fly for the children. On one occasion the tiny, impetuous Lotti jumped up to take the seat by the driver (this, by rights, would have been Henry's, as the eldest). When Elizabeth Goodman checked her by rapping her sharply over the knuckles with a parasol, Lotti is said to have seized the parasol and snapped it in half. She was intoxicated by the open air, the fields of standing corn, the estuary with ships made fast at the quay and the chequered lights and shadows of the Newport Downs. She wanted the driver to put on speed, or 'go bomewish' in the Island dialect which she knew perfectly well, but was not encouraged to speak.

During the holidays the children had the chance to tour the Island from Newfairlee. 'Past the white points of the Needles,' Charlotte wrote, 'over the Island sea, the pigeons of woods and other worlds flock home in autumn, dashing themselves sometimes at the end of the journey against the pane of St Catherine's light, dropping dazed and spent on the wet sand.' Shipwreck stories she could hardly have avoided, since they had more relations living 'back of the Wight', that graveyard of shipping; old Mrs Mew of Blackgang had once rowed out to take Christmas dinner to a crew stranded on what was left of their ship in Chale Bay. But Lotti's was the summer and early autumn sea, and the phosphorescent darkness of the summer beach at night.

> Tide be runnin' the great world over:
> T'was only last June month I mind that we
> Was thinkin' the toss and the call in the breast of the lover
> So everlastin' as the sea.

> Heer's the same little fishes that splutter and swim,
> Wi' the moon's old glim on the grey, wet sand;
> An' him no more to me nor me to him
> Than the wind goin' over my hand.

Ellen Mary was the farm cousin nearest to Charlotte in age, though not in temperament. In later years she joined an Anglo-Catholic community as Sister Mary Magdalen; she described Lotti as a child as 'full of the joy of life', and, less cautiously, as 'hard to manage'. But on Sundays the whole party walked by the field-path, thickly edged with dog-roses, to the new church of St Paul's, Barton, for Evensong. On the way they usually passed a blind man, who 'would put his fingers to his ears and tell me they were his peepers', with 'the piteous smile of one doomed to find no answer to it in the faces of his kind'. At St Paul's the vicar sometimes muddled up the responses, and Charlotte told, or more probably overheard, that he had been driven partly out of his wits by a young woman who was also pointed out, dressed in her white Sunday best, on the path to church. The blind man and the distracted priest, who would have been frightening to most children, fascinated her.

These were the days and nights, she said, 'of a short life when I could pray, years back in magical childhood'. But Sunday at Newfairlee, when she was not allowed to race through the cornfields or get soaked on the beach, was 'a day of eyes'. 'This was the thought that claimed my childhood,' she wrote in 1905, 'and in another fashion, claims it now. "A day of eyes", of transcendental vision, when the very roses . . . challenge the pureness of our gaze, and the grass marks the manner of our going, and the sky hangs like a gigantic curtain, veiling the face which, watching us invisibly, we somehow fail to see. It judged in those days my scamped and ill-done tasks. It viewed my childish cruelties and still, with wider range, it views and judges now.' From the age of six or seven Lotti, 'full of the joy of life', knew that she was guilty.

It seemed to her that she was self-convicted. But, strangely enough, it was the loyal and loving Elizabeth Goodman who had deeply imprinted on Lotti's mind the certainty of God's retribution. Every day she had to read a fixed number of pages from *Line Upon Line*, a book which re-tells the Bible stories extremely well, only after each one comes the sting. 'You remember how proud Absalom was of his hair. God let that very hair be fastened to the tree. We should pray to God not to let us be proud of anything we have.' Always we must be ready for judgement day, watch and prepare. 'Then you too will live with Jesus in heaven. You will sit down with Abraham, Isaac and Jacob and Joseph, and Moses and David.' This last prospect terrified Charlotte. But she did her best to prepare for it.

'In early years the rite and reality of daily prayers were for us strictly insisted on,' she wrote, 'and "Forgive us our trespasses" was no idle phrase when after it, each night at bedtime, we had to specify them.' Not only every sin (she was taught) but every moment of happiness has been given its fixed price in advance – though not by us – and must be paid for. That is why the roses and the grass, which she loved, seemed to challenge Lotti and 'mark the manner of her going'. Guilt of this nature can never be eradicated, a lifetime is not long enough. Unfortunately it will survive long after the belief in forgiveness is gone.

The Mew children sometimes stayed on till mid-September, long enough for the first of Newport's 'Bargain Zadderdays' or Saturday markets. These were hiring fairs, when hundreds of men and women farm servants, dressed up to the nines, crowded into Newport to get harvest work. The town was *en fête*, with stalls for ribbons and gingerbread. In the evening there was dancing, people got drunk, fighting raged up and down the High Street and if it was fine enough lovers rolled about the cornfields. Lotti was certainly kept clear of everything except an early look at the fairground and the stalls. But Saturday market 'grinning from end to end' remained with her as an image of terror.

Childhood has no escape from the random impact of images, however little wanted. They come before the emotions which will give them significance, as though lying in wait. As a child, and later as a writer, the idea of a coffin carried out at the door and a ship going down with all her lights, but without a sound, haunted Charlotte Mew. So too did church bells, a high wind, rooks flying, broad moonshine, and an ugly sight at Newfairlee.

I remember one evening of a long past Spring
Turning in at a gate, getting out of a cart, and finding
    a large dead rat in the mud of the drive.
I remember thinking: alive or dead, a rat was a godforsaken thing,
But at least, in May, that even a rat should be alive.

This rat was never exorcised and in her last, unfinished story she described it again, the dead bristling body, the finer texture inside the ears. The worst thing about it was its silence. It couldn't state its own case. And, as a poet, she was struck by the image's self-recall. She had remembered the rat many years afterwards, not for its own sake, but because she had seen a tree cut down.

At home in Doughty Street there was one picture in particular (although all the walls were hung with Fred's sketches) which fascinated Lotti. This was a drawing by her grandfather Henry Kendall, the picture of the Shining City. In the 1830s, when old H.E.K. had been developing the waterfront at Rosherville, on the Thames, in a modest and sober style, young Kendall had produced his own 'fancy composition' for the river entrance to the site. He could never have expected his father to take his design seriously, but in 1851 he developed it as a *dessin libre* and showed it, first at the Academy, and later in the

English section of the Paris Salon, where Baudelaire had raved over it. The drawing showed marble staircases and monuments dwarfing the tiny human beings, and whole fleets at anchor by the golden gates. To the Mew children this was Jerusalem, all the more because it was a Kendall image, hung in the drawing-room, and could only be seen on special occasions.

Certain colours, particularly white and red, always obsessed Charlotte Mew. She was more sensitive to colour than she wanted to be. She 'knew how jewels tasted'. There was also a favourite repeated movement, 'tossing'. In her poems there are tossed heads, 'tossed shadow of boughs in a great wind shaking', the toss in the breast of the lover, new-tossed hay, tossed trees, tossed beds. It can be active or passive – 'you will have smiled, I shall have tossed your hair'. Charlotte herself was a head-tosser. Everyone who knew her noticed this. Neat in all her movements, she could carry the gesture off, even in middle age. It expressed contradiction, relief from tension, and a defiance of what the tension meant. With 'tossing' went an obsession, which in itself seems mid-Victorian or Pre-Raphaelite, but probably had a more complex origin, with a woman's long hair. Her own hair was cut short; Miss Bolt, she had noticed, had 'only a small allowance'; Elizabeth Goodman's was decently hidden under her cap. Like nearly all her range of imagery, the vision of long, or rough, or flying hair came to her early, to be understood later. It was part of what she called 'the dazzling lights and colours of childhood's enchanted picture'.

CHAPTER 2

Love between Women

MISS BOLT had warned Lotti, from time to time, never to take
lemon juice in the hope of growing thinner, because dieting
would do no good – 'what you're made, that you will be'. Lotti
did not want to believe this last remark; in any case, what she
needed was something to make her stouter. She grew out of
early childhood still small-boned and tiny, with her face a
perfect oval, the 'moon-faced darling of all', but given to sudden
withdrawals. She had become a reading and writing child,
retreating under the nursery table and producing 'sheets of
pathetically laboured MSS'. These Elizabeth Goodman swept
into her dustpan. Much of the faithful servant's time was spent
in planning small treats and great careers for the four children,
but she didn't hold with this writing rubbish. Poetry, in fact,
she maintained, was 'injurious to the brain'. Lotti turned to
imagination's refuge. Evidently, she deduced, she was mis-
placed and alien, her father and mother were not her real
parents. 'Never, I know, but half your child' she wrote in *The
Changeling*:

> Times I pleased you, dear Father, dear Mother,
>   Learned all my lessons and liked to play,
> And dearly I loved the little pale brother
>   Whom some other bird must have called away.
> Why did They bring me here to make me,
>   Not quite bad and not quite good,
> Why, unless They're wicked, do They want, in spite, to take me
>   Back to their wet, wild wood?

These are verses for children, written in 1912. Charlotte used
to read them aloud, when the time came, to children of her
acquaintance, giving no explanation, because she believed

27

(quite rightly) that none would be needed. They understood her at once.

Anne was taller and prettier, but in spite of her brilliant violet-blue eyes, more usual-looking. She hadn't Lotti's strangely arched eyebrows, or her disconcerting look of astonishment, which might be sarcasm. Anne never wrote anything, but drew, or painted; she was the little sister, quicker to make friends than Lotti, but quite contentedly under her influence. Freda, the youngest, was the most striking of all. She was 'like a flame'. Anna Maria took pride in this youngest, and, determined to live through her daughter, liked to take little Freda about herself, particularly to dancing classes. For these Anna Maria dressed elaborately, appearing, for example, in a pale blue boa, an awkward thing for a very short woman to wear.

Henry, four years older than Charlotte, at a time of life when four years make the most difference, was the looked-up-to elder brother. In the room reserved as an office, he worked away at his drawing-board, but with an eye, quite naturally, to his own amusements. At the age of sixteen or so he began to go out dancing, and now, apparently, Elizabeth Goodman, 'when she was called upon to deliver the secret note or the unhallowed bouquet, would stand stiff-backed and sorrowful-eyed, holding it in her strong, beautifully-shaped rough hand to "receive instructions", with an impressive "Very well, sir", which was not convincing.' Why poor Henry shouldn't send a bouquet, which seems harmless enough, or why it should be unhallowed, is not explained. Possibly Goodman was doubtful of any form of communication between the sexes, as leading, in the end, to trouble.

In 1879 Lotti made her first venture beyond the family in Doughty Street and the cousins in the Isle of Wight. She was entered as a pupil in the Gower Street School. The school was not more than twenty minutes' walk away up Guildford Street and past the British Museum, so that she was able to come

Miss Lucy Harrison.

home for her mid-day dinner, but the headmistress, Miss Lucy Harrison, made a profound impression on her, which might be described as a revelation of a kind.

Lucy Harrison left a strong mark, in fact, on several thousands of young girls who passed through her hands. It couldn't be said of her – as it was of Miss Buss, at the North London Collegiate – that she was 'a great educator who should

29

never have been allowed to come into contact with children'. There are very many tributes to her good influence, intellectual and moral – she would never have distinguished between the two – but there was, in Octavia Hill's words, 'something Royal' about her which perhaps exempted her from criticism. She may not always have known what she was doing.

She had been born in 1844, in Yorkshire, of Quaker parents, the youngest of eight, and grew up into a top-whipping, boat-building tomboy, such as many large mid-Victorian families produced. A good shot with a stone, she felt, when she killed her first robin, 'after the first start of joy in the success of the action, a revulsion like the horrors of Cain' when she held the warm body in her hands. When she threw her favourite pocket-knife into the water (apparently by mistake) 'I felt' – she wrote – 'as if I had thrown my heart in.' Hers was the excess of guilt attributed to Maggie in *The Mill on the Floss*, or Cathy Earnshaw in *Wuthering Heights*, or Jo in *Little Women*, when their behaviour was not only passionate, but masculine. Lucy Harrison had to come to terms with it in order to control her own life and those of others.

She was educated in France and Germany and at the liberal and unsectarian Bedford College. Languages came easily to her, history and poetry were her passion. Coming as she did from a broadminded Ruskinian background, she prayed to be serviceable. This meant the Octavia Hill Settlement, temperance clubs, the Suffragists, prisoners, exiles. Mazzini, when she visited him in his wretched rooms, gave her a cigar which she kept as a souvenir till it fell to pieces. There was still a wealth of undirected energy which had to be worked off in heavy carpentry and amateur dramatics. Then, when she was twenty-two, she was asked to help out at the Bedford School, then attached to the college. In 1868 the college gave up the school, and it moved to Gower Street, with Lucy Harrison as assistant.

Children adored Miss Harrison. She kept them in order because she never expected to be disobeyed. All, apparently, felt when she stood in her favourite attitude, looking upwards with her hands clasped behind her, that what she said was 'given from above'. For these younger ones she evolved an effective question-and-answer method, which she later published as *Social Geography for Teachers and Infants*.

> Here is a picture of a *church*. Where is it standing? – 'In the middle of a *churchyard*' – Sometimes there is grass round the church, with trees and plants. How is the church separated from the street or road? – 'By *iron railings*' – When you walk up the steps or along the path, how do you get into the church? 'Through the *door*' – Sometimes when people die they are taken into the church which they attended while they were alive. How does the bell ring then? – 'Very slowly. It is said to *toll*.'

In 1875 the headmistress, Miss Bolton, retired, and Lucy Harrison took over. Worshipped by all the visiting staff, men as well as women, she had no problems of organization: concentrating now on the senior girls, she made them feel what education had meant to her – an uplifting emotional experience. 'You need not call anything a luxury that you can share.' They were to love music and poetry. A book, even a book's title, is a door into another mind, letting in light and fresh air, and in the pain and joy of poetry the soul has the chance to meet itself. As to what they read – and she read aloud to them untiringly – it must be what went deepest and lifted highest – Shakespeare, Dante in Cary's translation, Blake, Wordsworth, and her own favourites, Emily Brontë, Christina Rossetti, the Brownings, Coventry Patmore, Alice Meynell. Carlyle, describing the hero as poet, insists that we ourselves have Dante's imagination, though with a weaker faculty, when we shudder at the *Inferno*. This kind of thing gives endless scope to the teacher, and can end up as something like sentimentality. There was in fact a certain confusion in Miss Harrison's interpretations between the windswept heights which Dante and Shakespeare were then thought to share with the Authorised Version, and the indulgence of hot tears in the dark. A reading which all her pupils heard often, and never forgot, was from Alice Meynell's *Preludes* of 1875 – the sonnet *To a Daisy*, which ends

> Thou little veil for so great mystery
> When shall I penetrate all things and thee,
> And then look back? For this I must abide,
> Till thou shalt grow and fold and be unfurled

Literally between me and the world.
Then I shall drink from in beneath a spring,
And from a poet's side shall read his book.
O daisy mine, what will it be to look
From God's side even on such a simple thing?

This strange double perspective, – the poet's corpse buried beneath the daisy's roots and at the same time contemplating the earth from God's side, wouldn't have been strange to Ruskin (who called the last lines some of the finest in modern poetry) nor to Christina Rossetti, nor, evidently, to the Gower Street girls. With all Miss Harrison's liberality and fresh air went a certain morbidity. But hard work was called for, because it develops intellect, and intellect forms thought, and thought forms character. In this vein Miss Harrison returned to Carlyle, and to the idea of the heroic life as a model to imitate. She would speak of Sir Philip Sidney, and the girls sat and thought of Miss Harrison.

At the end of the summer term there was an Open Day, when the reports were read and there was music, and a French or German play. Miss Harrison approved of amateur dramatics, though not of low mimicry. Lotti, a born impersonator who could 'do' anybody, and did mimic, perhaps in a low way, Professor Kinkel, the venerable lecturer in geography, would not have been encouraged to take part. But as a brilliant pianist with a delicate touch she was needed for the concert, and, at this stage of her life, still frankly enjoyed being told that she played well.

The trouble was that she would only learn what interested her, and a number of things, including geography, didn't. But in spite of these failures her one motive was to please her headmistress. In her plain black jacket and waistcoat, with her short hair and calm gracious voice, Miss Harrison brought into the room 'the sense of august things'. Dissent would be shameful, and the 'inexpressible charm of her presence' made it impossible. There were no rules, as such, at Gower Street, although there were many precepts, from 'if a pudding is begun with a fork, the help of a spoon must not be called in half-way through' to Coventry Patmore's

Love wakes men once a lifetime each;
They lift their heavy heads and look;
And lo, what one sweet page can teach
They read with joy, then shut the book.

Lotti could not dress like Miss Harrison. She had of course, at the age of fourteen, no choice as to what she wore. She had a black-and-white checked dress, with a plain silver chain and cross, for weekdays, and a brown dress with a gold cross on Sundays. But she was allowed to keep her hair short, like Miss Harrison's.

Her best friends were sober, hard-working girls. The three Chicks – Elsie, Margaret, and Harriet, from Ealing – seemed set to become teachers. Ethel Oliver was the daughter of Professor Daniel Oliver, the curator of Kew Herbarium, and a friend of Ruskin and the painter Arthur Hughes. Maggie Browne, also a professor's daughter, was the dull one, always the last to be told anything, but the most faithful and stolid of friends. All these girls had good, quiet homes – the Olivers were Quakers – and were not much disposed to question things. Lotti amazed them. They saw at school her wild side, her inquisitive, flamboyant, head-tossing, parasol-snapping side. The beloved headmistress could not be disobeyed, but Lotti seemed to pass her days in a state of painful emotion, as though listening to something they could not hear.

In 1882, when Lotti was on the verge of adolescence, Miss Harrison, the undisputed centre of life in Gower Street, began to behave oddly. Her behaviour showed signs of overwork and strain. She was becoming what was then called (in reference to schoolmistresses) 'unhappy'. It was felt by the governors that she must leave the school, and try what a rest would do. She was going, it was decided, to retire for the time being and take rooms in Hampstead, half-way up Haverstock Hill. During the day-time she would work in the British Museum, grimly persevering with her *History of England*, never, as it turned out, to be published.

When Charlotte heard this news, she was practising the piano. She sprang up and 'in a wild state of grief began to bang

33

her head against the wall'. This recollection came from a much younger girl, Amice Macdonnell, a niece of Miss Harrison's. Amice was dismayed, and wondered whether she ought to bang her head, too.

Lotti was sick with one of the most cruel of all preparations for adolescence, the passion for a teacher, confusing intense sexual anxiety with the duty of loving the highest when we see it. Wisely or unwisely, Miss Harrison now offered to take some of the older girls from Gower Street as boarders, and to teach them English literature in the evenings, when their school day was over. Anna Maria was quite unable to face such a crisis, Lotti grieved wildly, Fred was called in to make a decision, and to put his foot down, and do something. He was frightened by his daughter's condition. He is described as 'going down on his knees' to persuade Lucy Harrison to take Lotti with her.

But if he had done the best he knew for Lotti, he can hardly be said to have understood her, for he believed the move would 'stabilize' her. For the next two years she was separated from her elder brother and her two sisters, Anne and the baby Freda. Anne continued placidly in the Gower Street junior school, 'good at art', giving no trouble of any kind. Miss Harrison's boarders, on the other hand, had to undertake, twice every day, the three-mile walk to and from Gower Street, down Haverstock Hill and Chalk Farm, through Camden High Street with its markets, down Hampstead Road to school. In the evening the walk was uphill. But Lotti's spirits were now so high, and she was so unpredictable, so entertaining, seeming sometimes to dance rather than walk, that the way seemed short.

Two of the Gower Street assistant teachers walked in front, as chaperones. Behind came the two sixteen-year-olds, Edith Oliver and Edith Scull, the daughter of an American professor. The two Ediths, then, walked ahead; next came Lotti, in the highest spirits, with the puzzled little Amice Macdonnell. When the little party arrived at Haverstock Hill there was a gracious reception, but also plain cooking of the cold meat and rice pudding variety. Mrs Newcombe, the Gower Street housekeeper, who regarded Miss Harrison with love and reverence, had come to Hampstead to look after her.

Eighteen months later, however, the situation totally altered when Miss Harrison herself fell passionately in love with Amy Greener, the teacher who had taken over the Gower Street School. When she recognized that her nerves had given way, Lucy Harrison had bought a piece of land, Cupples Field, near Wensleydale in her native Yorkshire. She had planted trees on the site at once, but waited for the right moment to build herself a house. Now, at one stroke she realized that the house must be shared. All the strength of 'the fairest hill and sweetest dell', she wrote to Miss Greener, 'without *you* leaves me longing', and again, in 1886, 'Oh, for one hour with you again!' and 'Dearest, I do not feel at home anywhere without you now . . . with the person you love comes a halo and glow over everything, however miserable and poor, and without that presence the light seems to leave the sun itself. This is a trite remark, I am afraid.' As she drove across the rough Yorkshire moors she recalled her walks with Miss Greener in the Tottenham Court Road. 'Dear, dear love, there is nothing in the world that could satisfy me or fill your place for me, but if separation by death had to come, I think one could fly to the hope and thought of meeting hereafter; it would, I think, be impossible to live without that hope at any rate . . . .'

These letters are quoted in Amy Greener's biography of her friend, which treats a delicate subject delicately. Miss Greener had asked herself whether some people, knowing that the idea of marriage had never attracted Miss Harrison, would wonder 'whether her life lacked the perfect rounding that love could bring'. 'Well!' commented a friend, who had been allowed to read the manuscript, 'the love she needed came!' And indeed the two of them were to live in perfect concord at Cupples Field for nearly thirty years. Lucy became the revered headmistress at the Mount School, York; Amy joined her staff. They retired together. On her deathbed Lucy asked Amy to read to her from Elizabeth Barrett Browning's *Catarina to Camoens*, in which Catarina, 'dying during the poet's absence abroad', tries to reconcile herself to the idea of his falling in love again. She wavers, but finally gives her blessing. It must have been painful for Miss Greener to read these words aloud in the whitewashed bedroom, among the plain oak furniture which her friend had knocked together.

Meanwhile the boarders at Haverstock Hill were left to face their entry into life without their headmistress. It was the end of Lotti's schooling, and part of her education had been to know what it was to be totally obsessed by the physical presence or absence of another woman. This for her was something more than the ordinary condition of being sixteen. It can be recognized in an early sonnet, *Left Behind*:

> I wait thy summons on a swaying floor,
> Within a room half darkness and half glare.
> I cannot stir – I cannot find the stair –
> Thrust hands upon my heart –; it clogs my feet,
> As drop by drop it drains. I stand and beat –
> I stand and beat my heart against the door.

Of course, large numbers of schoolgirls all over England, at the turn of the century, felt passionately about the teacher. *Schwärmerei* was a calculated risk for those who educated in Lucy Harrison's way. It passed, and was supposed to refine and ennoble. But for Lotti, the changeling, the odd one out, it proved to be an initiation into her life's pattern. She would always be physically attracted to women rather than to men, and she would always choose wrong. She was marked out to lose, with too much courage ever to accept it. From adolescence she was one of those whom Colette called 'restless ghosts, unrecovered from wounds sustained in the past, when they crashed headlong or sidelong against the barrier reef, mysterious and incomprehensible, the human body'.

36

CHAPTER 3

Lotti

LOTTI, everyone said, had changed. She was still unpredictable and passionate and could still, if she wanted to and was in the vein, make everybody laugh until they cried. But the innocent desire to show off had failed her. She was often fierce with strangers. Her wild impulses no longer turned all the same way, outwards, to meet the world. Once she had been driven to wild happiness at any kind of celebration; now, it seemed, she had hardened. 'It is a legend in my family', she wrote, 'that at festive seasons I am cynically indifferent to the pile of good wishes and parcels that come my way – but this may merely be a self-protective mask for the "emotional nature" which you insist on crediting me with . . . I am credited with a more or less indifferent front to these things – the fact is they cut me to the heart.' The storm within had to have an outlet. She needed exhausting music, not her piano pieces, but Wagner, *Tannhäuser* above all. Meanwhile the silver cross round her neck (and the gold one on Sundays) was an outward sign that she had entered an Anglo-Catholic phase, and, with her mother and Anne, was attending Christina Rossetti's church, Christ Church, Woburn Square. But whereas Anne continued in the same faith till death, Lotti suffered from all the spiritual nausea of belief and unbelief. Her family were at a loss, her friends still more so. They knew only that Lotti was very brilliant, and out of them all must be the one who would do great things. In appearance she was still a tough, delicate miniature – her boot size was number 2 – her smallness making an immediate appeal, wherever she went, to the toy-loving human race. Her voice had become rather chancy, sometimes hoarse, like a boy's breaking, but very flexible, and fascinating to listen to.

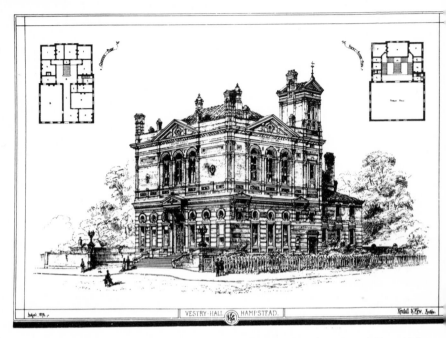

Vestry Hall, Hampstead (now the Old Town Hall) by Kendall and Mew.
A drawing by Fred Mew.

Freda was still a little girl, Anne continued placidly at the Gower Street School after Miss Harrison had left. Charlotte was now the daughter at home. Although Fred, as has been seen, was called upon as head of the household in all business matters, and when it was necessary for someone to be 'spoken to', it is doubtful if he saw much of his daughters. Still a complete failure from the point of view of gentlemanliness, he had had to put all his energy for some time past into the affairs of Kendall and Mew.

H.E.K. relied by now almost entirely on Fred. Old Kendall had died in 1875, leaving very little (he had entertained lavishly all his life) beyond the Brighton property, and in *The Builder*'s words, H.E.K. 'during his own later years, was greatly assisted in his professional engagements by his son-in-law Mr Frederick Mew'. The two of them were associated at Gordon House,

Isleworth, for the Earl of Kilmorey; at Madingley Hall, near Cambridge, at Staunton Harold, for Earl Ferrers; and, in 1876, in the new Hampstead Vestry Hall. So far, so good. This commission should have been the high point of the firm's success, ensuring a prosperous future for Anna Maria and the Mews.

Hampstead in the late 1870s was a rapidly extending rural suburb, with a population of 40,000. The Hall (now the Old Town Hall, Rosslyn Hill) was intended to house the sixty Vestry members in dignity and comfort, but it was also to be 'a centre of social life and healthful activity'. By this it was meant that the Vestry could recover some of the expenses by letting it out for concerts. From the outset it was stipulated that the main hall must hold 800, and, although the total costs were not to exceed £10,000, the building must be 'appropriate' and 'worthy'.

In April 1876 the contract was offered for competition. Kendall and Mew's entry, under the disarming motto *Cavendo tutus* (caution means safety) was accepted by a majority. Their design was for a handsome edifice in one of their 'Italian' styles, faced with red brick and dressings of Portland Stone, centrally heated and lit by gas. But almost at once the familiar unpleasantness began. 'Sir,' wrote an unsuccessful competitor, a few weeks after the award, to the *Hampstead & Highgate Express*, 'while inspecting the drawings for the above, prior to the decisions of the Vestry, my attention was called to a gentleman with a foot-rule, pointing out the merits (?) of the design marked 'Cavendo tutus' to all comers. Upon speaking to him, I discovered he was a vestryman, and he stated to me that he knew whose design it was, and had seen it prior to its being sent in . . . 'Cavendo tutus' appears to have ignored all the conditions – the large hall showing to hold about 400 people (if I mistake not) instead of the 800 required.' This was quite true, and nobody believed, either, in the accepted estimate of £9,375. The suggestion was that H.E.K., as Hampstead's district surveyor, had got his foot in first. Criticism grew louder when the work was held up for month after month. The Vestry, obliged to meet in one of the dining-halls of Hampstead

39

Workhouse, were restive. By midsummer the partners had to issue a statement 'that though the work had not been proceeded with so rapidly as it might have been, the architect was of the opinion that this was all the better for the building'. This sounds more like Fred than the suave and experienced Kendall, who in fact, at the age of seventy, had entered the slow deterioration of his last illness. Reports and certificates were no longer dated from his office, which was closed, but from 30 Doughty Street. With his wife Maria and daughter Mary Leonora, he had moved from expensive Brunswick Square to 34 Burlington Road, near Paddington railway station. Where had the money gone, from the long series of country mansions, Gothic parochial schools and Domestic Elizabethan lunatic asylums? On 10 August 1878 Fred was obliged to apply, on the partners' behalf, for '£100 on account', suggesting that they were operating on a very small margin.

By the end of the summer the main building was complete except for the boundary walls, and the Vestry, who had been 'crouching' in the half-finished rooms, emerged and passed a resolution that the money had been well spent. This, however, was in the face of public complaints about the delay, the small size of the hall, the bright red Bracknell brick which was 'brought before the eye to a painful degree' and which, without the stone dressings, would be 'unbearable' and make Hampstead's residents dizzy. Most unfortunate of all was the fact that the builder had already had the date carved over the entrance, 1877, whereas the grand opening had to be delayed until November 1878. At the celebration dinner a number of healths were drunk 'three times three', but not Kendall and Mew's.

It seems clear that the Kendall women, who had always treated Fred as an uncouth interloper, blamed him for this and every other misfortune, and refused to admit his difficulties at the end of twenty loyal years of partnership. Although Fred was only an executor of H.E.K.'s will and not a beneficiary (unless he survived Anna Maria), there was a strong feeling that he was after the money. This appears from Maria Kendall's will, made on 17 April 1883 to dispose of her legacy from her own family, the Cobhams. One-third was to go to Anna Maria 'for her sole

40

use and benefit separate and apart from and exclusive of her said husband Frederick Mew, and that she may hold and enjoy and dispose of such share in the same manner as if she were unmarried'. The legend that Fred was a monster of selfishness was now well established. Charlotte, sadly enough, the little girl for whom he had made the doll's house with bow windows, grew up to believe the legend, and repeat it.

In 1885 H.E.K. died, leaving a personal estate of £616 10s. His widow, with Mary Leonora, went to live permanently in Brighton, while Fred was confidently expected to keep the firm going, and maintain them all in comfort. Very likely the family did not know how things stood. Gissing's Dr Madden in *The Odd Women*, who considers that 'women, young and old, should never have to think about money', and fails to take out any insurance, was a not unusual type of professional man. And probably Fred could not bring himself to tell them the truth, which was that for all his size and presence he was a follower, not a leader. After the death of his beloved old master, he lost direction. For years he had been doing virtually all the work, in the office and on the sites, but always as Kendall wanted it.

During Kendall's long illness Fred had designed or part-designed a few private houses, a bank at Aldershot (1882), and (his most important commission) the Capital and Counties Bank in Bristol (1885), 'with details somewhat Greek in charac-ter'. In the same year the Hampstead Vestry, perhaps surpris-ingly, had asked the partners to undertake an extension to their Hall along the Belsize Park frontage. Fred in fact carried this out, but this is the last commission of his that I have been able to trace. The heart had gone out of him.

He was, admittedly, cowardly in not telling his wife that the firm's work had declined and that Elizabeth Goodman should be making do and patching even more, rather than less. After the commission for the Vestry Hall extension, he even agreed that the family should look for a larger house. Anna Maria no longer had Brunswick Square to fall back upon. She needed a 'better address'. In 1888 the Mews moved to 9 Gordon Street, just where the street joins, or once joined, Gordon Square. It was a much taller house than Doughty Street, four storeys

Gordon Square, Bloomsbury.
'Day follows day
The same, or now and then, a different grey . . .'

above the basement and its sunless area, and it had a *piano nobile* of spacious rooms, elegantly railed off with a wrought-iron balcony. The whole street had been built by Thomas Cubitt for the Bedford Estate before he moved on towards greater triumphs in London's West End. This would have recommended the house to Anna Maria, since Mrs Lewis Cubitt was the most distinguished of her aunts. It kept up the connection, and this was precious to her. Fred bought the end of the lease, with another twenty-four years to run.

Elizabeth Goodman settled them all in. The semi-invalid Anna Maria must of course be spared as much trouble as possible. Wek, her parrot, who had been with her since the days in Brunswick Square, was introduced, under protest, to his new home. Kendall's picture of the Shining City was hung in the front drawing-room, next to the portrait of Anna Maria as a young girl. Fred's office was on the ground floor. But Gordon Street was never either a happy or a lucky house. After the move, Fred pinned his hopes on Henry. The dashing, promising son must have been more than a help with the office routine, and a much-needed new life in the business. He was a refuge in a house full of women. But now, in his early twenties, Henry began to show unmistakable signs of mental breakdown. The illness was what was then known as *dementia praecox*, because it was thought to attack adolescents and young adults in particular. It would be called schizophrenia now. Fred was advised that there was no possibility of a cure, and for the rest of his life Henry was confined, with a private nurse, to Peckham Hospital.

The history of mental weakness was not on the Mew side, but the Kendall. Never mentioned in public was the reason why Edward Herne Kendall, Anna Maria's elder brother, had failed to join the partnership after his training, and why in fact he had no occupation of any kind. Edward was not a schizophrenic, simply a borderline case who might from time to time need looking after, and who could never be trusted with his own affairs. When he became completely irresponsible his money was saved up for him and invested until he 'came back'. Mary Leonora, also, was not strong in the wits, or, at least, foolish, and it was the constant fear of her mother, Mrs Kendall, that she might be 'got hold of' in some way, and left penniless. In all probability, Henry Mew's tragic illness had nothing to do with his Kendall uncle and aunt, and yet the suggestion remained that it had. Meanwhile the fact that there was no insanity to be traced in Fred's family was likely to make him more, and not less, to blame.

The family at 9 Gordon Street was reduced, after so many hopes, to three daughters. Elizabeth Goodman acted as the family's consoler. 'There was nothing conscious or masterful about this,' Charlotte wrote, 'it was simply the gentle, irresistible mastery of the strongest, clothed with an old-world deference.' The son was as good as lost, but the youngest, Freda, was doted upon. Even her name had been a romantic flight, distinguishing her from all the rest. Fred and Anna Maria, whatever their discords, both combined to love and spoil this exceptional little girl, who grew into adolescence still beautiful and brilliant. This would be about the time when Henry Mew made his sad exit into separation and silence.

Then, early in the 1890s, Freda followed him. She began to show recognizable symptoms of schizophrenia, then, like Henry, broke down beyond recall. Poor Fred asserted himself for almost the last time, and insisted that she must not be kept in London, but sent back to the Island, within reach of the Bugle Inn and the farm. Freda lived for another sixty-odd years as a paying patient at the Whitelands Hospital, Carisbrooke, without ever recovering her sanity.

CHAPTER 4

'These I Shall See'

CHARLOTTE MEW'S two asylum poems are *On the Asylum Road* and *Ken*. These, like the others from which I have quoted, were written at a distance of time from the first experience. Like Hardy and Housman, she was a poet of delayed shock.

Both *Ken* and *On The Asylum Road* are impersonations, written through, but not in, the first person. Mad people are described by a sane onlooker, but 'this I is not I'. In both poems the speaker, or spoken-through, is painfully indirect and breaks down at one point or another into a kind of dislocation, as though the subject of insanity could only be approached in that way. The guilt is obvious, but there is no solution for it, except refuge in the community's opinion.

Ken is not about a case of *dementia praecox*, but an amiable harmless local idiot. He lives and always has lived at a place which sounds very like Carisbrooke – 'the town is old, and very steep', leading up to the mental hospital, the castle and the convent (which in Carisbrooke would be St Dominic's). Ken means well, but is simply not like the rest of us, believing that all the children and all the deer in the park belong to him, and that a pile of broken feathers on the ground is really a living bird. He is hideous to look at, however,

> If in His image God made men
> Some other must have made poor Ken–

In time he becomes too much, not of a danger, but of a nuisance. Sometimes he stays in church too long, or points to the crucified Christ and says 'Take it away'; then everyone is embarrassed. The only thing to do is to pretend not to notice, 'You did not look at him as he sat there' and finally to lock him

45

up – and the speaker doesn't suggest that the authorities are wrong about this. What else could they have done? But the poem ends

> So, when they took
> Ken to that place, I did not look
> After he called and turned on me
> His eyes. These I shall see –

Charlotte claimed that in this poem she had tried to 'obscure the tragic side by tenderness of treatment'. Why she said this I cannot think. She must have known that she was emphasizing it.

On the Asylum Road is not localized, and might be anywhere where mental patients, at the end of the nineteenth century, were institutionalized and taken out for regular exercise. The first verse opens:

> Theirs is a house whose windows – every pane –
> Are made of darkly stained or clouded glass:
> Sometimes you come upon them in the lane,
> The saddest crowd that you will ever pass.

The horror of the darkly stained and clouded glass, the poem's one insistent detail, works very strongly. Surgeries, Christian churches and mortuaries, as well as asylums, shut themselves off in this way, with glass which is a denial of what glass should be. Behind their dark glass, the mad own nothing. 'Theirs is the house' – but we know it isn't, only it will be more convenient for us to pretend that it is. And 'you' (or in the next three verses 'we') have agreed that the best thing to do is to smile encouragingly at them,

> And think no shame to stop and crack a joke
> With the incarnate wages of man's sin.

The reader or listener is bound to ask what is happening here and why the inmates, the 'brother shadows in the lane', should (unless they are all syphilitics) be all classed together as 'the incarnate wages of man's sin'. This returns us to the wretched situation of 9 Gordon Street.

As ill-fortune would have it, the breakdown first of Henry, then of Freda, coincided with the years when the science or

46

apparent science of eugenics first took the field, and became a favourite subject of newspaper articles. Francis Galton's *Natural Inheritance* was published in 1889, and in 1894 he set up his research laboratory in University College. The belief of so many centuries that, given God's grace and human patience, there was a hope that mad wits could be restored, was superseded, for the time being, by what looked like conclusive scientific evidence. Eugenics dealt in statistics, family studies and the tabulation of 'morbid inheritance', setting out to show that transmission of this inheritance led to the gradual degeneration of a whole society. The improvement of society, then, depended on genetic politics. If any member of your family was 'different', no matter in what way, you were morally bound not to reproduce. If you did so, you contributed to the nation's decline and must expect 'the incarnate wages of man's sin'. In fact, the first editor to see *Ken* rejected it on the grounds that the magazine 'believed in the segregation of the feeble-minded'. Charlotte and Anne, living within the orbit of London University, both of them great readers of weeklies and attenders of lectures, came to the conclusion that they must never have children, and so had no right to marry. This decision was not the same thing for the two of them. For Charlotte, whether or not she ever came to terms with her own sexuality, all passion was destructive. She had learned that already, and never had reason to change her mind. Anne, on the other hand, three years younger, was the most normal or even 'the most human' of the family. There was some self-imposed guilt in regard to the persuadable Anne, although they must have made the decision together.

But both the Mew girls loved children, Charlotte in particular. Their great capacity for happiness and disappointment appealed to her, so did their detachment from adult affairs and their concentration on the far greater reality of a game. She was delighted when she saw a small girl and boy wait unconcernedly for a coffin to be carried down the stairs and out of the door, and then turn back at once to playing shops. Of walking on stilts she wrote: 'If you could go on doing it for ever, you need envy no-one, neither the angels nor the millionaires', and of

47

playing with water, 'The horse-trough is always there to sail your hat in and trail your arms in, until your elder sister sneaks up from behind, and cops you out of it by the neck'. She suffered, only half-unwillingly, from empty arms. If she did not want to bear children, she would have liked to want to. 'If there were fifty heavens God could not give us back the child who went or never came.' Absorbed as she always was, from her Gower Street days, with the Brontës, she was haunted by the story of Charlotte Brontë's dream as Mrs Gaskell tells it in her *Life*, a dream of holding a crying child, and knowing that nothing can save it.

There were the two daughters, then, in 9 Gordon Street, vowed to sterility, which would also mean devotion to each other. Three years' difference in age steadily came to be less and less important. Charlotte and Anne saw that they had been born to make head against their difficulties together, with this difference, that there were some things Charlotte would never tell, or feel it right to tell, the docile Anne. Their mother's role was established: she was a chronic invalid with no definable illness, a precious responsibility because so much had to be done for her. As to Fred, there is nothing to show what he felt about the fate of his youngest and oldest child, except his loss of interest in life. He ceased to do very much at all. There are no more records of him at the R.I.B.A., and his subscription to the newer Architectural Association lapsed altogether. In 1895 he wrote a dignified but pathetic letter to *The Builder*, pointing out that even the design for his Capital and Counties Bank at Bristol was now being attributed to another architect.

How did the Mews manage? In 1892 Anna Maria inherited a third of the estate from her grandfather, Thomas Cobham; this came to £2266 12s. 3d. Her mother died in this same year, again leaving her the correct third share, £1717 2s. 10d., and an annuity of £50. Anna Maria had also come into two legacies, a little earlier, from an uncle and aunt. All these sums of money were administered for her by Walter Barnes Mew, the son of Fred's sister Fanny, who was a solicitor with an office at 4 Harcourt Buildings, in the Temple. Fred evidently relied a good deal on Walter, and, writing to him as 'your affectionate uncle', was glad to leave matters in his capable hands. 'Anything that appears foggy to me will doubtless be clear enough to your legal eye,', he added, sounding a good deal older than his sixty years. Walter, with the approval of the trustees, invested the total sum in an annuity for Anna Maria, which would bring her in £300. It was a reasonable sum at a time when you could cling to respectability, even gentility, on £80 a year. The annuity, of course, would die with her, but Walter must have calculated that Charlotte and Anne, his two pretty cousins, would find husbands soon enough.

Or they might even earn their own livings. Anne, since she left the Gower Street School, had been enrolled at the Royal Female School of Art at 43 Queen Square, within easy walking distance of Gordon Street. The course offered two five-month terms at fifteen guineas a year, three times as much as the South Kensington Schools, which concentrated on design training for industry. The Female School, on the other hand, had in mind, from its first beginnings in the 1840s, the daughters of professional men 'unexpectedly compelled to earn a living', and at first the students had only been accepted at discretion, if they could show (preferably with a certificate from a clergyman) that they were genuine 'needy gentlewomen' who would be obliged to maintain themselves. Anne specialized in bird and flower painting. She was happy to do only that, hoping one day for an exhibition of her own, but if need arose she would be qualified to teach or to execute paid commissions, without ever ceasing to be a lady. Anna Maria need have no alarm on that score. Her younger daughter would still have the prestige of an amateur.

What about Charlotte, who had learned only what she chose to, but always did it well? She was, for instance, very good at embroidery, and she could have got an excellent training at the Royal School of Art Needlework, established with its workrooms in Kensington, or, if that was too far to go, there was a School of Mediaeval Embroidery, run by the sisterhood of St Katherine in Queen Square to supply church furnishings. She could then have worked at home, and sold discreetly, perhaps through the Association for the Sale of Work of Ladies of

Limited Means. She could, though this would have been more difficult to conceal from the neighbours, have given piano lessons. From Miss Harrison she had heard time and again a reading of Carlyle's 'Everlasting No' from *Sartor Resartus*. The 'No' is the certainty of death and the loss of faith which make life meaningless, followed by the answering Everlasting Yea, that in spite of this, man must work at what he is fit for. 'Were it but the pitifullest infinitesimal fragment of a product, produce it, in God's name!' But the truth was that Charlotte, in spite of Carlyle, hated steady work. It has to be admitted that she never applied herself systematically to anything.

It might be thought, however, that as a changeling and *enfant terrible*, only just grown up, she would have wanted independence at all costs. Here we come to the irreconcilables in Charlotte Mew. One side of her treated the other cruelly. She was secretly, and sometimes openly, impelled to let rip, to shock the shockable, and to turn her back on the lot of them.

> Please you, excuse me, good five o'clock people,
>   I've lost my last hatful of words

and yet she clung as desperately as Anna Maria herself to dear respectability. She never left home for long, never became – for example – a suffragette or even a suffragist, never made any attempt to claim political or sexual freedom or defend herself either against society or her own nature. On the contrary, with fierce self-suppression she inherited the fate of the world's minorities and suffered as an outsider, an outsider, that is, even to herself. She was determined to remain Miss Lotti – a lady, even if she made rather an odd one. There is pathos in this clinging to gentility by a free spirit, who seemed born to have nothing to do with it. But her home promised normality – its very dullness did that – and normality implies peace. As a five o'clock person, out of the shadow of the madhouse, a good daughter, devoted to her mother, she could treat the savage who threatened her from within as a stranger. To use her own image, she could stay as 'a blade of grass which dare not grow too high lest the world should snap it'.

However, she was also a writer. At the beginning of the 1890s

Elizabeth Goodman was still in charge of the household, since 'no-one dared to speak to her of rest', but she now no longer swept Charlotte's manuscripts into her dustpan. Alone in her room Charlotte sat down, partly to justify her friends' expectations – that always meant a great deal to her – partly to show herself what she could do, partly to earn money. Without money free will means very little. Though Charlotte never wanted to get rid of her responsibilities, she preferred not to be answerable to anyone. She needed, in fact, not independence but freedom.

There was a business-like side to Charlotte. She knew, at least, how to set out on a writer's career. Her manuscripts went out to a lady typewriter – they were still called that – who, herself, was a distressed gentlewoman. They came back neatly bound in brown paper, were lightly corrected in pencil and sent off with the stamps for return postage stuck to the front cover. As to where they should go, there was a wide choice in the nineties, the golden age of the English periodical. A hopeful writer, a beginner poised on the verge, must have been bewildered simply by the number of new and older publications. Although *Answers* and *Tit-Bits* had been started, with enormous success, to provide something lighter in the way of weeklies, they existed side by side with the older heavies, *The Athenaeum*, *The Sphere*, *The Academy*, *The Spectator*, *The Saturday Review* and a host of others, always increasing, literary or political or both, and joined every month by the closely printed ranks of magazines, led by *Blackwood's*, *The Strand* and the *Pall Mall*. These last specialized in fiction, and could count on the best-known names as contributors – Hardy, H. G. Wells, Rudyard Kipling, Conan Doyle, Conrad, Henry James, all of them valued in those days largely as spinners of yarns. The best seller had not yet parted company with literature. The yarns, whether they came from hacks or writers of genius, were set among feature and travel articles and pages of 'little-known facts' which linked the magazines with the earlier self-educational journals. The readers were loyal and persevering, ready to learn what the writers insisted on telling them.

In 1891, for example, when *The Strand* first appeared, George

Newnes 'respectfully placed his first number in the hands of the public', hoping, as he said, to justify its survival in spite of the 'vast number of existing monthlies'. Newnes opened with an absurd romance by Grant Allen in which the heroine faints on a railway line and the hero (called Ughtred Carnegie) has to decide whether to save her and derail the oncoming express, or to leave her to her fate. Next there are 'portraits of celebrities' (Tennyson, Swinburne, Rider Haggard, Sir John Lubbock, representing three parts of literature to one of science), notes from a sermon by Cardinal Manning, and a feature on the Metropolitan Fire Brigade, which opens:

> Fire! Fire! This startling cry aroused me one night as I was putting the finishing touches to some literary work. Rushing pen in hand to the window I could just perceive a dull red glare in the northern sky.

This leads to yet another rescue, when at the scene of the fire 'a female form appears at an upper window'. If it had not been a female form, or failing that, a child, it would have not been interesting enough for *The Strand*.

Charlotte's first venture, *The Minnow Fishers*, was in this 'curious personal experience' category, much in demand from editors and readers. It was based on a real incident during one of her walks along the canal towpath to Maida Vale, on the way to Kensal Green, where her grandfather Henry Kendall lay buried. The Minnow Fishers are small boys on this towpath, intent on their lines and hooks. They don't apparently notice that an even smaller child is struggling in the water 'or if they had it didn't detract them from the business in hand'. For this detachment Charlotte feels a kind of admiration. The drowning child is dragged out by a passer-by, and one of the boys has to admit to being the elder brother of this 'miserable object blinking palely out again at life, laboriously restored to the damp dusk, the cheerless outlook of the dingy stretches of the bank, the stagnant water and the impassive friends'. The brother is obliged to take the victim home, but gives him 'a vindictive cuff, which met with no response. The two remaining minnow fishers sat serenely on.'

In its sympathetic view of children hard, or hardened, as nails, this story makes a good introduction to Charlotte Mew's London. One detail, the bloated face of the rescued infant, 'a painful spectacle, suggestive of a crimson airball, a gruesome penny toy', shows that she is describing something actually seen. What is surprising is how little, after all, she seems to have learned from Miss Harrison's English lessons. Charlotte always had trouble with grammar and punctuation, but, apart from that, the presentation of the story is laborious in the extreme, opening with

> It was an after-dinner patter; someone had been generalizing on the elevating influence of sports, of angling in particular: 'And thereby,' interposed my friend, John Hilton, 'hangs a tale; it was when we lived near Maida Vale of Melancholy Memory: I was walking home one horribly damp afternoon by way of the canal'. . .

and so on. This very short story hardly needs the 'after-dinner patter' or John Hilton either: he is simply a device, or rather a gallant attempt to adapt to the fiction market. And he was not of much use to Charlotte, who was unable to place *The Minnow Fishers*, although she put it by and sent it later to *The Outlook*. She would have to try a different tack.

The epigraph to *The Minnow Fishers* is from Richard Jefferies, 'to be calm without mental fear is the ideal of nature'. Charlotte, from her school days, kept lists of quotations from favourite authors, copying out sentences that seemed to her helpful and true. In 1889 she had been reading Jefferies' *Field and Hedgerow*, his last essays, a book published after his death. 'It set my own heart beating,' she wrote, 'for I felt I discovered in it an undreamed-of universe.' Jefferies' large claims to have learned 'the spirit of earth and sea and the soul of the sun' answered to her own intimations, feelings beyond words that had come to her as a child on the Island.

> They come at evening with the home-flying rooks and the scent of hay,
> Over the fields. They come in spring.

Field and Hedgerow, like her own vision of nature's peace, was a relief from what she called 'pavement dreams – those thoughts that come sometimes in cities, of the weary length or terrible brevity of life'. The trouble was, and she knew this very well herself, that she was an incurable Londoner. The intimations would not hold. She wanted company, even when she was declaring she didn't, she loved hurrying from one appointment to another, and feeling all round her the pressure of a million unknown lives. Jefferies himself, in *Amaryllis at the Fair*, has a sudden glimpse of the 'terrible, beautiful thickness of people' in the London streets, 'so many, like the opulence of Nature itself'. How well she understood this Charlotte showed in one of her last poems, *The Shade-Catchers*.

At about this time Anne brought a new friend home to Gordon Street, a student from the Female School of Art, Elsie Millard. Elsie's father was elocution master at the City of London School; her elder sister, Evelyn, was on the stage. Evelyn had been rigorously trained in her father's personal system, based on a selection of speeches from Shakespeare arranged alphabetically to illustrate the whole range of emotions from Ambition and Anger to Unimpassioned speech, Violence, Wistfulness and Zeal. In 1891 she was appearing at the Grand Theatre, Islington, in *Joseph's Sweetheart*, but her speciality was in 'perfect lady' parts and her great successes were to be in Pinero's *The Second Mrs Tanqueray* and as Princess Flavia in *The Prisoner of Zenda*. Elsie, who preferred landscape painting, occasionally made sketching trips to the West of Ireland. The Millards were eminently respectable – they lived in Kensington, and were strict Catholics – but they did bring Charlotte, for the first time, into the fringe of the theatrical and studio world.

A break with the past came in 1893, with the death of Elizabeth Goodman. At the age of sixty-nine she contracted blood poisoning, as the result of running a needle into her hand. She had always wanted to die in harness, and she did. But after it was all over a strange group of Goodman relatives and in-laws, whom no-one had ever heard of before, turned up to take away her few belongings in a cab. They insisted on

arranging the funeral, 'not without some bitterness'. Charlotte
felt they made the house smell. 'Their moral and physical odour
seemed to cling about it long after they had left it.' An interesting point is her attitude to Elizabeth Goodman's 'plausible
greasy sister-in-law, who was alleged to be an artist's model
and when not sitting to someone or other was said to be nursing
an invalid gentleman at Boulogne or Worthing or Ostend.' In
short, she was a kept woman, 'always taking expensive medicines and borrowing railway fares', and this is what Charlotte
felt about such women when she actually met them. In contrast, she went on romanticizing the Magdalens and pale
harlots of the pavements and street lights, creatures of the
abyss, seen only in passing. In this matter Charlotte Mew was
truly a child of the 1890s.

Nothing of Elizabeth Goodman's was left at 9 Gordon Street
– not even her workbox, or her Queen Victoria Jubilee tea-pot.
How deeply and how confusedly Charlotte felt the loss can be
seen from a curious fantasy which she wrote, *A Wedding Day*.
The bride, in the excitement of her marriage, forgets the old
woman who has looked after her since she was a child. The old
woman, tired out by a lifetime's work, sits in her spotless cap
and apron, with her Bible and workbox on her knee, waiting in
vain for the expected visit. During the bridal night itself, when
for the lovers 'the present is eternity', the old woman dies. As a
corpse she is still sitting stiffly the next morning in her chair,
'alone and smiling'. She has remained on duty.

Charlotte was twenty-five. *The Minnow Fishers* had not been
accepted so far, nor had *A Wedding Day*. In 1894, in common
with most of London's hopeful writers, she saw the preliminary
announcement of yet another magazine, this time a new
quarterly. 'In many ways its contributors will employ a freer
hand than the limitations of the old-fashioned periodical can
permit. It will publish no serials; but its complete stories will
sometimes run to a considerable length in themselves.' The
notice was printed on bright yellow paper, with a bizarre
illustration by Aubrey Beardsley. 'And while *The Yellow Book*
will seek always to preserve a delicate, decorous and reticent
mien and conduct, it will at the same time have the courage of

its modernness, and not tremble at the frown of Mrs Grundy.'
Although John Lane, the publisher, was every bit as commer-
cially-minded as Newnes, the élitist tone of all this contrasted
boldly with *The Strand*, which had been 'respectfully placed' in
the hands of the public. *The Yellow Book* also promised to be
important, charming, daring and distinguished, and the editor
was prepared to consider contributions.

CHAPTER 5

A Yellow Book Woman

JOHN LANE, who launched *The Yellow Book* with his partner, Elkin Mathews, was (in Arthur Waugh's phrase) 'a sly newcomer', or, to put it another way, a publisher with a fine instinct for the right moment. In 1893–4 he sensed that the Aesthetes had still a little distance to go, and could contribute to the beautiful book-making which he loved. On the other hand, he could cautiously scent the new movements, women's independence in particular. He was projecting his *Eve's Library* (the title itself is a Lane-like compromise) which was to include a translation of Hansson's *Das Buch der Frauen* and studies called *The Ascent of Woman* and *Marriage Questions in Modern Fiction*. Meanwhile, when Aubrey Beardsley and Henry Harland came to him with their idea for the new quarterly, distinguished in contents and make-up, but bound in lemon-yellow, the colour of dubious French paperbacks, Lane realized that there was something in it for him. With the attention-catching *Yellow Book* he could trap new authors on to his list and publicize those he had already. 'Modernness', yes – no stirring yarns, no serials, no rescue from the railway-line – but Lane wanted Harland, while looking around for new talent and creating an agreeable stir, to keep his head. The down-and-out element on Lane's list, unfortunates like Ernest Dowson and Lionel Johnson, who was drinking himself to death on eau-de-cologne, all the pale infusion of French symbolism and post-Pre-Raphaelitism, even Aubrey Beardsley himself, could all be got rid of if necessary, and so indeed, before long, they were. Lane was the coming publisher, poised between the old century and the new, and making a profit from both.

Henry Harland, his editor, was a very different kind of

57

literary man, a garrulous flamboyant New Yorker, unpredictable except in his kindness. Although he wrote a great deal himself, favouring at this particular time a style half way between Maupassant and George du Maurier, his real talent lay in encouraging others. He was a champion of the short story, even a martyr to it, since underneath his party-giving geniality he was already mortally sick with tuberculosis.

Harland loved his contributors, whenever that was possible, and was loved. He was 'the Chief', with a rare editorial temperament, putting all his knowledge of the business at their disposal, and working passionately over their copy. Yet he allowed himself to be laughed at. He could in fact be quite childish, buttoning up his waistcoat over two cushions to appear unnaturally stout, or telling his guests – though always with great charm – that there was nothing to eat in the place and he could only conclude that he must have been drunk when he invited them. But the next step would be to some little French restaurant, where everyone could talk till the stars grew pale. When Aline, his wife, arrived from America, there might be arguments on a heroic scale, and a crockery-throwing element was added to the Harlands' true commitment to music and literature. The editorial desk was disorderly, and the Chief relied on his assistant, Ella d'Arcy (not really anything as grand as an assistant, she said, all she did was to tidy up the drawers and put the typescripts at the bottom to the top), to meet the printer's deadline. Before Ella volunteered for the job, however, and while there was still clear space on the desk, Harland and Beardsley brought out the first number of *The Yellow Book*.

All who paid their five shillings expected something extraordinary; most were outraged by Arthur Symons's *Stella Maris*, written a long way after Rossetti's *Jenny*, and glorifying the 'delicious shame' of some long past night with a prostitute, or, as he calls her, a 'Juliet of the Streets'. Symons's piece yearns back to the faint end-time of the last Romantics, and Beardsley's *Night Piece*, which does duty as an illustration, is precisely of the nineties. Ella d'Arcy's short story *Irremediable*, however, looks forward to the coming psychological novel. Understated, economical and subtle, the story is one of what she called her 'monochromes'. The husband no longer loves his intensely irritating wife who can't even shut the door properly, or 'do one mortal thing efficiently or well'. But in the end he accepts that she will always be the centre of his life, because hate is stronger than love.

Charlotte Mew seems not to have written her next story, *Passed*, until she had read *The Yellow Book*'s opening number. By this I don't mean that she was waiting to see what sort of thing would suit, rather that reading it set her imagination free. *Passed* bears every sign of being written at top speed, projected with not much conscious control from the level which her life as Miss Lotti suppressed. The narrator, who appears to be a well-off young woman, given, however, to ranging the London streets at the mercy of her own 'warring nature', suddenly rushes out of her comfortable home on a cold December evening. She enters a Roman Catholic church (which seems to be St James's, Spanish Place), and in the lamp-lit darkness sees a girl kneeling in 'unquestionable despair', a 'wildly tossed spirit' who appeals silently for help. 'Did she reach me, or was our advance mutual? It cannot be told. I suppose we neither know. [sic]' They hurry together through mean crowded streets to a wretched tenement, where the girl's sister lies dying; their last possessions, a chair and an inlaid work-box, have been put on the fire. We are to understand that they have come down in the world and the sister has been seduced by a lord, or at least by a clubman, as fragments of a letter on crested paper are lying on the quilt. The fragrance of a bunch of 'dearly-bought' violets, in a tea-cup at the bedside, strays through the room.

> Indisputably, I determined, something must be done for the half-frantic wanderer who was pressing a tiring weight against me. And there should be some kind hand to cover the cold limbs and close the wide eyes of the sleeper. . . . The dark eyes unwillingly open reached mine in an insistent stare. One hand lying out upon the coverlid, I could never again mistake for that of temporarily suspended life. My watch ticked loudly, but I dare not examine it, nor could I wrench my sight from the figure on the bed. . . .
>
> My gaze was chained: it could not get free. As the shapes of monsters of ever varying and increasing dreadfulness flit

through one's dreams, the images of those I loved crept round
me, with stark yet well-known features, their limbs borrowing
death's rigid outline, as they mocked my recognition with
soundless semblances of mirth. . . . The horribly familiar company began to dance at intervals in and out of a ring of white
gigantic bedsteads, set on end like tombstones, each of which
framed a huge and fearful travesty of the sad set face that was all
the while seeking vainly a pitiless stranger's care.

In spite of this Poe-like vision, the narrator harshly refuses to
stay. Suppressing her own conscience, she escapes (a cab
happens to be passing) to her own home and family. Her
brother's friends have arrived, there are lights and dancing,
and she waltzes all night. The next day, feeling uneasy, she goes
back to the church, where she is vexed by a 'mumbling priest'
and empty ritual. Then two children come in hand in hand, one
of them an idiot. 'Her shifting eyes and ceaseless imbecile
grimace chilled my blood. The other, who stood praying,
turned suddenly and kissed the dreadful creature by her side
. . . I shuddered, and yet her face wore no look of loathing nor of
pity. The expression was a divine one of habitual love.'
Snow is falling as the narrator (who is never given a name)
leaves the church, conscience-stricken. Her only chance of
peace is to find the girl she rejected so cruelly the night before
and make amends. But no one knows anything, no one can
direct her, the search is useless. 'Some months afterwards,' in a
large glittering shopping street, the girl walks past her, clinging
to the arm of a man. Obviously she is now a prostitute, or, as
Charlotte puts it, one of 'the dazzling wares of the human mart'.
And the man – the same man, of course, who seduced the sister
– is wearing a buttonhole of scented violets. The story ends with
'a laugh mounting to a cry. . . . Did it proceed from some
defeated angel? Or the woman's mouth? Or mine? God knows.'
Passed seems almost as over-written as a story can be,
hurrying along in distraught paragraphs, only just hanging on,
for decency's sake, to its rags of English grammar. Odd though
it is, the elements are familiar. The overwrought narrator has
something about her of Lucy Snow in *Villette*, and there are
echoes of Charlotte Brontë's 'flash-eliciting, truth-extorting'

style. The pathos of the bunch of violets suggests a number of popular novels, in particular Rhoda Broughton's *Not Wisely But Too Well*. The whole business of hurrying in desperation through a maze of mean streets is one of romance's standbys. Dickens, if he didn't invent it, used it to great effect for poor Florence Dombey and Little Dorrit. As to the blank encounter and the cry of despair at the end of *Passed*, not to mention the mumbling priest and the cynical seducer, they are part of the mythology of the nineteenth century's unreal city.

All the same, *Passed* makes its impact. Charlotte originally gave it the title *Violets*, but *Passed* gives a better sense of missed opportunity. Her story is impossible, but it is true. The real subject is guilt – the guilt of the provided-for towards the poor, the sane towards the mad, and the living towards the dead. The motive force is everything she had once half-understood about Miss Bolt and the disgraceful Fanny, all her feelings for her mad brother and sister, for her dead little brother and the dead Elizabeth Goodman, even for Anne. These had to be expressed in images, or they would have broken her.

Harland loved *Passed*. True, he favoured hurrying-through-the-mean-streets stories, and was to accept some particularly absurd examples. But *Passed* seemed to him not only a remarkable literary achievement, but original, and therefore bound to be violently abused, which was just what *The Yellow Book* wanted. He wrote (28 April 1894) a letter of acceptance, with two qualifications – he couldn't pay much, and he would like one or two 'very trifling' changes in the text. According to Harland, he had to read mountains of manuscripts every day, and nine hundred and ninety-nine out of a thousand were rubbish. When he picked one up at random he assumed it would be worthless, but this time he had a strange presentiment, and had turned to his sub-editor and told him he felt he was going to make a great find. This, of course, is the way editors talk, American ones in particular. It gave Harland the opportunity to ask Charlotte to call on him at his flat, 144 Cromwell Road, at 3 p.m. the following Monday.

Charlotte by this time had taken to wearing a mannish black velvet jacket and tweed skirt, as close as possible to Lucy

Harrison's style, but in a miniature version. Her manner was unpredictable, but it would have taken more than that to disconcert Harland, who was used to dealing with Aubrey Beardsley and his sister Mabel, 'Graham Tomson' and 'George Egerton' (who were both strong-minded women), the ambiguous Frederick Rolfe, and the novelist 'Victoria Crosse' who specialized in faintly moustached heroines. Charlotte, however, seems not to have set out to intrigue or amuse him, although she could have done both. She simply asked whether she could be paid at once. This in itself is an indication of how things were at 9 Gordon Street.

Harland sheltered behind his publishers, telling her that they normally paid on publication, but that if she was really in difficulties (most of his authors were, but he made it sound something quite unusual) he would 'speak to Mr Lane'. Lane, as he very well knew, was generous, but neither prompt nor just in making payments. (The only one of his writers who ever got the better of him was Laurence Housman, who wired: 'Dear Lane, my rascal of a publisher won't settle my account. Can you lend me £50?') Tactfully enough, Harland turned the subject to the trifling alterations. He wanted the story toned down, particularly 'the description of your almost delirious horror in the presence of the dead'. 'The starting eyeballs' ought to be cut out, too, and the 'stiffening limbs'. 'Of course the substance wouldn't be altered,' he told the protesting Charlotte, and he very much admired the psychology of the story and the strong sensual impressions; it was just that poignant subjects were best treated lightly and easily, and allowed to speak for themselves. This was very good advice, and Charlotte Mew always wrote at her best when she followed it.

He asked her to call again so that he could go over the whole piece with her, point by point. *Passed* was published in its revised form in the second volume of *The Yellow Book*, for July 1894. This meant that Charlotte made her first appearance in most distinguished company, alongside Henry James's *The Coxon Fund*, Ella d'Arcy's brilliant *Cousin Louis* and John Davidson's *Thirty Bob a Week*. There were six drawings by Beardsley, including one of the most striking he ever did, *Garçons de Café*, and Charlotte was placed well up the paper, at No. VI. She could hardly have made a better start.

That summer she entered the new world of the New Woman. It was an exhilarating place, which Netta Syrett describes in her autobiography *The Sheltering Tree* and Evelyn Sharp in *Unfinished Adventure*. Although the public, discreetly prompted by Lane, thought of *The Yellow Book* as bizarre and decadent, and though its male writers were often alcoholic, weak-willed and tired of life, its women were strong. Evelyn Sharp, who was one of them, wrote that they 'felt on the crest of the wave that was sweeping away the Victorian tradition', and that everything must go. Netta, Evelyn and Ella d'Arcy, like Charlotte, had seen *The Yellow Book* announcement and sent in their first contributions to Lane. They were also among Lane's Keynotes – that is, they contributed to a special 'advanced' series of stories, each with their own Keynote, designed by Beardsley. 'Petticoat' Lane liked to be seen with women round him, 'and we fell in and out of love,' said Evelyn, 'with or without disaster, like other people'. They would find time for marriage some day, but not yet, there was too much in hand. Everything was open for discussion. Netta Syrett, in particular, talked unconcernedly about sex, for her uncle, the writer Grant Allen, was a frank materialist and had brought her up to do so. But this was only one aspect of a world that had grown limitless, but still had to be put to rights. Skimming from one end of London to the other on their bicycles, without fear, without chaperones, they lodged two and two in flats, or in the newly opened Victorian Club in Sackville Street, which had small, cold, candle-lit bedrooms for professional women. If need arose they could emerge *soignées* and glittering, in the full evening dress of the nineties. These young women were not Bohemians, they were dandies. They complained when the down-and-out Frederick Rolfe, on his visits to Harland's flat, left lice on the furniture. Aubrey Beardsley was 'a dear boy' to them. They had no intention of drifting or failing, they meant to rise with the coming twentieth century.

All of them loved Henry Harland, who knew exactly how to

treat them. 'Darling of my heart!' he greeted them, 'Child of my editing!' When he had to give in, at last, to ill-health, and retired to Dieppe, they descended like a welcome flock of birds on his villa, and later at his boarding-house. There, according to Evelyn Sharp, the dying Harland was Harland still. Asked by the lady next to him to pass the salt, he exclaimed: 'Dear lady, it is yours! And may I not also pass you the mustard?'

Charlotte Mew certainly went to the Harlands' Saturday evenings in Cromwell Road, in the pink drawing-room with its Persian carpet, evenings to remember, when there were songs at the piano in French, Italian and German, and the young ones gazed in reverence at Henry James, who walked up and down the room, searching for a word to finish his sentence. Everyone knew what it was, but nobody dared to supply it. Harland himself, though often drunk, was never at a loss; the other young women had much more confidence than Charlotte in dealing with life, although her experience of suffering went quite as deep as theirs. Among unfamiliar faces, she was still uncertain of herself.

But to her old friends – the Olivers, the Chicks, dreary Maggie Browne, even the Millards – Charlotte seemed to have become precisely the New Woman of whom the newspapers complained. It was true that she was still living with her family, but now she ranged about London in her tailor-mades and close-cropped hair, dropping in on new acquaintances, or watching the street life. She used rough language which they had never heard from her before. She smoked continually, rolling her own cigarettes. Her head may have been turned a little in the summer of 1894. But if it was, and if she neglected Anne and these old friends a little, they made no protest. They had always known she would distinguish herself.

Of all *The Yellow Book* women whom Charlotte met during those months, the one who deeply impressed her was Harland's enigmatic, handsome 'office help', Ella D'Arcy. Ella (it was her real name, though publishers wouldn't believe it) was born in 1857, the daughter of an Irish grain merchant. She had been brought up in the Channel Islands, talked French fluently, and had once hoped to be painter. When she was just about to leave

Ella D'Arcy (P. Wilson Steer: *A Lady*)
'. . . a brutal portrait of me by Wilson Steer . . .'

the Slade, however, to study in Paris, her eyes began to trouble her, and she had taken, with a kind of casual energy, to writing. After sending out a quantity of short stories, with very few acceptances, she too had seen *The Yellow Book* announcement. Her *Irremediable*, which appeared in the first number, had already been turned down by *Blackwood's* because the editor thought it treated marriage with insufficient respect. Harland saw its quality at once, and begged her for more. She became *The Yellow Book*'s most frequent contributor, and all her stories are good, though they go back time and again to the subject of the ordinary decent man reduced to nothing by a stupid woman. This pity for men can only have come from her own good nature. She had a hard enough struggle to support herself, and took lovers as she chose, without drawing any particular attention to it. Frederick Rolfe, who could not stand her (it was Ella who had complained about his lice), called her a 'mouse-mannered piece of sex', probably Harland's mistress. What was more, he said, she had stolen two volumes of Harland's Encyclopaedia. But 'mouse-mannered' seems not quite right for this dark, handsome, untidy-looking, witty woman, who was more likely to give than to take. It was from her that Charlotte learned for the first time to read French literature, Flaubert in particular. Ella lent her the just-published four volumes of Flaubert's correspondence, and probably pressed on her, as she did on everyone, Rimbaud's *Illuminations*. But here Ella was ahead of her time and could not find, she said, in the whole of England, anyone to understand Rimbaud.

All the Keynotes worried over Ella's penniless state. It was no good asking her to stay, she was 'Goblin Ella', come and gone while your back was turned. Her worries at this time went deeper than most of them guessed. But she shrugged them off. About her entire behaviour there seemed to be a kind of heedless fascination which turned the whole current of Charlotte's being painfully towards her. Then, just as Charlotte was getting down to work on a new story, something longer, she hoped, and more ambitious, Ella disappeared. She went first to the Channel Islands, then to Juan les Pins, then took a room in Paris.

CHAPTER 6

The China Bowl

HARLAND is said to have told Charlotte Mew that if she gave up her family and friends, and shut herself away to write, she could do wonders. This may well have been one of his general stock of editor's remarks, and it shows that he knew nothing about the oppressive secrets of 9 Gordon Street, but if he had no means of understanding Charlotte, he certainly intended to encourage her. It was greatly to her credit that she didn't attempt another study in the style of *Passed*, which he had liked so much, or, indeed, in the style of anything else which had appeared in *The Yellow Book*.

She wanted a different setting and other lives than her own. *The China Bowl* is a long and tragic story of a Cornish fisherman, David Parris, torn between his proud mother and his savage wife. The wife, to assert her independence, sells a china bowl, the family heirloom, to an artistic 'lady visitor'. David for the only time in his life loses his temper and, although his wife is pregnant, hits her. She leaves home and in desperation he takes out his boat in a storm and is lost at sea.

It sounds like a regional play for radio and that, in fact, sixty years later, was what it became. But why did Charlotte Mew write it in 1895? She made her first visit to Cornwall in the nineties, and it left her, as she said, homesick to the end of her life for 'Newlyn lights'. Newlyn was then still a fishing village, whose street and harbour lights shone suddenly out of the darkness as you walked round the headland by the coast road, but since the 1880s a community of artists had settled in, with the doubtful approval of the locals, and formed a kind of *Plein Air* school of genre painting. In summer there were concerts and studio exhibitions and lodgings in the whitewashed cottages for Londoners, and it is significant that in Charlotte's story the 'artistic lady visitor' plays an ungrateful part. It is as though she was seeing herself, as she often did, with painful irony, from the outside.

In Cornwall Charlotte, who was a passionate reader of Thomas Hardy, recognized the truth of a passage in his preface to *A Pair of Blue Eyes*: 'The place is pre-eminently (for one person at least) the region of dream and mystery. The ghostly birds, the pall-like sea, the frothy wind, the eternal soliloquy of the waters, the bloom of dark purple cast that seems to exhale from the shoreward precipices, in themselves lend to the scene an atmosphere like the twilight of a night vision.' The women of her story, too, are Hardy-like in their strength, but in *A Pair of Blue Eyes* itself the only character who is actually Cornish is William Worm, described by Hardy as 'a dazed factotum' and brought in purely for comic relief.

Charlotte seems to have studied the dialect for herself, and tried to use it seriously. The starting-point of her story was probably the best-known picture of the whole Newlyn school, Frank Bramley's *Hopeless Dawn*. Bought by the Chantrey Bequest in 1888, it was a favourite with the public then, and still is. In this cottage scene the old mother and her daughter-in-law sit together as the first light breaks, waiting in vain for news of their man out at sea. On the table are two china bowls which Bramley, who specialized in cross-lights, put there to reflect the first gleam from the window. The bowls are much finer in quality than anything else in the room. They seem to suggest a story of their own.

But in spite of her commitment to *The China Bowl*, Charlotte could not quite bring it off. Her three main characters are stylized almost to the extent of the Aran islanders in *Riders to the Sea* (which, however, was written eight years later) but without Synge's lucky touch. They are stiff, as though they had learned their parts with an effort. David is absurdly noble, and although Susannah's fierce rebellion and her determination to be something on her own account are deeply felt, she is not too convincing either. The curious thing is that Charlotte had been familiar with storms and fishing-boats since she was a child,

Frank Bramley: *Hopeless Dawn* (Tate Gallery)

and if she had set her story in the Isle of Wight she would have had no trouble with the dialect at all, it would have come to her naturally. But clearly that was impossible. The Island was no longer picturesque to her. The Mews went there now only to visit Freda in the Whitelands Mental Hospital.

The fifteen thousand word manuscript arrived in Harland's flat in the January of 1895. The Chief seems to have been somewhat taken aback, but rose to the challenge, writing that it was the greatest literary experience he had enjoyed this long while. *The China Bowl* had 'supreme emotion and true tragic sense' and he compared the style to the rich and beautiful notes of 'cello music. He was confined to Cromwell Road at the moment, not being able to face the January fog, but he would tell his wife to write and propose a day for Charlotte to come to tea. One senses a note of caution here. Harland added that there was only one drawback. He had to admit that *The China Bowl*, as it stood, was too long for *The Yellow Book*.

But it was not as long as Henry James's *The Coxon Fund*, which Harland had printed in July 1894 alongside Charlotte's *Passed*, and he must have known this, and known that she knew it. He had, however, another suggestion – *The China Bowl* might go into a collection which he was anxious to make (presumably for publication by Lane). In fact, that was why he was so impatient for the tea-party. He had a million things to say, but he particularly wanted to discuss the collection.

Charlotte was hurt. She believed she had put her very best into her Cornish tragedy. Writers are not rational on the subject of their favourite work. But in any case it was character-istic of her that after a disappointment she closed up, and said no more about it. *The China Bowl* had not been thought good enough for *The Yellow Book*. She threw it into a drawer and left it there for three years.

After this she never contributed to *The Yellow Book* again. The reason for this, however, was peculiar to Miss Lotti. In April 1895 the scandal of Oscar Wilde's arrest became public news, and *The Yellow Book* (for which he had never written anything) was involved in his headlong fall to disgrace. The public's instinct connected Beardsley with Wilde, as someone much too clever and therefore unwholesome and expendable. Stones were thrown at the windows of John Lane's office in Vigo Street, Beardsley was dismissed and the magazine, after mis-sing one number, was reorganized without him. Lane himself was in America at the time and Ella D'Arcy always insisted that if he had been there things would have gone very differently. But they were left to Chapman, the office manager, who lost his head.

Charlotte felt the shock partly through Ella (who was in the Channel Islands at the time, trying to save money) but also through her friends the Millards. In February Evelyn Millard had opened at the St James's as Cecily Cardew in *The Importance of Being Earnest*. In April, after Wilde had been arrested, the management took his name off the programmes and the front of the theatre, and the run was cut short. The curious and pathetic side of Charlotte which felt even the faintest breath of scandal as a threat told her that she must have nothing more to do with *The Yellow Book*, even in its more sober form, or even with Harland and his million things to say. She was mistaken, because *The Yellow Book* circle was the one that suited her best, perhaps the only one, except for her own family, where she ever felt not at odds. After she left the Chief she did not find anyone to encourage her with the same whole-heartedness for another seventeen years. What was more, the break she had made was not complete, because she was in love with Ella D'Arcy.

CHAPTER 7

Nunhead and St Gildas

FOR A YEAR OR SO Charlotte had been in demand, always getting dressed to go and meet someone or other. Now she had serious duties at home. Poor Fred Mew showed no signs of getting any new commissions, and if he had he couldn't have undertaken them. By the end of the nineties he was very ill; the doctor diagnosed cancer of the stomach. He died on 13 September 1898, of cancer and extreme exhaustion. The certificate shows that Charlotte was with him at the end, and witnessed the death. By and large, he had not had much of a life of it. He had dropped out of his profession to such an extent that *The Builder* did not event print a memorial note until the following year.

Fred Mew left about £2000 in all. Anna Maria's contention was, as it always had been, that she had been betrayed and ill-treated, but that at all costs she must stay in Gordon Street, or her last hope of respectability would be gone. On the other hand, they could scarcely afford it. Fred, as was now quite clear, had been paying the rent and the bills out of capital. From Anna Maria's inheritance an annuity of £300 a year came in, but from that the Mews had Henry and Freda and their private nurses to support, as well as themselves.

Charlotte, taking charge, wrote to Walter Barnes Mew, and put it to him that her mother must not be separated from 'the few friends she has left to her'; and although Walter can't much have liked the implied criticism of his uncle, he was ready to give what help he could. Charlotte's idea was the last resort, which at all costs must be concealed from the world at large; lodgers. She had calculated that they could ask £100 p.a. for the six rooms on the two top floors and 'use of bathroom'. To find a tenant who would be unobtrusive enough to suit them she was looking for a good house-agent. As soon as she found one she wanted Walter to 'speak' to him. He also had to 'speak' to the Registrar, who had put 'Maw' instead of 'Mew' on the certificate, as though poor Fred had lost, in the end, even his own name.

The matter of men having to do the speaking divided Miss Lotti once again from the buoyant New Women, who did their own speaking for themselves and no longer felt a deep shame in letting off part of the house. Only a little while later Vanessa and Virginia Stephen divided up 46 Gordon Square, just round the corner from Gordon Street, into a kind of intellectual rooming-house, while in Doughty Street, the Mews' old home, both men and women were moving into the Havelock Ellises' communal house, the fellowship of the New Life. These hints of the coming twentieth century meant nothing to Charlotte and Anne, who were only concerned to see that their mother should have nothing to do with actually collecting the rent, and so would be spared as much as possible of the terrible humiliation. A long-term tenant, a widow, Mrs Caroline Gordon Lennox McHardy, moved in, and some arrangement must have been come to about the front stairs, on which she must never be met.

There were further possibilities. Anne might undertake small commissions at home, say screen-painting or furniture-painting of anything that, in 1900, needed to be decorated with birds and wreaths of flowers. Charlotte wrote (22nd June) to their landlords, the trustees of the Bedford Estate, to ask if they would grant permission for a studio to be built in the small piece of garden behind the house. She very sensibly thought it best not to make it clear how she and Anne proposed to make use of this studio, simply pointing out that they had been left in 'much reduced circumstances' by their father's death, and that with the help of friends (names not given) they believed they could increase the value of the property. If the studio was built, she hoped the trustees would see their way to extending the lease.

The trustees replied on the 25th June that they would have to see the plans and specifications of anything the Mews intended to build, but under no circumstances would they consider

73

extending the lease. As they no doubt calculated, nothing more was heard of the studio, and Anne, for the time being, continued to paint in her own room. She was also employed for a few hours every week at a ladylike – meaning badly paid – job with a guild of decorative artists. At the same time Charlotte began to place her work with another magazine, a monthly, *Temple Bar*; she had been recommended to it by a friend, Mrs Clement Parsons, who was a writer herself on educational subjects.

Temple Bar had been going since 1860, but its great days, if it had ever had any, had long been over. In its dull pink binding, with a forbidding print of the old Temple Bar, it made little attempt at either popular or aesthetic appeal. It had no illustrations, and was so closely printed that the readers must have risked eyestrain with each successive number. By the 1890s it was being passed from one editor to another. None of them had Henry Harland's flair, nor did they need it to put *Temple Bar* together. The fiction's main support was Maarten Maartens (Joost Marins Van der Poorten Schwartz) who wrote reliable tales on solid Dutch subjects. Strong digestions from the readership were needed for the dry masses of information in the feature pages, and the editor may well have been surprised to get in anything as lively and passionate as *The China Bowl*. Charlotte's story appeared in two parts in the September and October of 1899. After this, she became a regular contributor. But she must have missed Harland, and even more so when she wrote *The Governess in Fiction*, a somewhat tired little piece which she sent to *The Academy*. *The Academy*'s editor cut her article down and altered it, and all she could afford to do was to refuse to let it appear over her own name and to sign it simply M.

It was a cautious start into the new century, from which so much was expected, and which was majestically marked by the passing of the old Queen. For everyone who could afford them, there were hopes. From the anxious edge of the professional and artistic world Charlotte got her view of the gospels of Life and Joy, the new call to the open road ('going I know not where'), the commitment to self-purification and vegetarian diets, to the City Beautiful and to youth, energy, humanity and fresh air.

Lucy Harrison herself, calling on poetry to open the soul's windows, had guided her classes in the same direction; so had *The Yellow Book* women with their latchkeys and bicycles. Charlotte, just turned thirty, tried to prepare herself to be carried forward or, if necessary, to be left behind. Her face at this time took on its habitual curious expression, with her strong eyebrows raised in a perpetual half-moon, as though she had just heard a joke, or perhaps thought that if life is a joke it is not a very good one.

On the 22nd of March 1901 Henry Herne Mew died of pneumonia in the Peckham Hospital. He was thirty-five, and was registered as having 'no occupation or calling'. Charlotte made arrangements for the funeral in the nearby Nunhead Cemetery. For the second time her elder brother was lost, but this time much more terribly. She had come to terms with Henry's madness, but not with the idea of his dying mad.

'Her fears began with her brother's death. He had the same trouble as Freda. She was profoundly unhappy for many years.' This comment on Charlotte was from Professor A. G. Tansley, who married her old school friend Elsie Chick. Like most of her friends' husbands, he seems to have been half-fascinated, half-distressed by Charlotte. He was wrong in thinking that her 'fears' began in 1901, but right in guessing what the grim little private funeral meant to her.

> It is the clay that makes the earth stick to his spade;
> He fills in holes like this year after year;
> The others have gone; they were tired, and half-afraid
> But I would rather be standing here;

In *In Nunhead Cemetery*, which Charlotte wrote (like the asylum poems) ten years or more after the event, the elements of the real situation shift and re-arrange themselves, while the pity remains. The speaker here is a young man, most likely a city clerk, whose life has been totally transformed by his love for a girl. Before he met her he was a 'cheap, stale chap', but with her anything seemed possible; they didn't even mind the long wait before they could afford to get married, they walked about London together and were able to laugh 'like children'. Now she is dead, the funeral is over, he is standing in the cemetery

75

which he has seen time and again from the windows of the train, without thinking twice about it. The trains are still rattling past. As for children, the very idea of them nauseates him.

> One of the children hanging about
>   Pointed at the whole dreadful heap and smiled
> This morning, after *that* was carried out;
>   There is something terrible about a child.

The last fifty-four lines of the poem, Charlotte explained, were written first, and show 'the gradual lapse into insanity' as the clerk stands in the rain by the raw graveside.

> Now I will burn you back, I will burn you through,
>   Though I am damned for it, we two will lie
> And burn –

Sexual frustration can hardly be distinguished from fear as the twilight thickens: 'I am scared, I am staying with you to-night. Put me to sleep.' At last he has to admit that he has been cheated by Death in the shape of the Nunhead gravedigger. But if this man would only set about digging up all the mounds of rotting flowers, as he has it in his power to do, we should be able to see the faces of the dead again; and they might, after all, be alive.

In Nunhead Cemetery is a good example of Charlotte Mew's longer poems, giving 'the essence, never the solution of an idea . . . a psychological study that would have made a full six shilling novel if written by a novelist'. Her psychological study here, the speaker, that is, with whom she shows such ready sympathy, is the thirty-bob-a-weeker who appears so often in the period's fiction. He had been the hero (if he can ever be called that) of Ella's *Irremediable*, but he is also Kipling's young chemist's assistant possessed by the spirit of John Keats, and Forster's Leonard Bast, struggling to educate himself, and the 'pale bespectacled face' Edward Thomas described at the office window. Very few of these dreamers, beyond Wells's Kipps, ever get free from the desk and the counter, to finish up alive with the right woman. To aim so high seems to be destructive in itself.

But Charlotte Mew does more than pity the 'cheap, stale

chap'. She makes it clear that he is horribly aware of what has happened, but not of all his own motives, particularly his anger at the injustice done him after he has waited so long, and with such restraint. 'You never kissed me back.' He confuses the grave with her bed. The poem isn't about her suffering, but his own loss. That cannot be borne, and so there follows the 'lapse into insanity'.

It was felt, after Henry's death, that Charlotte ought to get away for a holiday. Her friends watched her changes of mood anxiously, though, to do her justice, she never asked them to, and was often taken aback by their kindness. In the June of 1901 they got together a party for a seaside holiday in Brittany. The convent of St Gildas de Rhuys, on the gulf of Morbihan, took in summer visitors, and they booked rooms there.

According to Charlotte's account the party consisted of 'six unmated females', all thirtyish, and all old school friends – a Botanist, a Zoologist, a Bacteriologist, a Vocalist, a Humorist and a Dilettante. The English party presented 'a bold un-chaperoned front' although a very different one from *The Yellow Book* women as they swooped untamed into Harland's villa in Dieppe. They had sixteen pieces of luggage between them. The Botanist was Edith Oliver, who had helped her father revise his official handbook to the Kew Gardens Museum. The Zoologist was Maggie Browne, the Vocalist was Florence Hughes, daughter of the painter Arthur Hughes, the Bacteriologist was Margaret Chick, the Dilettante was Anne (a painter without a studio), and Charlotte was, as she always had been at the Gower Street School, the Humorist. In the days when they had walked from Hampstead to Bloomsbury and back, she had 'carried on' and made the way seem short. Now, as they started out, she seemed in excellent spirits. Although they had a bad crossing she danced a can-can for them in the cabin, in her boots and silk directoire knickers. And no-one could dance as well as Charlotte, when she felt like it.

Charlotte's *Notes in a Brittany Convent* appeared in *Temple Bar*

(October 1901). It starts out in the approved lady journalist's style – stormy weather at Southampton, demanding cab-drivers at St Malo, 'spavined nags' (although there was no real reason for them to be any more spavined in France than in England), late arrival at the convent, which, they know, would be shut by nine o'clock.

> Thus we were rattled in procession through the grey, curious town like travellers in a dream, to be deposited opposite an unknown inn, in a dark street on the outskirts, into which hostelry our Jehu disappeared to have his supper . . . till the exasperated Botanist at length dashed in, and snatched the supping tyrant from his meal. Finally we jolted off, a huddled heap beneath a pyramid of oscillating trunks. After many stoppages, at some belated hour we drew up, got out and propped ourselves in an exhausted line against the convent wall. The great bell resounded with a startling clangour through the sleeping village. Two bright eyes and one soft voice behind a little *grille* at length examined us, and from our incoherent explanations rapidly concluded: '*Ah, les demoiselles anglaises!*' Who else, indeed, could such *drôles* be?
>
> The heavy gates clanked open, and our weird chaise clattered in; our *cocher* stacked our baggage in the sanctum of the little portress, who directed us to burrow for our nightgowns. Then with her lantern they led us across a courtyard and a stretch of garden, on through silent corridors, and paused: '*Vos chambres,*' said she, and vanished like an apparition. Whitewashed walls, a crucifix, a bed, a paradise in miniature! We staggered in, shut doors, and slept.

This is exactly what *Temple Bar*'s readers would expect. The French, they knew, are funny and untrustworthy, though controllable by anyone who is English and firm enough. At the same time the French language has a seductive effect which makes the writer put *drôles, cocher,* etc. far too often, and this gets worse and worse as the piece goes on. Again, there is something exotic about the heavy gates of the convent, and the 'soft voice and bright eyes' of the little portress suggest the wrong and un-English sacrifice of womanhood which the nuns are making in the name of religion. But their kindness and tranquillity, what about those? The unmated females are the champions of normality, putting up a good front against nonsense, but in a few days they are won over by a romantic and even sentimental vision of the whitecapped sisters. The church itself they still disapprove of sharply. A 'fat, damp, fatherly priest' who tries to convert them is easily routed, and a seminarist forgets his vows and listens dreamily to Florence Hughes singing 'Night of June' at the piano. This serves the priest and the seminarist right, but does not explain away the nuns, who have the tranquillity of the sunshine 'which suspends the breath of question'. Charlotte herself went to mass every day, and was uneasily impressed by the amount of work that had to be done in the convent to keep the holidaymakers going – washing, cooking, farm work, which would be even harder in winter. 'And then the winter sewing in the chill, dim rooms, where the high windows show a line of sea, or merely a grey patch of cloud cut by the cemetery crucifix, which stands out black against the sky.'

It is difficult to get a clear idea of Charlotte's religious position, and still more of her religious experience, at this point in her life. Her Isle of Wight cousin, Ellen Mary (who by this time had entered a convent), believed that Charlotte would have become a Roman Catholic if it hadn't been for the sacrament of confession. She could not bring herself to that. What is certain is that she had always had a devotion to the crucified, and a painful physical apprehension of the cross. 'He was alive to me, so hurt, so hurt!' But, as in everything else, she veered wildly from one position to another. In many people with divided natures the two selves, although they seem to be at odds, are really only surprised by each other, and even, as it were, congratulating each other. That was not so with Charlotte Mew, who always felt the wastefulness of conflict. Sometimes she blamed God for His negligence in not existing. At times she begged for peace at all costs, 'too sound for waking and for dreams too deep', sometimes she wanted, like Heine, to cling to this earth which, after all, is the best we can hope for. But unlike Heine she could not feel justified in this, or justified at all. She protested against suffering, but not against judgement. Her prayer, just as it was when she walked across the fields, as a small child, to Barton Church, was 'have mercy on us'.

The expedition to Brittany brought out the double nature and even the double-dealer in Charlotte. As the party's humorist, she was a success. There was, for example, a fellow-guest who could be heard praying loudly every night for the souls of 'the English party'. Charlotte did a good imitation of this woman. There were other 'coarse sallies', which upset the seminarist. These high spirits were just what her friends had hoped for. But there was something that escaped them. 'She could seem so gay and utterly without care that a friend of hers described her thus on a convent holiday in France, although all the time she was experiencing the great joy of being abroad she was writing letters to other friends recounting the misery and discontent she felt away from her normal surroundings.' From this time onwards she was usually careful to present edited versions of herself to those who were fond of her. This, I suppose, is not really double-dealing.

During the autumn and winter of 1901 Charlotte was under what she herself admitted was 'rather high pressure'. This pressure was then called 'nerves' (Edith Oliver called them 'the blues') and the advice given was usually to avoid morbid thoughts, and to pull oneself together. This was particularly necessary for 'unmated females'. In the spring of 1901 Elsie Millard, the most amusing of Charlotte's friends, got married, though not, as it happened, to anyone very amusing. She had chosen an Irish civil servant, James O'Keefe, who worked in the Treasury, and in his spare time edited old Irish texts. It was a Roman Catholic wedding with a bright, noisy child bridesmaid, Vivien Haigh-Wood (who grew up to be the first wife of T. S. Eliot). Charlotte must surely have had the same feelings as any other woman of thirty-two when her friends begin to settle down. Edith Oliver was still living at home in Kew, serenely occupied as a social worker and as deputy organist of St Mark's Church. Maggie Browne was never likely to change much, but two of the Chick girls were married by now, leaving only the eldest, Margaret, to write faithfully to the Mews. *The Yellow Book* women, of course, were survivors, although Henry Harland and Beardsley were in their graves.

But they had swept ahead in new directions, and Charlotte was no longer in step.

She set herself to work in a less haphazard way than usual, and placed her study of the old dressmaker, Miss Bolt, in *Temple Bar*, as well as the *Notes in a Brittany Convent*. In September she appeared for the first time in the *Pall Mall Magazine*, edited by Frederic Greenwood, with *Some Ways of Love*. This was a society romance, in the manner of Paul Bourget ('"And so you send me away unanswered," said the young man, rising reluctantly and taking his gloves from the table'). It shows, at least, a determined attempt to be professional, and also the course of Charlotte's thoughts. The heroine, who teaches the hero that there are many ways of love, is called Ella.

Ella D'Arcy was still in Paris. In the ordinary way Charlotte could hardly have afforded to go abroad again so soon, but early in 1902 the finances at 9 Gordon Street improved a little. Mary Kendall, the Brighton aunt, died, leaving her household furniture and jewellery to Anna Maria; another trust was set up for Edward Herne Kendall, who was never likely to be able to provide for himself, and the rest of the estate, invested in two small house properties, went to Charlotte and Anne. This meant about £20 a year more for each of them, and (though they had been fond of their aunt) it must have given them a sensation of freedom. Charlotte at once set off for Paris.

Apart from her own family she seems to have told no-one but Edith Oliver, though Elsie, she wrote to Edith, 'understands'. And the quiet Edith, for her part, seems to have made no comment, but lent Charlotte a spirit-stove for making tea, of the kind then used by English ladies travelling abroad.

CHAPTER 8

Rue Chateaubriand

SINCE the early *Yellow Book* days Ella had fallen on lean times. She was getting on for forty, and hard up as always – 'I *do* care for money,' she said, 'having none' – and she had greatly overestimated her power over her publisher, John Lane. Lane was, of course, hung about with female authors, but Ella had always been attractive to men and gambled on holding him. It is sad to think of a rash and generous nature like hers reduced to such straits.

When Lane sailed for America in 1895 Ella had hoped to see him off at Euston, 'but no-one invited me to do so', she wrote to him, 'and I hadn't the cheek to come unasked'. She could send him letters, however. About the Oscar Wilde scandal she wrote surprisingly little – 'various little contretemps have arisen', as she put it – but stuck to her main point. 'Of course you won't answer this letter – you are Napoleonic even in trifles – so I don't ask you to do so; but I think it a pity you didn't take me with you as secretary, for then I could have answered it for you, couldn't I?' Her *Monochromes* in Lane's Keynotes had had more quality than almost anything else in the series; he knew she could write, and shouldn't have been deaf to her appeals. Scarcely able to pay her way, she flitted from one boarding-house to another, at one point lodging with a Spanish count who, she said, had reduced her meals to bread and water, and threatened to knock off the bread. Lane seems to have owed her small sums of money – small to him, but not to her – and he had the copyright of 'a brutal portrait of me by Wilson Steer' which he refused to destroy. She could never trust him. He would be expected and not turn up, or come, but leave by an early train. Ella had more than enough experience to recognize a man on the run, but she could not give up. 'That I ever dined with my publisher at the Crawford Hotel seems like a bygone dream,' she wrote. She was still good-looking, and had plenty to offer, but Lane, for the sake of peace, preferred to do without it. In 1898 he settled the question by marrying a wealthy American widow.

This new wife, as it happened, was interested, and interested Lane, in translations from the French, which were Ella's speciality. But Ella made no further appeals. She had wanted Lane, and hadn't got him. With her usual stoicism she accepted this, and left London for Paris. In 1902 she was still there, still broke (she reckoned to be able to live on £90 a year, but rarely had it) and was in danger of falling into the melancholy inertia which always lay in wait for her. She knew a number of French writers and publishers, and sometimes got a little literary work, but she was capable of sitting for hours over a book at a café table, or staying all day in bed. A French bed, because she had always said you couldn't find a decent one in England.

Charlotte, who seems to have been expected, arrived in Paris in April, but did not date her first letter to Edith Oliver beyond 'Thursday: 1 p.m.'. There is an atmosphere of uncontrolled excitement. Nothing could be more unlike the *Notes in a Brittany Convent*. In Brittany Charlotte (according to her own account) had been talking calmly, in fluent French, to the sisters, asking them the secret of tranquillity. Now it turns out that her French was so poor that she couldn't be understood when she asked the way. She had never been to Paris, had never been abroad by herself before, didn't know where to go first, was dazzled by the lights and in danger of being run over by motor-cars and the French two-decker steam trams. She was supposed to be sightseeing. It was the Paris of the Expo, with new pavilions, new Guimard-style entrances to the Metros, and all the illuminations stepped up to give a dazzling enchantment to the violet evening sky. Charlotte, though she normally had a sharp eye for colour and architecture, noticed very little of all this. She was in a state of passionate agitation. 'My dear, I scarcely know where to begin and start at random,' she wrote to Edith. She was beyond doing justice even to Notre Dame. 'My head was stupid and my eyes livid – I couldn't look up.'

For some reason she had booked into a *pension* at 26 rue de Turin, which was then a noisy business quarter. However, she had a room with a balcony, and was able not to take notice of the other *pensionnaires*, which was exactly what she wanted. The arrangement was that she should take her meals at Ella's place in rue Chateaubriand, about half-an-hour's walk away. It would, surely, have been more convenient to find somewhere nearer, but it was typical of Charlotte that she had to hold herself, at first, at a distance. 'Up to now I have had no impressions or sensations worth recording – perhaps I have worn them all out – and then I have been living at rather high pressure but physically I am better – mentally still tired – but if I wished to get my nerves under control, I have done it – and hope that it will last. I can't transport my thoughts to England and the things left behind with any sense of reality – and perhaps it is better so – but it makes me seem very egotistic – which I'm not really – it is a queer uncertain mind this of mine – and claims are being made on it at the moment which I find difficult to meet.' The claims on her mind were being made by her body, and Ella, although she took other people's behaviour easily enough, must have been somewhat puzzled. In the morning, when they were supposed to meet at Parc Monceau, half-way between the two *pensions*, Charlotte suddenly defaulted. 'E. d'A wished me to meet her but as it was wet I did not feel inclined – and waiting for a break started off by myself in the direction . . . and prowled about the Quartier Latin.' In her jacket, collar and tie she must have looked like a tiny, rather out-of-date *lionne* among the large hats and sumptuous fashions of the Expo. But her courage only went so far and no further. In this Paris of 1902, where lesbians met by mutual understanding at the *Chat Noir*, where Willy had already published Colette's *Claudine à l'Ecole*, and in rue Georges-Ville the Marquise de Belboeuf, dressed in mechanic's overalls, reigned mildly over her circle as 'Missy', Charlotte could not summon up the nerve to go into a café by herself. She looked for a *crêmerie*, and as she couldn't find one she went without her chocolate for that day.

To maintain her independence she needed to feel that she had come to Paris to help Ella. This was an insurance against loss of self-respect, if not against unhappiness. 'I found E. D'A somewhat in need of someone to look after her,' she told Edith. 'The details I am not free to enter into.' Ella was probably between lovers; certainly she needed to pull herself together to receive Caroline Grout, Flaubert's niece, who wished to discuss the translation of her *Souvenirs Intimes*. Ella's room was in a mess, and she had made no preparation of any kind. Charlotte hurried out to buy 'the little necessaries for the occasion – flowers – cakes – &c. – and we arranged the room (one lives in one's bedroom here and hers is a very charming one).' Ella, of course, asked her to stay and meet Mme Grout, but Charlotte once again suddenly retreated. 'As I was timid I didn't stay to see the lady but came back here – and then found myself too restless to keep quiet and went for a walk till about 5 when I dressed for dinner and started off again in pouring rain.' Passionately interested as she was in Flaubert, Charlotte would have liked above all things to meet this favourite niece who was at work on an edition of the letters he had written to her since childhood, yet she threw away the chance when it was offered from a morbid fear of being one too many. A few hours later she was back in rue Chateaubriand, smoking one cigarette after another over a wood-fire which Ella made the *concierge* light in her room. (Wherever she lived and whatever she did, the *concierges* always put themselves out for Ella.) And then 'I saw E. D'A was rather done up and came home along the Champs Elysées looking wonderful with innumerable lights and nearly lost my way coming home as it is difficult to see the names of the streets at night – the omnibus men either cannot or will not help you. They are very surly – sometimes one finds a pleasant work-girl who directs you – very kindly – but my French is so bad – it's not easy to understand or to make oneself understood. This afternoon I shall take it easy – and not go to the rue Chat perhaps till dinner though Ella will wonder where I am as I promised to turn up for déjeuner.' One more attempt to show to herself, and to Edith Oliver, and above all to Ella, that she could take it or leave it, and was at no-one's disposition. But how much did Ella care, or even notice? She was not homo-erotic, and had none of Charlotte's self-tormenting, self-doubting temperament, over-anxious to give, but too nervous to receive. As her letters to John Lane show, Ella went straight for what she wanted and shrugged off the consequences. She was not likely to understand in Charlotte the nervous lover's painful superstition or perversion which backs away from what it most wants. In any case, it was a losing battle. By the end of the week Charlotte had to turn out of her room in rue de Turin and asked for all letters to be forwarded to her at rue Chateaubriand.

After this the letters stop short, or more likely were destroyed by Edith, who cannot have approved of the way things were going. Ten years later, when Charlotte fell in love again with yet more humiliating results, she repeated almost exactly the same pattern – the wild dash, the hungry need to offer help, the withdrawal, the embarrassment, and the pathetic attempt not to commit herself. In both cases, whatever she had to offer was rejected.

When Charlotte left Paris, she felt as though she had been spat upon. She had made a fool of herself, but she had acted from the heart, without calculation as to what kind of woman Ella was, though that was not hard to find out. Thirty years later, to be sure, Ella, as an old woman with hair dyed 'a dreadful red orange' was said to look 'a little masculine', but in 1902 she was patently a warm-blooded, clever, unreliable man's woman, too generous, and in the end too lazy, to take much advantage of men. And easy-going as she was, she didn't want anything as inconvenient, or, perhaps, as absurd, as Charlotte's love. The point was put as kindly as she knew how. 'Ella once said to me, "One acts foolishly in order to write wisely – *non è vero?*"'

Whether this advice was sound or not, Charlotte's Paris poems are not wisely written. *Le Sacré-Coeur* ('Dear Paris of the hot white hands, the scarlet lips, the scented hair') is keyed up to hysterical pitch, so is *Monsieur Qui Passe – Quai Voltaire*. But on all the impulses which were frustrated or done to death in her, she wrote a lyrical epitaph.

I remember rooms that have had their part
In the steady slowing down of the heart.
The room in Paris, the room at Geneva,
The little damp room with the seaweed smell,
And that ceaseless maddening sound of the tide –
    Rooms where for good or ill – things died.

Charlotte had told Edith that she had no idea how long she would be away, she might be back in a week. In the event she seems to have stayed long enough to improve her French a good deal, but she could not leave Anne for week after week with the responsibility of Anna Maria. By June she was back in 9 Gordon Street. Ella continued to write, whenever a fit for letter-writing took her. But there is no record that she ever met Charlotte again.

CHAPTER 9

The Quiet House

When we were children Old Nurse used to say
  The house was like an auction or a fair
  Until the lot of us were safe in bed.
  It has been quiet as the countryside
  Since Ted and Janey and then Mother died.
And Tom crossed Father and was sent away.
After the lawsuit he could not hold up his head,
  Poor Father, and he does not care
  For people here, or to go anywhere.

To get away to Aunt's for that week-end
  Was hard enough; (since then, a year ago,
  He scarcely lets me slip out of his sight –)
At first I did not like my cousin's friend,
  I did not think I should remember him
  His voice has gone, his face is growing dim
And if I like him now I do not know.
  He frightened me before he smiled –
  He did not ask me if he might –
  He said that he would come one Sunday night,
  He spoke to me as if I were a child.

The Quiet House (these are the first two verses) was written in
1913 and out of all her poems was, Charlotte said, 'to me the
most subjective of the lot'. The transpositions here from her
own life are as strange, but just as readily understandable, as *In
Nunhead Cemetery*. Once again the story has to be made out from
the fits and starts of a sick mind confessing to itself. In verse 1
Elizabeth Goodman appears almost unchanged, saying the
things that 'Old Nurse used to say'. The mother, not the father,
has died, and the father, not the mother sits at home and is
pitied for his disgrace. The brother and sister are dead, the

Cumberland Market, N.W.1, near Gordon Square.
Charlotte Mew's 'Hay-market.'
'It is a place of carts and the sky . . .
on the map you will find it very small, though it is more important
than Piccadilly; it is in the real world.'

elder brother is lost, but whatever he has done is his own fault, and he is blamed for being 'sent away'. There is no role in this story (or in any of Charlotte's poems) for Anne. The speaker is left alone in the house with her father and the shut room 'where Mother died'. During her one escape to her aunt's she has had an experience for which nothing had prepared her. 'At first I did not like my cousin's friend.' And in fact the incident meant nothing, the cousin's friend treated her like a child, and his promise to call on her meant nothing either. But as the empty months pass it has become an obsession with her. 'Everything has burned, and not quite through.' The guilt of wanting and not being wanted is so intense that the house itself seems to accuse her. The red light through the stained-glass window on the staircase landing seems to accuse her, or perhaps to wound her, 'as if, coming down, you had spilt your life'. This is a child's fantasy, not an adult's, a regression which Charlotte Mew always shows as the borderline of insanity.

> The things that kill us seem
>   Blind to the death they give:
> It is only in our dream
>   The things that kill us live.

There are two sorts of things, then – more usually called two sorts of people – who 'kill'; those who destroy us quite casually, without even seeing what they're doing, and those whom we loved but who are dead or mad, and can come back to us as they were only in dreams.

In *The Quiet House* these are daytime thoughts. In the early evening comes the perpetually hopeful and exciting time, *l'heure bleue*, represented in autumn Bloomsbury by fog and drizzle. The front-door bell rings, the servant comes up from the basement to answer it, but there is nothing to hope for.

> To-night I heard a bell again –
> Outside it was the same mist of fine rain,
> The lamps just lighted down the long, dim street,
>   No one for me –
> I think it is myself I go to meet:
>   I do not care; some day I *shall* not think; I shall not *be*!

Without doubt Charlotte was living from day to day *à rebours*, in the dark thrill of her own sexuality and the frustration she had inflicted on herself. For this condition there was no hope of peace, except in total extinction. But 'life goes on the same outside'. Gordon Street was, in fact, not particularly quiet at all – the gates which Cubitt had installed at one end to keep out 'omnibuses and low persons' were no longer effective against traffic, and Charlotte complains in one of her letters of emerging from 'the noise of Gordon Street' as though stunned. But inside the quiet house life circulated slowly, as though stagnant. Preserved on her invalid's sofa by her daughters' loyalty and care, Anna Maria had shrivelled away even further and was

addressed by both of them as 'Ma'. The Mews now had only
one maid-of-all-work, Jane Elnswick; she was the last girl to be
trained by Elizabeth Goodman, but very different in character,
a cheerful resilient Londoner. Jane and Charlotte between
them somehow got through everything that had to be done. The
house, in those days, dictated its own terms in a kind of
conspiracy with the seasons. It 'made work'. In summer it
demanded different curtains and floral chintz covers, while the
soot-darkened winter ones were washed and put away. In
winter the 'brights' needed daily polishing to counteract the
fog, and together with the doorstep (which needed whitening)
and the fireplaces (which needed blackening), they represented
woman's hard-won triumph over nature. Charlotte always
represented herself and Jane at work as a kind of Quixote and
Sancho Panza. Once when they were making the beds together
she looked out of the window at the plane trees in Gordon
Square and observed that it was nearly summer, to which Jane
replied that was a good thing as the kippers were much better in
warm weather, fatter and oilier. When Charlotte sat down at
her desk Jane, pitying her, as the brisk and efficient always pity
a writer, came in frequently to ask whether she should finish up
the rice pudding for her dinner, and should she run out to the
shops, or would Miss Lotti mind going out herself? All this was
to keep the young mistress on the go and take her mind off all
this reading and scribbling.

Perhaps partly to satisfy Jane, Charlotte began to do some
voluntary social work for Miss Paget's Girls' Club, at 26
Cartwright Gardens, a few streets away from home. The object
of the whole Federation of Working Girls' Clubs, founded
under the auspices of the YMCA, was to train the home-makers
of the future on a missionary basis, since 'no nation can
permanently rise above the level of its womanhood', and some
centres promoted the Snowdrop Bands, which encouraged
purity and discouraged the wrong kind of conversation. The
Federation's handbooks, however, emphasized the danger of
'emphasization of personality with young and impressionable
natures' and 'the subtle temptation in the leader's heart to
rejoice in her power and to draw closer round her a following of

girls'. In club language, the girls tended to get a crush on their 'ladies', so that Charlotte, with her magnetic appeal for some young women (while she made others uncomfortable), was warned from the start from exerting all her power. But as an excellent pianist and, for that matter, a good dancer, she could be of great use to Miss Paget, who was opening several more clubs in the St Pancras area. She also did district visiting, sorting out troubles with doctor's and oculist's prescriptions, and rent arrears. Gratitude was not what she was looking for; she was delighted to recognize the defiant spirit of Miss Bolt among the crowded poor families who were supposed to be pleased to see her when she came. Once, when she was asking for directions, the ground-floor tenant shouted up to the top, 'Tell the lady upstairs there's a person here who wants to see her.' This was a shock for Miss Lotti, but Charlotte was delighted.

Although she continued to send in something every month or so to *Temple Bar*, Charlotte seemed, since her visit to Ella, to' have lost her first confidence. Whatever may be wrong with *Passed* and *The China Bowl* they are hers and no-one else's, but her short stories between 1903 and 1905 suggest that she was studying the market simply with the object of finding a style which would sell. *Mademoiselle* (1904) is, sadly enough, in the style of Henry Harland's *P'tit Bleu*, while *Mark Stafford's Wife* (1905) is a good imitation of Henry James. All this might be considered as a useful apprenticeship, and perhaps, if it had come earlier, it would have been. From time to time she thought of writing a novel, but her friends discouraged her.

Feature articles, which she also tried (*The Governess in Fiction, The Country Sunday, The London Sunday, Mary Stuart in Fiction*), meant, as it did for so many other women writers, 'the descent into the valley of the shadow of the books'. This is George Gissing's phrase for the British Museum Reading Room, though he also calls it 'the blessed refuge of the great dome', where hacks and scribblers could pass the day without spending money on heating, and whose peculiar atmosphere, 'at first a cause of headache', soon became delightful. The heroine of his *New Grub Street* (1891), who works there from 9.30 in the morning till dusk, with one break for a cup of tea, is 'getting up' French authoresses of the seventeenth century from the entries in Larousse, and Charlotte's articles show that she was probably doing the same thing, copying bits out of Bible concordances and histories of world literature and the notebooks which she had kept since her schooldays. As Gissing makes only too plain, the Museum was (as it still is) a place of slavery. The habitués talked and laughed in a strange, muted fashion 'as a result of long years of mirth subdued in the Reading Room'. If Charlotte was too unsystematic to make a regular feature writer, at least it meant that she was spared this fate.

What she really wanted to write about was the poetry of Emily Brontë. For Emily herself she had always felt something stronger than an attraction, more, perhaps, a religious devotion. About Haworth Parsonage and the Yorkshire moors she had heard first of all from Miss Harrison, but apart from that she had nothing to go on in the early 1900s beyond Mrs Gaskell's *Life of Charlotte Brontë* (1857) and a curious book, *Emily Brontë*, by Mary Robinson, published in W. H. Allen's *Eminent Women* series in 1883. Miss Robinson had been up to Haworth and consulted local people who knew the family. Her version of the story stressed 'the vulgar tragedy of Branwell's woes' and the dual nature of Emily's faith, touching ecstasy on the one hand and on the other 'terrible theories of doomed incurable sin and predestined loss' which warned her that 'an evil streak will only beget contamination and the children of the mad must be liable to madness; the children of the depraved bent on depravity'. Whether Emily really believed anything like this or not, for Charlotte Mew these words struck home. Miss Robinson went on to discuss the source of Emily's strength. How could a woman write anything as violent as *Wuthering Heights*? But informants in Haworth parish had told her that Emily, though often severe, was 'something quite jovial, like a boy' and 'so genial and kind, a little masculine'. The suggestion, put forward here for the first time, that Emily Brontë's nature was ambiguous or ambisexual, did not attract Charlotte Mew, or, if it did, it frightened her. For reasons that she would scarcely have defined to herself, she wanted to show that Emily was apart from and above sexuality altogether. 'It is said that her genius was masculine,' she wrote, 'but surely it was merely spiritual, strangely and exquisitely severed from embodiment and freed from any accident of sex.' Charlotte wanted to see in Emily a reconciliation of opposites. The parsonage daughter who baked the bread and worked 'in the narrow channels prescribed for her by dreary circumstances' was also one of Nature's outcasts, a noble spirit who 'lived long enough to lift such a cry for liberty as few women have ever lifted'. In this passionately admiring piece Charlotte scarcely even tries to disentangle her own feelings from her subject. Death, she says, was not a terror for Emily, 'this girl who mused habitually upon facts and mysteries more terrible. It was not a problem, because it was the end of problems.' In this interpretation, death meant rest, and the peaceful involuntary resolution of all the abnormalities and discordant elements which had tormented her in life. And Charlotte gives way to the temptation of misquoting the last sentence of *Wuthering Heights*, ' "There can be" – it is her final word – "no unquiet slumbers for the sleepers in that quiet earth." '

Her essay, she hoped, would stand as an introduction to the poems. More than fifty years after Emily's death, there was still no complete edition. Collecting and arranging that would make the headache-inducing visits to the Reading Room worthwhile. Who would publish it? John Lane, who had treated Ella so ignobly, was obviously impossible, but Charlotte thought of Lane's old partner, Elkin Mathews. Mathews had been ousted by Lane and shoved back into the antiquarian book business, but he was still in publishing on his own account, and he specialized in poetry. He was an approachable man, fussy, but mild and considerate. She had no luck, however. Mathews, although he had only kept on a small business, had not lost his touch, and he must have known, though Charlotte did not, that there were two editions of Emily Brontë's poems in the offing; one was from Heinemann with an introduction by Arthur Symons, the other a *Complete Works* from Hodder, edited by the all-purpose journalist Clement Shorter, with the poems as Volume I. Charlotte had chosen the right subject – or rather it had chosen her, since she loved Emily, as she says, 'with something of her own intensity' – but several months too late. It seems doubtful, in any case, whether Charlotte had the patience or the temperament to make a good editor, and her wild essay on 'the passionate child of storm and cloud' was not quite the sort of thing to appeal to Elkin Mathews.

There was always *Temple Bar*, which printed it in August 1904. Charlotte had, at least, the comfort of being the magazine's regular contributor. Between 1899 and 1905 it had taken twelve of her pieces, almost all, in fact, that she had managed to write. But in 1905 *Temple Bar* quietly folded. It ceased publication in December, tried flounderingly to revive itself with a new series in 1906, and then collapsed for ever.

There were plenty of magazines and weeklies left on the market, more, indeed, than ever, and much more attractive ones, but Charlotte hadn't the resilience of ten years back. The *Temple Bar* contributors scattered, and her friend Mrs Clement Parsons gave up journalism altogether. During the next three years Charlotte seems to have written hardly anything, or, at least, had hardly anything accepted. She possessed two large trunks which nobody, not even Anne, was allowed to look into. Possibly they were full of unread or rejected manuscripts; no-one could say.

For any kind of break from their routine the two girls relied on their friends: the Chicks, who had a house at Branscombe in Devonshire, and the Brownes, who now lived in a largeish dull house called 'Anglefield' at Berkhamsted in Hertfordshire. Here Mrs Browne, Maggie's mother, talked of nothing but the price of vegetables and the difficulty of getting servants, and her father about nothing but marine biology. Maggie had become set in her ways, and it was not likely she would get married now.

1909 brought a distinct improvement. Anne had been able, with the small extra income left her by Aunt Mary Kendall, to rent a studio of her own – 6 Hogarth Studios, 64 Charlotte Street, off Fitzroy Street in Soho. This was a true artists' quarter, and both Anne and Charlotte breathed freer air. You couldn't cook there, but you could ask friends in and boil a kettle. For the first time Anne had one of her flower paintings accepted by the Royal Academy. Charlotte, for her part, wrote a poem, the first she had produced since her twenties. She sent it to *The Nation*, which was then a sixpenny radical weekly under the editorship of H. W. Massingham. Massingham accepted it.

The poem, *Requiescat*, is an elegy for a dead woman,

> At the road's end your strip of blue
> Beyond that line of naked trees –
> Strange that we should remember you
> As if you would remember these!

which ends with an elegant variation:

> Beyond the line of naked trees
> At the road's end, your stretch of blue –
> Strange if you should remember these
> As we, ah! God! remember you!

What is striking is the professional neatness and ease of this. Nothing could be more different from the intensely-felt but often ragged *Quiet House*, *Rooms* and *Ken*. Charlotte herself did not put her poem very high and when Ella D'Arcy wrote to her about it, had mixed feelings. 'Looking through some of Ella's old letters,' she wrote in 1914, 'I find she wrote to me 3 about the Requiescat . . . she had seen it in *The Nation* and wrote at first ironically – Thanking me for sending it to her (very likely! as she'd always spit on everything I'd done –!) and adding "it goes into my private anthology". And in the next, "But you are a poet which I did not know and I beg you *very earnestly* – not to neglect this finest of all gifts. The poem was a sight realer and more beautiful than any by the Brontë sisters whose poetical genius you think so much of – go on producing."' Ella, idling at a café table with her letters and the English papers, had insulted Emily Brontë, whom she thought much inferior to Shelley and Rimbaud, and yet Charlotte felt the warmth of encouragement. But, most characteristically, she did not write another poem for three years.

That summer, as soon as the Academy's summer show was over, she and Anne were to go to Brittany for two weeks. Charlotte had managed to get to France two or three times with

Edith Oliver – once they went as far as Aix – and her French was now fluent. But she had never, since 1901, been away with Anne. This, as always, depended not only on Anna Maria but on the whims of the tough old parrot. Wek and Mrs Mew, close as they were to each other, often refused to be looked after by the same attendant. But in July some sort of compromise had been reached. Then Anne, who was never very strong, caught cold, and Elsie O'Keefe took her place.

Charlotte would rather have gone with Edith Oliver, since Elsie, particularly since she'd got used to the moral support of a husband, was a faint-hearted traveller and easily 'gave way'. But it was understood that Charlotte was the man of the party. At Quimper Elsie, upset by the crossing and the queer foreign food, had to be left guarding the luggage while Charlotte braved Madame at the Hôtel Lion d'Or and tried to get the cheapest rooms possible. But it was, of course, very good of Elsie to come at all, since by now she had two children, who had to be left with their nurse.

Ancient chapels, Breton costume, stone Calvaries, seaweed burners, clattering sabots, quaint processions, the Benediction of the Sea – more typical lady tourist's letters couldn't be imagined, as though Charlotte had sat down deliberately to write them as Miss Lotti. She adds that the way to see Brittany is off the beaten track, and resents the idea that 'the old faith is dying out'. This is no longer the tough-romantic journalist of *Notes in a Brittany Convent*, and certainly not the restless, excited woman in a 'queer uncertain mind' who prowled round the streets of Paris. Two English ladies, no longer young, with their guide-books in their hands, they went to Audierne and walked over the rocks to Lauderneau, which looked, Charlotte thought, like a penal settlement. They just got back to Le Quendé in time for a cup of tea. 'A gentleman' at the hotel had recommended this outing and she now decided that all personal recommendations on holiday were useless and that she herself would never make any. Back at Audierne there was a plague of children and beggars, complained of by all the lady visitors. A dozen of the boys buried Charlotte's umbrella in the sand, and it was a piece of luck that the woman at the semaphore station on the beach had noticed what was happening and had marked the spot.

This is the first we hear of Charlotte's horn-handled umbrella, which was said to be almost as tall as she was herself, and was carried defiantly at her side as a defence (possibly an attack) against the rest of the world. Even when she and Elsie had to get a lift from a courier's cart, riding on the roof with the luggage, she carried her umbrella at the familiar angle. It was, needless to say, part of her equipment as Miss Lotti.

In the process of getting as much value as possible out of their special French Railway tickets, she and Elsie went out from Dinan to the Crozon peninsula. They were lucky in being able to see the Chapelle de Rocamadour, which was burned down less than a year later; after a good blow in the sea air, they stayed the night at Camaret-sur-Mer, or, as Charlotte spelled it, Cameret.

PÉRI EN MER
(Cameret)

One day the friends who stand about my bed
    Will slowly turn from it to speak of me
Indulgently, as of the newly dead,
    Not knowing how I perished by the sea,
      That night in summer when the gulls topped white
    The crowded masts cut black against the sky
Of fading rose – where suddenly the light
    Of Youth went out, and I, no longer I,
Climbed home, the homeless ghost that was to be.
    Yet as I passed, they sped me up the heights –
Old seamen round the door of the Abri
    De la Tempête. Even on quiet nights
    So may some ship go down with all her lights
Beyond the sight of watchers on the quay!

Charlotte never reprinted this sonnet, perhaps because of the frightful French/English rhyme *be/abri/quay* (she used these quite often, however). But the subject is simple enough, and universal – in November, when she got back from her holiday, she would be forty. When she wasn't ill or depressed, she still looked much younger than her real age. Still, she would be forty. After a brilliant start, she knew she had failed to meet her friends' expectations. Her nature stood in fear of itself, and when she had given way to it she had twice been painfully rejected. In front of her lay the Quiet House, and a money situation which was getting no easier. Her favourite image of the ship with all her riding lights turns, in the last lines, into a shipwreck without trace. Like Emily Dickinson, she felt her life closing before its close.

The temptation would be either to a more consoling religious faith than she had ever had, or to no faith at all. But in 1910, when Alfred Noyes's *Collected Poems* came out, she read his *The Old Sceptic* and reflected that as far as sentiment went, she might have written the poem herself.

> I pierced my father's heart with a murmur of unbelief,
>   He only looked in my face as I spoke, but his mute eyes cried
> Night after night in my dreams, and he died
>   In grief, in grief.

The point of Noyes's poem is that the sceptic has taught himself to doubt so efficiently that he finds he is beginning to doubt doubt and disbelieve in disbelief. This, it seems, was also Charlotte Mew's case. She turned back, as she had done before, to her childhood's faith, with its moments of intense joy and its persistent sense of guilt. She accepted that this was a personal matter. 'Religion is like music, one must have an ear for it,' she wrote. 'Some people have none at all.'

She had felt anxious about leaving Anne at home in 1909 and Edith Oliver had been enlisted to call at Gordon Street and see that the cold didn't turn into a sore throat, or anything worse. The drains, as usual, were suspected, and in 1910 the Mews spent £100 in having them resited. At last, in 1911, the two sisters had a chance to go away together. Yet another companion had been found for Anna Maria, and Wek, so far, had not attacked her. Anne would sketch and paint, and Charlotte, perhaps, would write.

This time they went to Boulogne, booking into quite modest rooms over the Café Belle Vue, 10 Place Frédéric Sauvage. There was a good view, and the price was only 40 francs a week, but the rooms were not too clean, and the water in the tap, they found, was 'lazy'. Charlotte, gathering her courage together, made Madame have the whole place scrubbed out, and when that was done Madame, recognizing strength when she saw it, smiled. They went to the circus and the cinema, and (accompanied by some Scottish ladies from one of the hotels) to the casino. There Charlotte and Anne 'lost a franc or two', but they both felt they needed peace. Gordon Street seemed 'ten thousand miles away', and they could relax in the old part of Boulogne, where the milk-carts were pulled by large dogs, and cars went by 'at the pace of a hearse from a house of mourning'. Anne sketched in the fish market, Charlotte wished she too was a painter, but she was far more relaxed, far more herself, or one of her selves, than she had been with Elsie in Brittany. She lounged about the fishermen's quarter, talking to them as they mended their nets, and offering her hand-rolled cigarettes. This time she admitted openly that she was a confirmed quay-haunter, and a watcher of ships and seamen. Her ambiguous stride, unexpected in such a tiny creature, and her hoarse little voice marked her out this time from every other lady tourist. The Boulogne fishermen accepted her, it seems, and asked her into their houses. She felt suspended between two worlds. 'I have not told Maggie I am here,' she wrote to Edith, 'as I said I couldn't go to Berkhamsted and haven't heard anything of her for ages'. At night she went down to the quays again, to see the lights. It would be very easy to get to Paris. But she did not go. She told Edith that she was 'too tired to face the racket'.

CHAPTER 10

The Farmer's Bride

BETWEEN 1909, when she published *Requiescat*, and the beginning of 1912, Charlotte Mew wrote no poetry at all. Then on 3 February 1912 another poem of hers appeared in *The Nation*. Anyone who could say what prompted her to write it, at the age of forty-two, would be able to understand the nature of the poetic impulse itself.

She gave it the title *The Farmer's Bride*, though it is the farmer, not the bride, who speaks, in a voice which might be from anywhere between the Isle of Wight and Hardy's Wessex.

> Three summers since I chose a maid,
> Too young may be – but more's to do
> At harvest-time than bide and woo.
>   When us was wed she turned afraid
> Of love and me and all things human;
> Like the shut of a winter's day.
> Her smile went out, and 'twasn't a woman –
>   More like a little frightened fay.
>   One night, in the Fall, she runned away.
>
> 'Out 'mong the sheep, her be,' they said,
>   Should properly have been abed;
>   But sure enough she wasn't there
>   Lying awake with her wide brown stare.
>   So over seven-acre field and up-along across the down
>   We chased her, flying like a hare
>   Before our lanterns. To Church-Town
>   All in a shiver and a scare
>   We caught her, fetched her home at last
>   And turned the key upon her, fast.

She does the work about the house
As well as most, but like a mouse:
    Happy enough to chat and play
    With birds and rabbits and such as they,
    So long as men-folk keep away.
'Not near, not near!' her eyes beseech
When one of us comes within reach.
    The women say that beasts in stall
    Look round like children at her call.
    I've hardly heard her speak at all.

Shy as a leveret, swift as he,
Straight and slight as a young larch tree,
Sweet as the first wild violets, she,
To her wild self. But what to me?

The short days shorten and the oaks are brown,
    The blue smoke rises to the low grey sky,
One leaf in the still air falls slowly down,
    A magpie's spotted feathers lie
On the black earth spread white with rime,
The berries redden up to Christmas-time.
    What's Christmas-time without there be
    Some other in the house than we!

She sleeps up in the attic there
Alone, poor maid. 'Tis but a stair
Betwixt us. Oh! my God! the down,
    The soft young down of her, the brown,
The brown of her – her eyes, her hair! her hair!

With these six verses Charlotte for the first time attracted notice and respect as a poet. Some readers were reminded of Sue Brideshead's leap out of the window to get away from her husband in *Jude the Obscure*, or possibly Hardy's *The Homecoming*, although in that poem the farmer stands no nonense on his wedding-night:

Now don't ye rub your eyes so red; we're home and have no cares;
Here's a skimmer-cake for supper, peckled onions, and some pears;
I've got a little keg o'summat strong, too, under stairs:
What, slight your husband's victuals? Other brides can tackle theirs.

But poetry is what it sounds like, and *The Farmer's Bride*, Wessex dialect or not, doesn't sound like Hardy. The change in metre, racing along in the first four verses and breaking down, with 'the short days shorten, and the oaks are brown' into a dragging, faltering close, is Charlotte Mew's own. Nor was Hardy, great situation-man as he was, likely to hit on such an improbable, inhibited, tantalizing but touching story, once again an entire life's emotional history in a short space.

The objections are there for anyone to make, and they were made. What kind of farmer is this? Not like Hardy's brute with a little keg o'summat strong, and, for the matter of that, not much like Charlotte's Uncle Richard on the farm at Newfairlee. H. W. Nevinson, *The Nation*'s literary critic, was only one of many to find the farmer 'much too sympathetic. A man can hardly imagine why the most sensitive of women should run out into the night to avoid him.' A man can hardly imagine it, but Charlotte could. She knew perfectly well that a farmer was unlikely to compare his wife – say her Aunt Maggie Mew – to a violet, but she didn't believe either that farmers never looked at wild violets, or that they couldn't recognize a season which is beautiful because it only offers promise and cannot, by natural means, be forced into anything more. There is a curious dissociation in the poem because we are asked to pity both parties, the sweating farmer and the frightened girl, and even to see why it is that she has to be caught. 'So . . . we chased her, flying like a hare'. The 'so' is powerful, meaning that it was the obvious next step to take, but so is the 'we'. It is the whole community that turns out with their lighted lanterns, because things, after all, can only be allowed to go so far and no farther, just as they were in *Ken*:

> So, when they took
> Ken to that place, I did not look
> After he called and turned on me
> His eyes. These I shall see –

The girl, 'too young, may be', is one of those magic figures of the pre-1914 years (Kipling's *Jungle Book*, W. H. Hudson's *Green Mansions*), a talker to birds and animals. But this gives her (unlike Mowgli and Rima) no kind of power or advantage, it only makes her seem odd. She gets more understanding, but not much more sympathy, from the women than the men. In any case, these women have their own work to do, and certainly they make no objection to her being brought back. And once she is trapped, and 'about the house' again, but sleeping on her own in the attic, the subject of the poem, its whole weight and impetus, is quite clear; it is frustration. In the same way that the clerk in *In Nunhead Cemetery* watches the train, and the clay on the gravedigger's spade, so this bewildered farmer sees the magpie's feathers fall. One verse more, and he will lose his grip, tear upstairs and break down the door, and then what kind of wretchedness will ensue? The poem remains as an intolerable situation, perhaps just (at the end of three years) on the point of resolution. Meanwhile 'the brown of her – her eyes, her hair! her hair!'

The Farmer's Bride and all the poems which were to follow it, where Charlotte Mew speaks in different voices, raise the question – why do poets impersonate at all? They may do it because they have a great deal to hide, or because (like Browning) they haven't quite enough. They may (like Byron) be too energetic or too self-indulgent to contain themselves, they may (like Eliot) want to escape from emotion, or (like Yeats) from the unsatisfactory limitation of self. To Charlotte Mew impersonation was necessary, rather than helpful. 'The quality of emotion', she thought, was 'the first requirement of poetry . . . for good work one must accept the discipline that can be got, while the emotion is given to one.' And what she needed to give a voice to, as she also explained, was the *cri de coeur* – that is, the moment when the emotion unmistakably concentrates itself into a few words. Examples which she gave are Marguérite Gautier's '*Je veux vivre*' and Mrs Gamp's 'Drink fair, Betsy, wotever you do.' 'One has not only the cry but the gesture and the accent – and so one goes on – calling up witnesses to the real thing.' A cry has to be extorted, that is its test of truth. It might make a poem, or it might not. Charlotte once saw a woman walking across Cumberland Market, in Camden Town, 'with a tiny child holding on to her skirt, trying to keep up with her and chattering in a rather tired treble, like a chirpy little sparrow, as they went along. Suddenly the woman stopped and struck the child, with a thickly spoken "Now go and make yer bloody 'appy life miserable and stop yer bloody jaw."' This too was a *cri de coeur*. As to the farmer, she believed that 'as far as I had the use of words, they did express my idea of a rough countryman feeling and saying things differently from the more sophisticated townsman – at once more clearly and more confusedly.'

The Nation's readers, even if they thought the farmer's restraint unlikely, responded to the raw sensation of wanting and not getting, against the background of the season's return. Among these readers there was a Mrs Dawson Scott, a doctor's wife from Southall, who wrote herself, and was a most generous and determined, not to say ruthless, patron of writers. Charlotte first met her on the 30th of May 1912. Mrs Dawson Scott wasted no time. She never did. Taking at once to the new poet, whom she described in her diary as 'an Imp with brains', she invited her to tea immediately. Charlotte now had the curious experience which she had just glimpsed for a short while in her *Yellow Book* days, of being 'taken up'.

CHAPTER 11
Mrs Sappho

To take up Charlotte Mew was not an easy matter, but Mrs Dawson Scott never gave way to difficulties. Firmness was all that was needed. And yet 'she was entirely deluded' (according to someone who knew her well) 'in thinking that she was fundamentally hard and lacking in affection'. She was capable of sudden infatuations and bitter disappointments, like the rest of us, but was sustained by her trust in the future and her great competence in dealing with the present. Arriving in London at the end of the 1880s, quite unheard-of and not knowing anyone, she had soon become one of Heinemann's 'young authors' (though this, disappointingly, never came to much) and she made herself, over the next twenty years, into a celebrity in the world of letters. One of her most successful ideas, in later years, was International P.E.N., which brought together writers from all over the world. Mrs Dawson Scott had noticed that writing was a lonely occupation, and loneliness was something that she did not permit.

She is described as a 'dumpy, energetic little woman', with a round peasant face and round blue eyes. Her name was Catherine, but she was always known as Sappho (to Charlotte Mew, who got onto Christian-name terms with difficulty, as 'Mrs Sappho'.) The nick-name came from the title of a long poem, *Sappho*, her first published work. There was some irony in this, for Mrs Dawson Scott, through marriage, childbirth and miscarriages, was not much interested in sex or in the female psychology, and though she considered herself, and was considered, an advanced feminist, she knew and cared little about such things. Her poem was not on the subject of lesbianism; it claimed social, but not sexual, freedom for woman. Her own

Mrs 'Sappho' Dawson Scott

energy went into organization. She was a wonderful friend, but her friends, too, must allow themselves to be organized.

Her husband, Dr Scott (who avoided, as far as he could, her literary friends), had his practice in Southall, half an hour out of London, so that Sappho could not exactly hold a salon; still, the strength of her personality was such that people felt themselves compelled to take the train from Paddington and stay as long as they were bidden. They felt the warmth of her genuine concern. In June or July they were summoned to one of a series of cottages in Cornwall in which 'sanitation was not a successful feature', but there was enthusiasm, red wine, and bracing sea air on the cliff-paths, up which Mrs Dawson Scott walked barefoot, wearing a long velvet tea-gown. It is easy to criticize such people, difficult to do without them. To Sappho's enthusiasm a surprising number of people, some of them resistant at first to any kind of patronage, owed a great deal.

It was part of her strength that she treated both celebrities and beginners in exactly the same way, and she was not daunted by Charlotte Mew. She was surprised, however, that this poet, who at forty-three was only four years younger than herself, looked at times almost like a child, with a clear, pale, unlined skin and tiny hands and feet, shod in doll's boots. This child, or doll, often broke into rapid ungrammatical French, and then, as though dissatisfied, back into English, and swore in both languages. Her poetry was disturbing and strange, and Sappho was determined that as many people as possible should hear it. Charlotte must collect up *The Farmer's Bride* and whatever else she was writing, come down at once to 'Harden', 6 King Street, Southall, and give a reading. The Dawson Scott principle was never to take 'no' for an answer, although it met on occasions Charlotte's own everlasting no, as fiery as Carlyle's. And even when she did come Charlotte could be farouche, or even 'inexcusably rude' to the company, or walk out abruptly. Privately she was half-pleased to have what she called 'my jingles' or 'my damned immortal work' recognized, and at the same time furious at something like a threat to her independence. Did Sappho, she wondered, think she was Little Tich (that is, the tiny music-hall comic, who made his entrance in enormously large shoes) or perhaps a monkey – was she supposed to perform to order? To this kind of thing Sappho, who loved a battle, stood up gallantly, saying that if Charlotte didn't accept she'd be damned if she asked her down again. Only on one point did she lose – Charlotte absolutely refused to come down to Cornwall. The only Cornwall for her was 'Newlyn lights', the stormy coast of *The China Bowl*.

The effect of the readings was astonishing. Only a few were asked at a time. They sat facing the little collared and jacketed figure, with her typescripts and cigarettes, who would never begin until she felt like it. Once she got started (everyone agreed) Charlotte seemed possessed, and seemed not so much to be acting or reciting as a medium's body taken over by a distinct personality. She made slight gestures and used strange intonations at times, tones that were not in her usual speaking range. During *In Nunhead Cemetery* Sappho had 'to pinch herself black and blue', so she wrote in her diary, to keep back the tears. Evelyn Underhill, the religious poet and mystic, felt as though she was 'having whisky with my tea – my feet were clean off the floor'. At the end Charlotte gave her characteristic toss of the head. A great friend of the Dawson Scotts, the painter Kathy Giles, took this as a signal and asked some questions, but Charlotte, looking over her head into the distance, seemed hardly conscious of them, and Miss Giles was told 'she's not here yet'. She seemed, quite literally, to have been carried away by the experience of reading. But the audience made no complaint, they were content to 'receive'. Florence May Parsons, who had known Charlotte since the *Temple Bar* days, but had never dreamed she could do anything like this, told Sappho that she would cancel every other appointment if Charlotte was going to read, it was the 'heart of life' to her. Even Mrs Dawson Scott was somewhat taken aback by this. She suggested, in her straightforward way, that Charlotte was a lonely eccentric genius, like Sappho of Lesbos. 'Is that how she strikes you?' asked Mrs Parsons doubtfully.

These small chosen audiences were used to readings from Swinburne, Tennyson, Francis Thompson and early Yeats – 'the silver apples of the moon, the golden apples of the sun'; to them *The Farmer's Bride* and *In Nunhead Cemetery* were something new and undreamed-of. By this time the avant-garde had declared itself in London, Wyndham Lewis and Ezra Pound were on the point of launching *Blast*, and John Lane, ever watchful, was considering whether to publish it, and, if he did, where to give the first Vorticist dinner. But neither Pound nor Lewis had made any impression as yet on Sappho's circle. And her guests, after all, were right. Charlotte's poems were not like anyone else's.

Although the regular visitors at 'Harden' were not as distinguished as they later became – Sappho was really just starting and it was only in 1910 that she had persuaded her husband to live near London – they represented an expansion in Charlotte's horizon. Sappho, at her innumerable tea-parties, was 'full of mercurial energy, darting from guest to guest, breaking up parties which had clung together too long for her liking, leading the unknown to the known, and removing them when she thought the known had had enough'. Propelled by this unexpected force, Charlotte, by the end of 1912, was in a modest way becoming one of the known.

FAME

Sometimes in the over-heated house, but not for long,
   Smirking and speaking rather loud,
I see myself among the crowd,
Where no one fits the singer to his song,
Or sifts the unpainted from the painted faces
Of the people who are always on my stair;
They were not with me when I walked in heavenly places;
   But could I spare
In the blind Earth's great silences and spaces,
   The din, the scuffle, the long stare
   If I went back and it was not there?
Back to the old known things that are the new,
The folded glory of the gorse, the sweet-briar air,
To the larks that cannot praise us, knowing nothing of what
                          we do
   And the divine, wise trees that do not care.
Yet, to leave Fame, still with such eyes and that bright hair!
God! if I might! And before I go hence
   Take in her stead
   To our tossed bed,
One little dream, no matter how small, how wild.
Just now, I think I found it in a field, under a fence –
A frail, dead, new-born lamb, ghostly and pitiful and white,
   A blot upon the night,
   The moon's dropped child!

At the literary party, perhaps, even, in the drawing-room at 'Harden', Charlotte sees herself 'smirking and speaking rather loud', but, as she admits with appalling frankness, 'not for long'. A divided nature, it seems, can't bear the sight of itself for more than a short time. But neither can it bear the English poet's accepted flight to the country. In *Fame* Charlotte uses for the first time the images of pregnancy and stillbirth which were to recur in her later poetry, notably in *Madeleine in Church* and *Saturday Market*. The dislocation and sterility are complete. No-one fits the singer to the song, earth's spaces are 'blind', Nature wisely cares nothing for us and the dream, whatever it might have been, is not only dead but huddled away under a fence in the staring moon-light, a raw abortion.

    The guilt seems more profound than any reason given for it.

But Charlotte wrote the poem in 1913, when she had to contrast her own success (though she never exaggerated this) with what was happening to Anne. The fixed expenses of the Gordon Street household were Freda's maintenance in the mental home, the rent, and the rent of the studio, and it was probably to keep the studio going that Anne now took a disagreeable job. It was in a workshop which 're-decorated' – that is, faked up – seventeenth- and eighteenth-century furniture, and the conditions were no longer ladylike. It was sweated labour among the paints and varnishes. The boss, Charlotte considered, was 'a first-class devil'. Anne had always been delicate and subject to backache, and the work left her too tired to paint anything of her own. 'She was perfectly heroic at having no work of her own to send in anywhere, but I feel it rather keenly,' Charlotte wrote, and, in another letter, 'and though I am credited with a more or less indifferent front to these things – the fact is that they cut me to the heart'. This was the background of *Fame*. It was also why she told Sappho that 'you made me feel rather a vampire the other evening and as if you were eventually going to present me with a heavy bill for something I never much wanted to buy – i.e. the world's faint praise. Please let me have the estimate now, as I mayn't be able to pay it after all.'

These brusque remarks show Charlotte's usual method of protecting herself. In each new environment she adapted to the expected image and produced a somewhat different personality, so that at first Mrs Dawson Scott's Charlotte was only partly like Anne's, or Edith Oliver's, or Ella D'Arcy's. At Southall she was not only somewhat fierce, but defiantly not an intellectual: 'I read next to no poetry and understand less,' she wrote to Sappho, and again, 'I am a loafer and should really die of exhaustion if I had even to try to keep up with complicated people: the fishermen on the Boulogne quay are more in my way.' When Sappho pressed a volume of Evelyn Underhill's poems on her she said she would 'attack it' after a cup of Bovril and some strong nerve pills. Charlotte, in fact, was reading Flaubert as always, Chekhov, Conrad and Verlaine; the 'only artists' for her at the moment were Chardin, John Martin and Hogarth, and, in music, Wagner and Schubert. This suggests, as we might expect, a need to go from one extreme to the other, but not someone who has to take strong drugs before tackling a little religious verse. She wanted to be seen as a little rougher and a little more simple than she was, someone who had to brace herself up in dread before the next 'intellectual orgy'. Sometimes she let go a little, but when she suddenly burst out one day that she didn't know why they were all so good to her and 'a severe silence' fell on the company, she concluded that it served her right. On the occasions when she left abruptly, or said conspicuously the wrong thing, she felt the next day as though she would like to cut her own head off.

But when things were not running smoothly – and the Dawson Scott marriage had its difficulties – no-one could be more quietly understanding than Charlotte Mew. 'We only have about half-an-hour' (on this earth), she wrote to her new friend. 'Let's do what we can.'

Through all these months, Charlotte was, as she put it, 'dog-tired with poisonous business and other diverzions'. 'The doctor won't give me sleeping-stuff,' she wrote to a friend, 'so I am fighting it out myself with the selfish resolution to put business and domestic cares behind me for a while.' The domestic cares were the same as always, with trouble from the kitchen range and the boiler and heavy doctor's bills for Anna Maria. The 'diverzions' were probably one of Charlotte's greatest disappointments as a writer – her failure to get *The China Bowl* on to the stage. She had re-written it as a one-acter (by this time she had seen Synge's *Riders to the Sea*), completely ruining it in the process, but she had great hopes of it, and, of course, of making money. The London managements gave their usual replies – Frederic Whelen at Wyndham's liked the play but unfortunately his lease of the theatre was just coming to an end etc. etc., Violet Vanbrugh was also complimentary, but nothing came of it. Evelyn Millard had gone into management on her own account at the Garrick a few years earlier, and might have been ready to help, but the experiment had not been much of a success, and she had gone back to touring. Charlotte, in her usual way, flung the script into a drawer, and is said never to have looked at it again. The theatre was not her *métier*, but there are very few writers who don't believe that they can do a play, and none who don't take the rejection of a play as a personal insult.

The first of Charlotte's poems in print after *The Farmer's Bride* were *The Changeling* and *The Pedlar*. They appeared in *The Englishwoman*, a short-lived monthly edited by Elisaveta Allen, the discarded wife of the publisher Grant Allen. The contributors formed a sympathetic genteel artistic group of their own. 'I have a studio At Home on Saturday,' Charlotte wrote in March 1913, 'to see new people, which invitation I owe to the English-woman things.' What these At Homes were like she described in an article published that March; one of the guests, she says, was a blind man.

> We had talked mechanically over the tea-cups: éclairs, Maeter-linck, Vesta Tilley; I would rather have asked him what he made of us from the studio patter, how we 'saw' this or didn't 'see' it, our poses and our pictures, while the picture framed by the window which wasn't going to be hung anywhere made no claim. The greys and greens were deepening there; the line of lamps, just lit, cut the broken mass of trees in the garden opposite; a light rain was beginning to freshen the dusty leaves.

The Changeling and *The Pedlar* were both written as children's poems, although she sometimes read them to adults, and they needed children to listen to them. One of the great attractions of the Dawson Scott household was the growing family there. These Charlotte described as 'a delightful girl of 14 who does the housekeeping and leaves the mother free for literary work – a boy of 10, and a footpad some years younger.' Marjorie, wise for her years, was a support to Charlotte as well, the only one she could turn to when she needed to relax her nerves at the end of a reading. The footpad, Christopher, reminded her of Elsie O'Keefe's two boys, a couple of 'Irish rascals'. He once offered her sixpence to make him laugh, which she appreciated, be-cause 'any blighter can make you cry, but only the very elect can make you laugh'. Nothing made her happier than to take

Mrs Dawson Scott and her daughter Marjorie.
'A delightful girl of 14 who does the housekeeping . . . .'

Marjorie to a concert or the whole lot of them to the Zoo, with
tea at the studio afterwards. Then she could be a cross between
a 'blighter' and a kind aunt. She never let them down; she
remembered too vividly what it had been like to develop
mumps just before the pantomime, and to be told by Elizabeth
Goodman that this would teach her submission to God's will.
And at the Zoo she was a privileged person, being on confidential terms with the parrot-house keeper, whom she consulted
from time to time about Wek.

Mrs Dawson Scott herself became fascinated by Charlotte,
perhaps more so than she had bargained for. She herself had no
lesbian sensibilities, and understood the dictionary meaning of
the word without the least notion of the reality, or of anything of
the kind ever being connected with anyone she knew or was
likely to know. Still, she felt an unexplained attraction. The
truth was, as she noted in her diary, that she longed for

Charlotte's 'stimulating, irritating, interesting company, her rough ways, her genius, often rude, her little pointed face and shining waves of hair'. Once when she was sitting in the Edgware Line train, absorbed in thinking about Charlotte, both the Mew sisters unexpectedly got into the carriage, as though thought-willed, at Golders Green. 'She is tiny, like a French Marquise,' Sappho reflected, 'uses amazing slang, and has ungainly movements – a queer mixture. Has a wonderful young soul, neither quite boy nor quite girl. Under the curious husk is a peculiarly sweet, humble nature.'

In a spirit of true generosity, Sappho determined to push Charlotte a little farther in the right direction. She must meet the best-known and most influential of all the visitors to Southall, May Sinclair. In 1913 Miss Sinclair was at the height of her success as a novelist, a talented professional, kindly, enthusiastic and *affairée*, bustling from the Women Writers' Suffrage League to the Society of Women Authors to the Women's Social and Political Union, and courted by pub-

May Sinclair outside the 'Votes for Women' shop
in Kensington, 1910.

115

lishers on both sides of the Atlantic. She was always moving house, and yet was never without what she called 'a writing retreat' and a devoted servant of some kind to look after her. In this respect she was even better organized than Sappho, and could always make time for one more book (she had published eight in the last seven years) or one more introduction. Where Charlotte was awkward and uncertain, May was sophisticated and firm. She would do Charlotte all the good in the world.

CHAPTER 12

May Sinclair

SIMONE DE BEAUVOIR called lesbianism a choice of life, but this is scarcely comprehensible. 'We are what we are,' wrote Charlotte Mew, 'the spirit afterwards, but first the touch.' She did not choose to fall in love with Lucy Harrison, or with Ella D'Arcy, and certainly not with May Sinclair.

In 1913 May was fifty. In appearance she was small, plump and neat – Ezra Pound compared her to an acorn – with a straight nose and a fine head of hair, which made her look to advantage when photographed in profile. She looked at first sight like a nice little homebody who would make someone an excellent wife. Her eyes were dark, with a peculiar golden glow in them, but although she was charming and friendly there was a certain coldness in her manner which was disconcerting at times. May was also formidably clever, and had trained herself, under Miss Dorothea Beale of Cheltenham Ladies' College, in philosophy.

> She came to dinner sometimes [wrote the novelist I. A. R. Wylie] and talked mainly about cats . . . . Once I asked J. D. Beresford to join us. He too was a philosopher and I thought between the two of them we should have a feast of reason. But philosophers, like pugilists, are wary of each other in the opening rounds and the feast threatened to be a complete frost until suddenly May Sinclair, rousing herself to the direct attack, leaned across the table and fixing her opponent with her eye demanded sternly, "And what, Mr Beresford, do you think of the ultimate reality?" After which they were off.

May had come up the hard way, with little money, a drunken father, a clinging 'little Mamma' and a pack of spoiled brothers. It is doubtful whether after her mother's death she cared intensely for any living creature except her black cats Tommy (d. 1914) and Jerry (d. 1927). After the primary emotional experience she seems, although she was always surrounded with friends, to have withdrawn precisely into herself. Here there was a mystery. She worked meticulously at the backgrounds of her books, and it was said (quite wrongly) that the first time she had to write a drunk scene she sat down and got drunk herself. But all her novels are concerned with the damage men and women do to each other, and the mutual destruction of flesh and spirit. How did refined, cosy-looking Miss Sinclair (once described as 'a small piece of upholstery rising from its seat') know about such things? How could she write for instance (as she had in *Mr and Mrs Nevill Tyson*) about the feelings of a woman who has to stop feeding her baby because her jealous husband wants sex? The question was naïve, perhaps. But it corresponded to May's own firm belief that a writer creates not from personal experience, but from imagination and knowledge of human psychology. 'Genius has little need of personal experience as the man in the street understands it,' she declared. Psychology she had studied since her days with Miss Beale, Freud she read in German as soon as *The Psychopathology of Everyday Life* and the *Three Essays on Sexuality* were available. Her method, in fact, was clinical. She allowed herself to indicate whether her characters were acting wisely or unwisely, but her main concern was to show how and why they behaved as they did.

The cost of this clear-sightedness to a woman writer might, she felt, be very great. In *The Creators* (1910) a woman novelist insists that virginity means a concentration of power which can be expended in art. 'Genius is giving you another sex inside you, and a stronger one, to plague you with,' but this too can be liberated in words. No need to go through marriage or childbirth, the writer is 'born knowing'. Experience, in fact, is a disadvantage, 'because it blinds you to everything but your own reactions'.

Whether or not all this could possibly be true of say, Mary Shelley, or of Ella D'Arcy (whom she had met), May did not discuss. She knew it was true of herself, and passionately believed it was true of the Brontës. They were self-sufficient, needing nothing outside the walls of Haworth Parsonage. When four of Charlotte Brontë's letters to M. Héger were printed in *The Times* (July 29, 1913) May felt them as a heavy personal blow. Like every other novelist who writes on the novel, her message had been: do it as I do it. This single vision admitted no qualification. Still, it could be misunderstood, and Charlotte Mew did misunderstand it. She was a totally different kind of writer, more different than she could possibly have guessed, registering only what corresponded to her own acute inner tension, while May looked outward, with a kind of keen placidity, to observe what she called 'the psychological mystery of human behaviour'.

Charlotte didn't want to be introduced to May Sinclair. She was never anxious to be introduced to anyone if it meant being produced as some kind of discovery, and she was quite genuinely afraid of May's reputation as a brilliant and highly educated woman, busy at the moment on her *Defence of Idealism*. What was more, Charlotte had particularly disliked what she had written about Emily Brontë in *The Three Brontës* (1912). May had interpreted Emily (from *Wuthering Heights*) as mentally and physically 'virile', and (from inquiries at Haworth) said that she had tramped the moors 'with the form and step of a virile adolescent'. Charlotte, as we have seen, profoundly believed that Emily was not like herself, but was above and apart from sexuality. *The Combined Maze*, however, which appeared in February 1913, was a different matter altogether, and by this latest novel of May's Charlotte felt stunned. 'It has completely got and kept hold of me – by what it is,' she told Sappho.

The Combined Maze is a psychological novel whose symbolism is drawn, rather unexpectedly, from the mixed gymnastics class at the Marylebone Polytechnic. May attended the institute evening after evening to get the details right. As it happened, she was, in spite of her demure roly-poly appearance, an excellent runner and jumper, and had even been taught by her brothers to be a good footballer. From an expert's point of view, then, she watched the Polytechnic's show piece, a combined formation march for both sexes, and saw it as an image of the wheel of life. In her novel the tramp of the approaching P.T. students is 'an unheard measure, secret and restrained, the murmur of life in the blood, the rhythm of the soundless will'. The elaborate exercise is a form of interpenetration,

> and as the radiant and vehement life rose in them like a tide, their gravity and shyness and severity passed from them; here and there hair was loosened; combs were shed and nobody stopped to gather them; for frenzy seized on the young men as their arms pressed on the girls' shoulders, urging the pace faster and faster . . . so divine was the madness of their running, so inspired the whirling of the wheel . . . so wise and powerful was the London Polytechnic.

But the central figure, a thirty-bob-a-weeker (a clerk, this time, in an Oxford Street store) is doomed by his own decency to act out the wrong pattern, sacrificing himself to the coarse and fleshly girl who sets out to get hold of him. (Self-sacrifice was always, in May Sinclair's view, a solution of a sort, but a mistaken one.) It is not hard to see why the story got and kept hold of Charlotte.

In the early spring of 1913 Sappho wrote in her diary:

> I went to Evelyn Underhill's and met May Sinclair and asked her to come and see me. She agreed and I then asked Charlotte, who resisted, saying she didn't want to meet clever people. Eventually agreed to come. May arrived first and was annoyed, as she had wanted to talk to me. However, when Charlotte came I persuaded her to read to us *The Farmer's Bride*, and May was so won over that she deserted me and they went away together.

It was a curious position that Charlotte should be seduced by a novel, and May 'won over' by a poem. The friendship, however, found its way slowly. May, at the beginning of 1913, was very much occupied with the organization of a favourite project, the Medico-Psychological Clinic of London. Into this she had sunk £500 and a considerable amount of time, for the excellent reason that she wanted to share with others what had

May Sinclair in 1913.

been of help to her. She had looked to Freud, and later to Jung, to exorcise the unhappiness of her own childhood. Once that was done, she had been able to tranquillize it into fiction. Now she wanted, with her medical colleagues, to open to the public the first clinic in England offering psycho-analysis as a treatment. In June, while she was still drumming up support and looking for clerical help, Charlotte took her summer holiday.

She went to Dieppe, apparently by herself, and also apparently on her own, she went to the circus. When she took children on this kind of outing, Charlotte enjoyed it just as they

did, and just as she had when she was six – that was one of the
reasons they liked going out with her. But in Dieppe that June
she imagined what it must be like to be an adolescent French
schoolboy, cooped up in the *internat* and let out for the day, with
nowhere to go or to amuse himself except the *fête* and this same
circus. If it was spring-time instead of summer, that would be
the hardest time of all for him, when even the rain sounded as if
it were 'starving'. He would have to sit with his friends on the
wooden benches, watching the clown, the dancing bear, and
the pretty lady on horseback.

> 'The good nights are not made for sleep, nor the good days
>   for dreaming in,
>   And at the end in the big circus tent we sat and shook and
>   stewed like sin . . . .'

The boy must be young enough to idealize his mother, who
has told him 'nothing is true that is not good' and old enough to
'stew' at the sight of the pretty lady with the white breasts.
'Charlotte is writing a poem about the soul of a boy of 17,' Mrs
Dawson Scott noted in her diary on September 13th. This
description had to do for the time being.

When she came back from France Charlotte had at first seen
a good deal of May Sinclair, who asked her to a woman writers'
dinner, and then wrote (4th July): 'My dear Miss Mew . . . I do
so want to see you and know you better. I was more grieved
than I can say at having to let you go the other evening. I was
steward at that terrible dinner, and had to leave to see that
everything was in order . . . . But I know you have forgiven me.'
There was something dazzling about May's ceaseless activity,
which always seemed to leave her time to do more than anyone
else. Two weeks later Charlotte was asked to bring her poems
round, and May eagerly made copies of everything. To her
mind they had 'profound vitality', and Charlotte mustn't mind
their lack of 'metrical technique'. She hadn't at all understood
Charlotte's experiments in free rhyming verse, following line by
line the impulses of the speaker, like jets of blood from a wound.
She simply felt that they needed tidying up. Never mind, she
would show them to Ezra Pound, for May knew Pound, as she

knew everybody. (She had in fact been one of the first people he marked down when he arrived in London from America five years earlier, ready to declare war on English literature.) Pound suggested the *English Review*, or, no, *Poetry* might pay better. 'Dear Charlotte,' May wrote, determined to drop formalities. But Charlotte still hung back.

She wanted to be on equal terms, and to repay hospitality – as Miss Lotti had been brought up to do – was difficult. May gave brilliant dinner parties and confidential tête-à-têtes at her flat in Edwardes Square, in leafy Kensington. Charlotte could manage tea at Anne's studio, but if they asked anyone to Gordon Street it was necessary to transfer old Mrs Mew discreetly upstairs, otherwise she tended to wreck the conversation with querulous interruptions. The solution would have been to join a club where guests could be invited – the Lyceum, for example, which was specifically intended for artistic and thinking women. But Charlotte could not have afforded the subscription.

In the late summer May suddenly disappeared to North Yorkshire. She had discovered (she was a great discoverer of places) a small guest house at Reeth which was quiet and comfortable enough to write in. To Charlotte this seemed a withdrawal, almost a snub. She began to fret – how much is clear enough from a letter from May saying that she had never dreamed that 'good-bye, good luck' would be taken as meaning 'good-bye for ever'. She was sorry she couldn't ask Charlotte up to Reeth, but it was impossible, she had been immensely busy, had had to pay a long visit to Scotland, had to rush to the deathbed of a dear old friend who had sent for her, had at all costs to catch up with her writing, on which, after all, her livelihood depended. May had a certain amount of time apportioned to each book, and made a summary of exactly what was to go in each chapter. Nothing was left to chance.

'All verse gains by being spoken, and mine particularly – I suppose because it's rough – though my *ideal* is beauty,' Charlotte told Sappho. Left behind in London, she wrote more poems than at any other time in her life, though some of them were left half way to be finished later. The 'soul of a boy of 17' was given the ironic title *Fête*. Another, *The Forest Road*, is almost impossible to follow; Dr Scott read it and said it was so deeply realized that he felt the author must be mad – 'a professional opinion', as Charlotte remarked. She knew she was tackling things which might prove too much for her, 'as in this form I am only a beginner'.

Possibly too much for her, certainly the longest, was *Madeleine in Church*. A woman is kneeling in the darkness in a side chapel, before the image of a homely saint 'with his tin-pot crown' – because the crucified Christ seems too remote from her. She is willing to believe and willing to disbelieve, but not able to do either. Madeleine isn't, in the late Victorian sense, a 'magdalen'. She is a demi-mondaine who has knocked about through marriage and divorce and has (like Pinero's Mrs Tanqueray) the capacity for good, but knows she has done harm.

> . . . The hateful day of the divorce:
> Stuart got his, hands down, of course
> Crowing like twenty cocks and grinning like a horse:
> But Monty took it hard. All said and done, I liked him best,
> He was the first, he stands out clearer than the rest.

But Pinero had made the guilty Mrs Tanqueray repent and, very properly, sacrifice herself (otherwise it would never have been a favourite part of Evelyn Millard's). Charlotte's Madeleine, with greater realism, asks not for less, but for more. She is prepared to have faith in heaven, but only in terms of this earth, because she was born to live through her senses – so much so that as an adolescent she couldn't bear even the shadows on the grass or the scent of white geraniums in the dusk, 'or, sometimes, my own hands about me anywhere'. And what is God going to do with the sensualists he created? He doesn't even reward the pure or the faithful, who have to pay out in suffering for what they never had.

> No one cannot see
> How it shall be made up to them in some serene eternity.
> If there were fifty heavens God could not give us back the child
> who went or never came.

But Madeleine is largely concerned with herself. She never wanted peace, only a body that would stay young, and hers has begun to age. On the verge of loneliness, she demands justice:

> There must be someone. Christ! there must,
> Tell me there *will* be some one. Who?
> If there were no one else, could it be You?

This, if it is a prayer at all, is prayer in very unflattering terms. God's peace in any case, she considers, is a last resort. He breaks us down and reduces us to nothing before he lets us come to him. 'I do not envy him his victories. His arms are full of broken things.' The only way Madeleine can form some conception of the love of God is through remembering a man who never touched her all night, except for one kiss. 'We slept with it, but face to face, the whole night through.' This is the best her imagination can do. 'We are what we are' and

> You can change the things for which we care
> But even You, unless You kill us, not the way.

Madeleine, like the clerk in Nunhead Cemetery, and the girl in the Quiet House, lets her life come back to her in fragments which her mind hardly wants to recognize. Some of these feel like Charlotte's own autobiography, in particular the 'little portress at the Convent School' and the mother, 'yoked to the man my father was', free of him now, but shrivelled in old age to a sapless mask while her portrait on the wall, 'her portrait at nineteen', seems to mock her. But Madeleine herself is a complex creation, something very different from the prostitute in *Passed*, or the 'sinner' in *Pécheresse*. We can't tell, and neither can she, how much of her agony is the protest of someone whose 'body is her soul' and how much is simply the terror of growing old.

Having got to the last two verses, Charlotte could not think how to end the poem. Her nerves were bad, and not made any better by one of her many attempts to give up smoking. These efforts reduced her to tears. Without cigarettes, she said, 'I want to die.' Where was May? But all that autumn and winter May could only be caught on the wing. She was in London in

October, on Medico-Psychological business. After the inaugural meeting she realized that her money was getting low, and with admirable efficiency shut herself up again with her cat to write four saleable short stories.

Charlotte relied very much at this point on the household at Southall. Although Sappho declared frankly that she had neither honour nor decency and let her friends see everything that was sent to her, Charlotte went on posting parcels of new poems for her to look at. She only asked not to be made to look too much of a damned fool. Then there were the children. She was teaching Christopher to repeat *The Golden Vanity*, and she wrote out *The Pedlar* and *The Changeling* for him. These copies, in her strong black dashing handwriting, are still in the family's possession.

Poor Anne was busy with rush orders at the workshop and was not given an hour off even on Christmas Eve. When she got home at last she was 'dreadfully fagged and [with] a chill from working in a freezing room'. The two sisters sat together on Christmas morning among piles of nightdress-cases, hat pins, pen-wipers and scent-bottles, tokens with an old-fashioned air which suggests they were from old school friends. Mrs Dawson Scott sent a nice antique sugar basin. Charlotte acknowledged this first of all, in case Judgement Day intervened before she thanked her for it. She had few wishes, she said, and not many needs, 'but real china of that particular kind is a (hereditary) passion, and I suppose the chief "need" of all of us is just that generous remembrance of our real selves that you have sent me'. Christmas letters can't be held in evidence against anyone. But what did Charlotte think of as her real self?

In the New Year May Sinclair was back in Edwardes Square. She was 'swallowed up', she said, in activities, but she must see Charlotte, or would Charlotte come to her?

CHAPTER 13

'Never Confess'

MAY WAS in two minds about *Fête*. Once again she was doubtful about the agitated long lines and the broken short ones. The poem had passion and vision, to be sure, but it was 'something about the form'. When Charlotte read it aloud, in her appealing boy's voice, just on the point of breaking, it was a different thing altogether. Privately May told Sappho that it was 'wonderfully achieved, but it absolutely needed her voice, her face, her intonation and vehemence, to make it carry. I think she's got to find a form which will be right without these outside aids.' But *Fête* must be published. Harriet Monroe's *Poetry* (which had rejected everything that Charlotte sent in) was condemned. Ezra Pound, too, was disgusted with *Poetry*. Perhaps he would consider it himself for *The Egoist*, on which he was the temporary literary editor. Only, May warned, there was no money to pay the contributors, and both Pound and Richard Aldington, the acting editor, were fastidious about what they called 'the metric' and 'intolerant with the implacable intolerance of youth'. Charlotte interpreted this to Sappho by telling her that they were 'choosy young gents'. Pound, however, was a connoisseur of metamorphosis, of speaking through and being spoken through, and, what was more, he understood the broken rhythm. He made no objection to *Fête*. He offered to print it in *The Egoist* as soon as there was room in the literary section. As he was also taking Joyce's *Portrait of the Artist as a Young Man* as a serial, Charlotte (as in her *Yellow Book* days) had for a while a place among the front runners.

But if this looked like success, what about Anne, still toiling away for six days of the week? This was the old situation, no better for being old. 'I simply hate telling [Anne] about these verses – because she's had no chance whatever, and has 100 times my pluck and patience – and her own very definite gift – all going to seed – and to me it's heart-breaking – and she would be furious if she knew I was saying it – and hasn't the least idea that I feel it acutely – so little do we people who spend our days together know each other.'

Charlotte meant more by this than the waste of a professional career. She saw the uncomplaining Anne, 'my little sister', cut off from the resources of her imagination. Thinking over Charlotte Brontë's question, whether the imagination is a greater blessing or a greater curse, she came out unhesitatingly on imagination's side, preferring to suffer (as she certainly did) with the tormented creatures who spoke for her. Her audience knew this when she sat exhausted after her readings, lost to them and to herself. With artists like Charlotte Mew it is truly not possible to tell the dancer from the dance. Whether Anne's painting meant as much to her there is no way of telling, but Charlotte believed that it could have done, and Anne was now forty years old.

It was at this point that something in Charlotte seemed to break free, and she began to behave to May Sinclair exactly as she had done ten years before to Ella D'Arcy. She fell in love, as before, with a woman older than she was, partly from physical attraction, but partly because, in each case, she had been helped and taught. One of her most endearing characteristics was her capacity for gratitude, a kind of bewilderment that anyone should take so much trouble over 'this dreary little person'.

The first thing was to make herself useful to May. She offered to address circulars for the Medico-Psychological Clinic (May's niece had come to help her, but had got sick of it after sticking on seven stamps). May refused, on the grounds that she couldn't put such a burden on any of her friends. Soon there was another opportunity. Amateur musicians next door were making life intolerable in Edwardes Square. May loved music, but preferred to choose when and where she heard it. She must move at once, preferably to Hampstead or better still to Bloomsbury, where she had heard there were no musicians. Charlotte accordingly threw herself, beyond the call of duty, into house-hunting.

May, who had a number of other friends on the job, was aghast at Charlotte's exhaustion. 'And all my days I shall be haunted by a vision of you, small, and too fragile by far for the hideous task, going up and down those infernal houses.' None of the places Charlotte suggested would suit, either. The rents were all too high. But May's relations were 'scouring' in all directions. They would probably find her somewhere in St John's Wood. 'Of course I know you were angelic enough too – perhaps – like running round to House Agents for me – but can't you see that your time ought to be given to poems, and not to lazy friends?'

Charlotte had meant to be indispensable, instead she was an object of pity. 'I shall simply have to bolt,' she wrote to the Dawson Scotts, though without saying why. At first it looked difficult, since Jane Elnswick had suddenly announced she was going home to look after her mother, something that the Mews, of all people, could hardly object to. But a cleaning-woman descended 'like Manna from the clouds' on Gordon Street, and it was possible, after all, to go.

On the 6th of April she was in Dieppe again, at the Hôtel du Commerce, where they knew her, and gave her a small room at the top of the house, looking out over red roofs and grey tiles and clouds which seemed ready to drift in at the window. 'It makes all the difference to me to be in the right place,' she wrote to Edith Oliver. 'And I should never have done *Fête* if I hadn't been here last year. One realizes the place much more alone I think – it is all there – you don't feel it through another mind which mixes up things – I wonder if Art – as they say, is rather an inhuman thing?'

She hadn't brought any books with her, only the tea-making machine. The first morning she always spent as Miss Lotti, getting methylated spirits from somewhere or other to make the wretched thing work. In the afternoon she went down to the harbour and watched a furniture auction, in an odd state of mind. Just before she left London she had heard that two more of her 'jingles', *Fame* and *Pécheresse*, had been accepted by the *New Weekly*. But she felt 'in a mild state of stupor', as though she didn't care whether they were published or not. The next day she was at the street corner in the fishermen's quarter, watching the old women mend the nets and go off 'with dreadful loads of them on their bent shoulders'. Nobody noticed her, it seemed; she might just as well have been invisible. 'I think born quay-loafers are taken for what they are.' The 'fisher-children', in their black school overalls, took to her particularly well, and showed her how to chalk out the pavement for a game of *pelote*. She was half-way towards becoming a 'rambling sailor'. (The Rambling Sailor was an inn-sign which had stuck in her memory. Rambling is more spirited than wandering, and more innocent than roving.)

But a letter came to say that Anne was ill from overwork. Charlotte hurried back. She had always thought that Anne should give notice – even if it meant starvation – and, not long afterwards, Anne did. The idea was that from now on she would not go out to work, but give lessons in the studio, though at the moment she had only one pupil, a music-hall singer, magnificent in her hat and sealskin coat but, Charlotte thought, very dirty underneath them.

May was now installed in St John's Wood, at 1 Blenheim Road, where there was a courtyard with trees behind the house. But during Charlotte's absence the doted-upon black cat, Tommy, had died, and May was only just recovering from the shock. She was in a vulnerable, affectionate mood. Charlotte opened cautiously by asking her to tea; Sappho would also be there. 'I'd ever so much rather see you by yourself (though I like Mrs Dawson Scott very much),' May replied, and a week later, calling her 'My dear', she begged her to come to supper with Evelyn Underhill and the Richard Aldingtons. No. 1 Blenheim Road, she added, would be 'honoured and blessed' by Charlotte's crossing the threshold. In the few weeks since the two of them had met again a curious situation had developed, a tenseness where the smallest misunderstanding might be a declaration of love or war.

130

Not by way of an answer [May wrote on 14 May] but as a general statement, may I assure you that I really have *not* a complicated mind, but in some ways rather a simple one, and when I say 'I want to walk with you to Baker Street Station', I mean to *walk*, and I want to walk with *you*, and I want to walk to Baker Street Station. The act of walking is a pleasure in itself, that has no ulterior purpose or significance.

Better to take things simply and never go back on them, or analyse them, is not it?

I (who am so complicated) took it all quite simply and was glad of it – of you being here, of you talking to me – well, why can't you do the same?

May Sinclair had, apparently, no idea why Charlotte could not do the same, and after several more meetings asked Charlotte to come and read whatever it was she had been writing. Charlotte read the first verse of *Madeleine in Church* 'so furiously well' that May said she wouldn't dare give her anything of her own afterwards, as it would sound totally dead. 'Finish – finish your courtisan, she's magnificent. The last verses are all there – coiled up in a lobe of your brain asleep and waiting to be waked, like Tommy in his basket.' And Charlotte did finish it. Madeleine, in the published version, drops her defiance and remembers her childhood, when she lay awake at night, unable to bear the thought of the Crucifixion. 'When I was small I never quite believed he was dead.' And yet she could have borne the pain if Christ had seemed, even for one moment, to notice her.

At this point in the summer Charlotte herself was thinking of writing a novel (though Mrs Dawson Scott was emphatically against it) – 'in Russia they are producing the very short and impressionistic variety just now'. She was also reading Conrad's *Chance*, taking it very slowly so as to make it last as long as possible.

In *Chance* she marked a passage on page 193, where Marlow, Conrad's self-questioning narrator, discusses whether it makes sense to confess.

Never confess! never! never – a confession of whatever sort is always untimely. The only thing which makes it supportable for a while is curiosity. You smile? Ah, but it is so, or else people would be sent to the rightabout at the second sentence. How many sympathetic souls can you reckon on in the world? One in ten, one in a hundred – in a thousand – in ten thousand? . . . For a confession, whatever it may be, stirs the secret depths of the hearer's character. Often depths that he himself is but dimly aware of.

If Charlotte could have had her time over again, she would not have confessed what she felt to May Sinclair. But at the end of June a feverish gaiety seemed to have taken hold of May. She wanted to talk French with Charlotte, and to discuss Verlaine. Then it came out that she had written a poem in French herself, which she wanted read through and corrected. The subject was *La Morte* (the Dead Woman).

Qu'avez-vous fait de vos beaux jours, ma chère,
Les jours qui sont passés,
Et de vos joies, les âpres, les amères,
Qu'avez-vous fait?

Du petit corps, si tendre, si frileux,
Des bras qui se tordaient,
Du petit coeur malin et les yeux
Qui ont tant pleurés?

De l'âme sauvage, qui se tourne et se brise
(Ma pauvre bien-aimée!)
De la petite âme fuyante, fragile, exquise –
Qu'avez-vous fait?

O mon enfant, tout ce que tu as souffert
Tu ne saurais jamais –
Et moi, je ne donnerais mon enfer
D'être ce que tu es.

My dear, what have you done with the best days of your life, the days which are past and gone, and what have you done with your harsh and bitter joys?

(What have you done) with your little body, so tender, so sensitive to the cold, your writhing arms, your wicked little heart, and those eyes which shed so many tears?

What have you done with that wild soul, which is twisting and breaking itself, my poor beloved, that little, fleeting, fragile, exquisite soul?

Oh my child, you will never understand how much you have
suffered, and as for me, I wouldn't give up my share of
hell to be what you are now.

May Sinclair was a strange woman. There is no accounting
for the warmth, even the extravagance of her letters and the
demureness of her actual presence. Very probably it was
writing this odd and morbid poem in itself that excited her.
'Wicked little heart' (and 'wicked little smile') were phrases
used often, though always affectionately, about Charlotte. We
have to take it that May didn't intend, or not seriously, any
personal reference to the little body and the self-tormenting
soul. But it is understandable that Charlotte thought that she
did.

'Charlotte has been bothering and annoying May,' Sappho
entered in her diary at the beginning of July. 'Charlotte is
evidently a pervert.' 'Are all geniuses perverts?' she added, in
bewildered indignation. She recalled Ella D'Arcy's reputation
with men. She could not understand it. She could not come to
terms with it. May had asked her to tea 'so that we can talk',
and told her what had happened.

It seems rather unlucky – but Charlotte was hardly ever
lucky – that this incident, like Shelley's first wedding and
Swinburne's decline, has only been recorded in terms of farce.
Rebecca West sent to May Sinclair's biographer, Dr Theophilus Boll, a copy of a letter from the novelist G. B. Stern ('Peter').
The letter recalled, at a distance of time, how May had told
both of them 'in her neat, precise little voice' that 'a lesbian
poetess, Charlotte M., had chased her upstairs into the bedroom – "And I assure you, Peter, and I assure you, Rebecca, I
had to leap the bed five times!"' And Dr Boll, a most painstak-
ing American academic, was left to calculate, as he tells us,
whether May, at the age of fifty-one, would really have been
able to do all this leaping, and if she did, how she could have
managed after the fifth leap, which would have trapped her
against the wall. I am not sure how Dr Boll could tell whether,

in the summer of 1914, May's bed was against the wall or not. What is certain is that there was an uncontrolled physical confession of furious longing, desiring and touching which terrified May, and perhaps also terrified Miss Lotti.

'My mother told me the detailed story,' wrote Marjorie Dawson Scott (Mrs Marjorie Watts), 'when I was about 17 and asked why we never saw Charlotte. She also recorded in her journal that when she and that attractive gossip and novelist, Netta Syrett, were discussing Margaret Radclyffe Hall and Una, Lady Troubridge, with May, the latter said: "I don't believe what is said of them is true," to which Netta replied: "I believe it, but I don't mind." And May countered this with: "You wouldn't like it if it happened to *you*. It did happen to me," but I said, "My good woman, you are simply wasting your perfectly good passion."' This phrase of May's is the final insult to Charlotte's love, the nursery phrase, recalling from childhood the 'perfectly good' knickers that can be worn again, and the 'perfectly good' bread and butter that someone else would be grateful for. It was as though Elizabeth Goodman was watching still.

What could Charlotte possibly have hoped for? A physical response certainly, but even so she and May could never have lived together as loving friends. Even if May was free of family ties, Charlotte decidedly was not. Whatever happened she must lose (this, of course, is the moment for taking risks). She didn't want, and for Anne's sake couldn't afford, to leave the society of 'five o'clock people'. Hans Andersen, another homo-erotic writer, told children (among others) that his Little Mermaid did not suffer and die because she wanted to leave the human community, but because she wanted to join it at any cost. Charlotte, the unwilling outsider, was left with a deep capacity for love, even a vocation, but May had pitied it with even less understanding than Ella D'Arcy.

'Blindest of all the things that I have cared for very much In the whole gay, unbearable, amazing show.' Was it necessary for May Sinclair to tell so many other people about it – Charlotte had no way of knowing how many? 'I don't think there's anything quite so deadly as "giving people away",' she had told

9 Gordon Street W.C.1.
June 24: [1917]

Dear Mrs Scott

    If adjective are powerless, I'm afraid
there's nothing to be done with people
deaf to the Sacred Call & to whom
the prospect of being 'snowed under'
is a tranquil one - with - let us hope -
some sense of humour & proportion
still creating jents beneath the drift.
    People are only 'disappointing'
when one makes a wrong diagnosis
- but they char come the sole beget of
a ~~~~~~ Tomorrow Club to be
babbling o' green fields 's yesterday's

            w Sincerely yours

            Charlotte Mew.

course it's nice to know that up to
June 21. 1917) you still liked the
old jungle: C.M.

Letter from Charlotte Mew to Mrs Dawson Scott, 24 June 1917.
'People are only "disappointing" when one makes
a wrong diagnosis . . . .'

Mrs Dawson Scott a few months earlier, 'but it never seems they are given away to me – because I think I see beyond their weakness and their poses – "we are all stricken men" one way or another – and the only thing I have no mercy for is hardness and deadness.' She had made herself 'dam ridiculous', in her own phrase, and more so than she had ever dreaded. Perhaps she felt that Mrs Sappho, to whom she owed so much, might have made more allowances for her. Something was broken between them that could never be mended. Three years later, when Sappho had founded the first of her writers' organizations, the Tomorrow Club, she was disappointed because Charlotte refused formally (though not very politely) to come and read to them, in the old way. 'People are only "disappointing"', Charlotte wrote in this letter, 'when one makes a wrong diagnosis.'

In August 1914 the outbreak of war separated them all. Dr Scott joined the RAMC, Mrs Dawson Scott set to work on plans for a Women's Defence League, Edith Oliver began training in Queen Alexandra's Nursing Yeomanry, Evelyn Millard, who had been appearing as Cho-Cho San in *Madam Butterfly*, switched to a patriotic Queen Elizabeth in *Drake* at the Coliseum. Charlotte, who was home-bound, and had what was then called 'no men to give', extended her visiting to the volunteers' wives who had for several months no idea when and where to collect their allowance of three shillings a week. Very soon, too, there were the widows of some of the first 32,000 casualties.

But in the almost unbelievable early anxiety to be in the thick of 'the show' May Sinclair seemed to be well ahead of the field. From September to October she was in Belgium with an ambulance team sent out by the Medico-Psychological Unit and working with the Belgian Red Cross. The commandant was Dr Hector Munro, the clinic's consultant. May acted as secretary and contributed a good deal of the funds. But she was used to organizing things in her own way, and perhaps showed this a little too plainly. The first weeks of inactivity, before the refugees from the German advance arrived, were the worst. 'I began to feel like a large and useless parcel which the commandant had brought with him in sheer absence of mind.' A few days later, according to her *Journal of Impressions of Belgium*, she was 'coldly and quietly angry' with the commandant. 'I don't quite know what I said to him, but I think I said he ought to be ashamed of himself.' Even Dr Boll, her sympathetic biographer, says that 'she did not subordinate her strongly critical mind to the disciplinary phase of the military machine'. In October Dr Munro asked her to go home and appeal for more funds. While she was in England he sent a message to the War Office, telling them that on no account was Miss Sinclair to be allowed back to Belgium.

With what disappointment and humiliation we can't tell, but, with all her energies intact, May came back to St John's Wood. She had not seen Charlotte since July. The first thing she wrote (before even her *Journal of Impressions*) was a story for *Harper's* which she called *The Pinprick*. It was a tale of studio life. The male narrator describes an enigmatic figure, a woman artist, May Blissett. Mrs Blissett (she is a widow) gives 'the illusion of fragility – an exquisite person in spite of her queerness'. He is amazed at 'the tiny scale of the whole phenomenon', but thinks of her 'God forgive me, as malign'. She is shy and touchy and furiously anxious not to be 'in the way'. Nobody wants her to take the empty studio in the block, but she moves in, and his fiancée, Frances Archdale, explains 'she's not like a woman. She was trying to tell you that she wasn't. She isn't. She isn't – really – quite human.' The reason, Frances thinks, is that May Blissett has been through so much. Her father had gone mad, the family had lost all their money, her baby died. 'She's come through it all, my dear. She's utterly beyond. Immune.' But one afternoon the strange little woman calls on Frances, who has an old friend in for tea, and doesn't much want any other visitors. May Blissett, however, stays and stays. It must, they think, be simply her obstinacy and her '*quand même*'. But when at last she takes her leave she goes up to her studio, locks the door, and asphyxiates herself. After all she has suffered, she is driven to despair, in the end, by a 'pinprick'. She had not been wanted, and she knew it. What they had taken for malignity was loneliness.

The 'malignity' of the tiny woman suggests 'ton petit coeur malin', and it can hardly be doubted that *The Pinprick* is an analysis of Charlotte, which was also intended to set May's mind at rest. This was her long-tried method. Neither here nor anywhere else in her work, however, does she discuss homosexuality, and in 1914 she had very little guidance on the subject, and none at all on homosexuality in women, since Freud had declared that their 'erotic life was still veiled in an impenetrable obscurity'. May Blissett is presented as the victim of a trauma, the result of a series of tragic deaths in the family and sudden poverty. The shock has been suppressed, and the victim seems to be 'immune'. But in fact there has been no release of the long-buried emotional material, and when she makes a last appeal to be allowed back into normal human contact, and is rejected, she sees no point in living any longer. In Charlotte's case, there had been an alternative ending. May had overcome the early diffidence and touchiness and 'talked out' the sad history – as far as she knew it – of the Mew family. The result, according to Freud's earlier studies, on which May relied so heavily, would be the transference or investment of love to the doctor or sympathetic friend. This explanation, or what seemed to be explanation, would make Charlotte's behaviour understandable. This doesn't mean that May condoned it. Indeed, she differed sharply from both Freud and Jung over the value of repression, considering it good for everyone, and for the writer in particular.

Charlotte, between 1914 and 1918, wrote a group of poems about shameful exposures and betrayal. *Ne Me Tangito* (by which I think Charlotte meant *Nolle me tangere*) is the strangest of the lot; the beloved, who 'fears her touch' and tries to hide the ugly doubt 'behind that hurried puzzled little smile' turns, in her dream, into a baby at the breast

> The child for which I had not looked or ever cared
> Of whom, before, I had never dreamed.

There are free associations here of a frightening kind, and they connect with *Saturday Market*, which is one of the most successful things Charlotte Mew ever wrote. In this poem a wretched woman has to walk through the open market, hiding her pregnancy or abortion, we can't tell which, under her ragged shawl – a nightmare experience, while the crowd is 'grinning from end to end'. This is an image from the Mews' childhood, the old rough Saturday markets at Newport, which were always forbidden ground. There is, in fact, a ballad-singer's jaunty air to the poem. The speaker gives the woman her orders, being able to see through all her efforts at conceal-ment. 'Cover it close', 'hasten you home with the laugh behind you', 'fasten your door', 'take out the red, dead thing'.

> In the white of the moon
>   On the flags does it stir again? Well, and no wonder!
> Best make an end of it; bury it soon.

Lie down, don't waste too much time crying, kill yourself. The joke of it is that none of this matters, because 'in Saturday market nobody cares'.

In *Ken* and *The Farmer's Bride*, however much we pity the outcasts, we have to suppose that the small community rejects them because it must protect itself. In *Saturday Market* the pressure of the outside world is felt for the first time as entirely cruel and hostile. But the poet's voice is also cruel, offering no hope to the disgraced. The woman who carries and buries the 'red, dead thing' is advised to forget the sea, the swallows and the trees. Nature doesn't want her either, there is no refuge there.

Between Charlotte and May, however, there was no definite break. Indeed, after she got back from Belgium, it was May who seemed unwilling to let go. She went on sending affection-ate notes, asking Charlotte to meet useful people, and to walk round the streets of London, now darkened against a possible Zeppelin raid. On 9 June 1915 she wrote Charlotte a long letter about the Imagist poets Pound, Flint, Aldington and Hilda Doolittle. She had two points to make – first, what would the imagists do if the presentation of a concentrated moment, without comment, wasn't sufficient to 'carry' or express the strength of their emotions? 'Poets shouldn't be ridiculed, however, for doing something else,' she went on. 'You don't despise Meleager because he isn't Sappho, although if you had to choose between them, you know which you would let go.' Secondly, had the Imagists strong human emotions to express at all, or was their passion just 'hair-tearing'? The hearts and souls of the Imagists, she had come to the conclusion, weren't strong enough to carry them to 'great heights and depths . . . .' But 'I know one poet whose breast beats like a dynamo under an iron-grey tailor-made suit (I *think* one of her suits is iron-grey) and when she publishes her poems she will give me something to say that I *cannot* and do not say of my Imagists'.

This letter, meant to be persuasive, strikes one as tactless in the extreme. The reference to Sappho seems unfortunate, but then so too is the reference to Meleager, about whom Charlotte knew nothing. As to the remarks about poor Charlotte's heart and her grey suit, they are an attempt to strike May's old sensible, rallying tone, but without success.

Dame Rebecca West told me that May (whom she had known as a young woman) managed to persuade herself that Charlotte's passion was nothing but *Schwärmerei*, an inconvenience. 'You wouldn't like it if it happened to *you*.' Another viewpoint comes from the American poet Virginia Moore, who interviewed May at the end of the 1920s, when she was over in England working on a study of the Brontës. In her book, when it was eventually published, Virginia Moore noted that May had described Emily, in *The Three Brontës*, as having 'the form and step of a virile adolescent', and she added a footnote on Charlotte Mew. 'Her voice, manner, taste in clothes, walk and physical appearance, though she was small and delicate, hinted faintly of masculinity. She could not change. She did not know what to do about the instincts in her. She was half-appalled, half-loyal to them.' If this represents May's final judgement, it is a more thoughtful one. After that blankness descends, for in the 1930s May Sinclair entered a long mental twilight during which she could neither recognize nor care about any other human being, except her housekeeper.

In 1915, however, she was generous enough to tell Charlotte that if only her income hadn't been down to bedrock (largely through supporting the ambulance unit) she would have liked to publish *The Farmer's Bride* and all the other poems herself. Fortunately, Charlotte was soon to come across a publisher, and at the same time a place, where she could venture to feel welcome without being altogether ridiculous. This place was the Poetry Bookshop.

CHAPTER 14

The Poetry Bookshop

❧

THE POETRY BOOKSHOP (in its first premises) existed from 1913 to 1926. It was in a squalid bit of Bloomsbury, full of small workshops, dustbins and cats – 35 Devonshire Street (now Boswell Street). It opened from 11 a.m. to 6.30 p.m., never had many paying customers at any time, and, right from the start, was usually in financial difficulties. But it was there, and even the fact that it was there was of real importance.

The shop itself was on the ground floor of a dilapidated eighteenth-century house, with only one cold-water tap for the whole building. However, as you came through the swing door you felt the warmth of a coal fire burning at the other end of the room. There was a dog stretched out there and a cat, which sometimes sprang about the shelves, apparently deliberately, knocking down piles of books. The furniture had been made by the Fabian master-carpenter Romney Green, and was exceptionally solid, the curtains were of sacking, and there were cushions in 'jolly' colours. Across the walls rhyme sheets were displayed in rows, a penny plain, twopence coloured, and bought mostly for children. A whole generation learned to love poetry from these rhyme sheets. On the table by the fire were the shop's latest publications, for anyone to sit down and read. Everything was for anyone to sit down and read. The stock included all the poetry in print by every living English poet, and living poets were there themselves, particularly if they were young and poor. It was the first place they made for when they got to London, and if they had nowhere to live there were rooms for them in the attics, at a very low rent. Robert Frost brought the whole of his family there in 1913, Wilfred Owen was squeezed out, but given a room over the coffee shop opposite,

Wilfrid Gibson lived in a kind of cupboard, marked 'in case of fire, access to the roof is through this room'. 'They have underneath the house a shop where they sell poetry by the pound,' according to the sculptor Gaudier-Brzĕska, 'and talk to the intellectuals.' In a small office on the first floor, in front of a heavy Barlock typewriter, sat a conventional-looking business man with a dark moustache and a diffident smile. This was Harold Monro, the proprietor, harassed, but easily persuaded to come out and give advice, with his sudden warm smile, to the customers.

Monro was the awkward product of a new century's gospel of Joy, Hope, Freedom and Simplicity at work on a dour, practical Scot who drew a reasonable income from his family's private

Harold Monro in the Poetry Bookshop.

143

The Poetry Bookshop in 1913.

lunatic asylum. Some business caution he always retained, but the romantic idealist in him had made him waver, until he was nearly thirty-five, between the choices in life. In 1908, for example, he had been training himself to join the Samurai, a society vowed to clean living, vegetarian diet, exercise, and meditation 'with the object of evolving a higher human type'. His diary (not for the only time) recorded nightmares. He dreamed that he was a corpse watching the worms eating him, or that he was falling down the inside of a narrow tower lined with bookshelves, which he clutched at for support. In another dream John Galsworthy was eating an enormous beef steak which covered the whole table – 'finally he chases and be-labours me with it'. This mixture of the ideal, the sinister and the grotesque was to haunt Harold Monro to the end of his life.

But although he tried various occupations, nothing mattered more to him than poetry. He was addicted to poetry as others are addicted to drink – indeed, as Monro himself was addicted to drink, for he found life a tormenting business. 'I can't learn to know men,' he wrote,

144

'or conceal
How strange they are to me.'

'He was slow to react,' according to C. H. Sisson, 'for the best reasons, because he was all the time trying to eject something which lay at the bottom of his mind.' But at length, in 1911, he arrived back from his European travels to England and devoted himself to 'doing something about poetry'. No groups, no cliques, nothing doctrinaire, but a meeting-place (he called it a 'depôt') for poets of all persuasions, and every kind of reader. He would publish, too, but at the 'depôt' poetry must be heard read aloud, because to him a book was a printed score, brought alive only by the human voice. It was a brave ambition for a shy and only moderately well-off man. (Even the unsavoury Devonshire Street had been partly chosen in the hope that the poor would come into the shop and read; they didn't, however, but looked on him as a source of free drinks after hours.) Going about the affair with Scottish good sense and competence, he acquired his own magazine, and found small firms who could print up to his standard. In September 1912 he was asked by Eddie Marsh to publish the first volume of *Georgian Poetry*.

Marsh was Winston Churchill's private secretary, a generous patron of modern painting, and, in an innocent way, of young men, who eventually led him towards poetry. With Rupert Brooke and Monro (who shared the financial risk) Marsh felt he was making a decisive step forward with his anthology of up-to-date Georgians, the point being that they were not Victorians. Fortunately, in 1912 he could count on a general *disposition* to read poetry. There were many other circles like Mrs Dawson Scott's, and beyond this it was the great time for small, thin-paper, verse anthologies, with a ribbon for a bookmark, which went easily into the side-pocket, and were taken for long tramps in the fresh air, returning with grass and pressed flowers between the pages. *The Golden Treasury* (1897) was one of the first of these, and there was no sign of their running out. It was true that these little volumes, even when they were by the newer poets, were often not very demanding. John Drinkwater, for example, in *Poems of Love and Earth* (1912) thanks God for (1) sleep; (2) clear day through the little leaded panes; (3) shining well water; (4) warm golden light; (5) rain and wind (apparently at the same time as (2); (6) swallows; (7) wallflowers, tulips, primroses and 'crowded orchard boughs'; (8) good bread; (9) honey-comb; (10) brown-shelled eggs; (11) kind-faced women with shapely mothering arms; (12) tall strong-thewed young men; (13) an old man bent above his scythe; (14) the great glad earth and 'Heaven's trackless ways'. There was a great deal of this kind of thing at the lower and easier end of the repertoire, where eggs were always brown, the women always kind, and the earth always glad. But the poetry was meant to give pleasure and it was, after all, the last body of English poetry to be actually read, by ordinary people, for pleasure.

To this easy-going public Marsh now wanted to introduce his new voices – Rupert Brooke, Walter de la Mare, Ralph Hodgson, W. H. Davies, D. H. Lawrence. There was no question of any women poets, and it was not until his third volume that Marsh ever enquired as to whether there were any. Monro told him that if the voices were to be new they must include Ezra Pound. But Pound refused permission to include his early poem on Christ, *The Goodly Fere*, because he was reprinting it himself. No Pound, then, but this did not disturb Marsh, who thought of him as a wild creature, an outsider rampaging through Kensington. The grand old man, to whom all looked up, was Thomas Hardy, who was known to be suspicious of the Georgians, but might be won over. Neither Marsh nor even Monro realized how soon English poetry was going to be taken over by powerful aliens.

Meanwhile they printed 5,000 copies of *Georgian Poetry 1911–12* and sold, in the end, 15,000. With only an office boy and a lady secretary to help him at the Bookshop, Monro had more work than he could manage. The office-boy was so absent-minded that the kettle, which was a slow boiler, was named after him; then Wilfrid Gibson, the simplest and most delightful of poets, disorganized the business by eloping with the secretary. Still Monro was unwilling to give up any part of the work, least of all the Bookshop. At this point he had the good fortune to meet Alida Klementaski.

Alida Monro

Alida was a beautiful girl from a Hampstead-Polish refugee family, looking for a way to make the world a better place. She was twenty years old, and at the back of her mind (she said) she seemed to hear a voice repeating 'Life is expecting much of thee.' She might be a doctor, she thought, or an actress, or a leader in the women's suffrage movement. She might go out and rescue prostitutes from the street, but at all costs she must not be 'an encumberer of the ground'. This sounds as though Alida had no sense of humour; she had, but she took serious things seriously.

She and Harold Monro first met at a poets' club dinner at the Café Monico on 14 March 1913. The subject was the nineties poet John Davidson (the author of *Thirty Bob a Week*). The soup was Velouté Shakespeare. Alida, in a borrowed Liberty dress, was the reader, and Harold Monro realized, when he heard her, that there were women, as well as men, for whom poetry was life. His own wife, from whom he was separated, had frowned if the word 'soul' was mentioned. Almost immediately Alida found herself a bed-sitter and began to work, at a salary of five pounds a month, in the Bookshop. In a fit of conscience Monro warned her that to 'join the ranks of the emancipated' would cause eyebrows to be raised. Alida gloried in the idea. Her energy and devotion were so great that he soon admitted he was 'at sea' without her.

From 'Dear Miss Klementaski' she rapidly became 'Dear Alida' and then 'Dear child'. They were deeply in love, but not lovers. Alida felt herself one of the free, and longed to bear his child, or at least to live under the same roof. But Monro could not bring himself to admit to her outright, either then or ever, that he had been homosexual since his school days at Radley. In an attempt to lead up to an explanation he told her that it was possible to love one person for their mind, another for their body, and, once, that he felt he was doing her 'a great, sad wrong' which it was impossible to explain. He can be seen as afraid to lose her, and even more afraid to hurt her. Alida was an impressionable, but not a complicated, person. One day for her could be torture, the next joy unspeakable. She had no idea what he was talking about.

It was no secret, however, to some of the Bookshop's regulars, who liked Harold, but felt Alida needed consolation. Ralph Hodgson, a pipe-smoking, bull-terrier-fancying poet, not a man of many words, came into the shop one evening and kissed her. 'I couldn't help it and couldn't prevent it,' she wrote. 'He knew that and apologized after. It is very curious the terrible repulsion I have to the feel of anyone besides you near me. I don't suppose that you have it, do you?' Harold replied, disappointingly, that he could not set up to be a protector of women. But he loved her, he said, as he loved the earth itself, without always remembering it was there.

To this trust Alida responded with noble loyalty. Her great concern was to keep to the ideal of their first friendship, those moments which she thought of as 'beaten into white heat'. With those in mind, she sustained herself during his frequent ab-

sences on lecture tours and hard-working business trips. With
the declaration of war in 1914 her responsibilities doubled. At
first Monro thought the Bookshop would have to close at once,
but in a few weeks it was business as usual. He relied on her to
keep him in touch day by day. That was hard enough for a girl
who was training herself as she went along, and even harder
were some of the letters she had to write. On April 26 1915, for
example, she had to break the news to him that Rupert Brooke
had died in the Dardanelles. 'I'm so glad he wasn't shot, aren't
you?' she offered as the one consolation.

On most things, certainly on political principles, they were
absolutely agreed. After the war all colonies must be handed
back to their inhabitants and all governments must become
democracies. No prisons, no slaughterhouses. As to the Bookshop, it must stay open for the duration, as poetry's shelter.
Monro (who had volunteered as a despatch rider and been
turned down) refused to make money out of the 'patriotic
anthologies' which were rushed into print during the first
recruiting drive. The most he would do was to end the shop's
poetry readings with a war poem, often Laurence Binyon's
'They shall grow not old'.

These famous Bookshop readings, famous, that is, out of all
proportion to the size of the audience, were on Tuesdays and
Thursdays. They took place in an attic up a flight of stairs, steep
as a ladder, so that Alida sometimes made a note 'No falls
to-night'. In front of the curtain and the softly-shaded light,
Monro welcomed all comers with 'stiff, soldierly little bows',
concealing an agony of nerves. He often had to get drunk
afterwards – particularly, for some reason, on Thursdays – and
had nightmares of suffocation. He never read his own poems
aloud himself, but left this to Alida, who slipped them quietly
into the programme on the 'twentieth-century' evenings. For
one of these, in the late autumn of 1915, she arranged to read
from Monro, John Masefield, James Joyce, Eleanor Farjeon,
D. H. Lawrence and Charlotte Mew.

Alida, like Mrs Dawson Scott, had read *The Farmer's Bride* in
1912, and had not forgotten it. No-one seemed to know Charlotte Mew's address, but Monro suggested that they might get

it through *The Nation*. Alida, who by this time had undertaken most of the secretarial work for the shop, accordingly wrote off, and asked if there were any more poems to be got together to make a small book. A reply arrived from Charlotte, thanking Miss Klementaski, but pointing out that if her poems *were* published, nobody would want to read them. Enclosed, however, was a copy of *The Changeling*.

Both *The Changeling* and *The Farmer's Bride* were in the programme for a Tuesday in November 1915. Alida had written once again to 9 Gordon Street, asking the author whether she wouldn't like to come and hear her verses read aloud? There was, of course, no way of knowing what this newcomer would look like. About twelve or fifteen people used to drop in on the modern poetry evenings, most of them young, some of them in uniform. At about five minutes to six the swing door opened and out of the autumn fog came a tiny figure, apparently a maiden aunt, dressed in a hard felt hat and a small-sized man's overcoat. She was asked, 'Are you Charlotte Mew?' and replied, with a slight smile, 'I am sorry to say I am.'

CHAPTER 15

Alida

CHARLOTTE was telling neither less nor more than the truth. Her confidence was at its very lowest. Although in the autumn of 1915 May Sinclair continued to press cheerful invitations and offers of help upon her, she could only see these as the long-drawn-out end of a miserable mistake. The poem she had sent to the Bookshop, *The Changeling*, was not associated with May or May's enthusiasm. It had been written before Charlotte met her.

The Changeling ('I shall grow up, but never grow old') was not readily suited to Alida's voice, which was a rich young contralto. Charlotte might have had mixed feelings at hearing a reading by some one else of this poem, with which she had disturbed Sappho and beguiled Sappho's children. But she liked Alida's interpretation, comparing it later to the wind, which changes the colour of the cornfields as it passes across them.

When Alida sat down thirteen years later to describe what she remembered of this first encounter, she found it very difficult. To begin with, there was Charlotte's oddness. Fashions had changed during the first year of war, and Charlotte's long coat, red knitted stockings and clutched umbrella looked much more old-fashioned than they would have done even a year earlier. She had 'quantities of white hair'. This is the first time we hear of Charlotte's hair having turned white, and evidently she no longer looked much younger than her age. When introductions were made she had a defensive air, anticipating an enemy. 'She did not have any illusions about herself,' Alida wrote, 'and what people might think of her when they first met her and heard her speak in her rather strident voice and her *méfiant* manner.' Knowing what people might think made her talk not less stridently, but more so. This, too, was a habit of maiden aunts. It was called 'bristling'.

It was as 'Aunty Mew' that Alida first got to know her, after the first mistrust and suspicion were over. Charlotte had two cousins living in London, Ethel Louisa, an art teacher at Notting Hill High School, and Florence Ellen, but neither of them had married and there was no younger generation, so that the relationship with a grown-up niece was something quite new. Alida, of course, made nothing of the difference of age. When she gave her friendship (or, it must be said, her dislike) she put her whole heart into it.

In her room in Red Lion Square Alida spent 7s. 6d. a week for rent, 2s. for gas and had £1 left to cover everything else, but she asked Charlotte to come and see her whenever she liked. Every week's bills were a crisis ('it doesn't matter at all', she wrote to Monro, 'if you haven't any money') but Alida was not in the least ashamed of this. It was studio life, but without any of the gentilities of the Hogarth Studios, where a cake and flowers were provided just as Charlotte had once provided them for Ella D'Arcy. Alida simply threw a length of orange sacking, *Ballets Russes* style, over the coal-box, sat down, offered a cigarette, and talked into the small hours. In return, she was asked to 9 Gordon Street, where even Sappho had never been invited. The lodgers, however, were still never mentioned, and it was years before Alida knew they existed. She was shown Henry Kendall's prize picture – the city of shining towers – and the portrait of Anna Maria as a young girl. The old lady herself, 'Ma', was a frightening sight – withered like a dried specimen, with little claw-like hands. Alida was also presented – there is no other word for it – to Wek, under his everyday name of Willie (he was William Edward Kendall). Alida, who later became a successful dog-breeder, had no fear of any kind of bird or animal, and the hateful old parrot recognized his match.

Both at Gordon Street and Fitzroy Street Alida had the chance to get to know Anne. There seemed to be more than three years between the two sisters, and Anne was always ready for company, and 'much less weighed down by the sorrows of their lives'. The responsibility was always Charlotte's. A sort of loving conspiracy grew up between Alida and Anne to make Charlotte a little less diffident and farouche and to get her to show them more of what they felt sure she must have written. In her room she still kept the two mysterious trunks, apparently full of papers; sometimes she would take out one or two and roll them up into spills, either for her cigarettes or to give them to Wek to chew to pieces. This was done casually, with the remark that she couldn't think what else to do with her manuscripts. Then Alida and Anne drew together a little, aware that she might be laughing at them.

Alida's memoir of Charlotte Mew shows that some things were kept from her, others altered, and a few suppressed. She never knew about Freda, for example, or indeed that there was madness in the family. Fred Mew was presented as the villain of the piece, 'a man who took his responsibilities very lightly' and 'died, leaving nothing, having spent all his available capital on living'. Something was said about May Sinclair, but Alida got the misleading impression that there had been 'a very complete friendship, until something she heard about Miss Sinclair destroyed it forever'. She was also told about a lawyer who had made away with a sum of money left to Charlotte by an aunt, 'destroying her faith in Man completely'. This lawyer, if he ever existed, left no traces, but it was some kind of explanation of Charlotte's deep distrust of men, including, as it turned out, Harold Monro himself. As to the mystery of the manuscripts, it remains unsolved to this day. Under the terms of Charlotte's will, Alida was allowed to select one of the two trunks for her own, but 'without the contents'.

Charlotte did not fall physically in love with Alida Klementaski. She never fell in love with another woman after May Sinclair. She was most scrupulous, too, in her treatment of those who were attracted to her. One young girl cared for her so passionately that both the poetry and Charlotte Mew herself became an obsession. The girl, the daughter of Mrs Clement Parsons, was tubercular. During what proved to be her last illness she lay there trying to recite to the nurse 'in her own trembling, weak, ill voice' from *Pêcheresse*. Charlotte was a friend to this girl and helped her, gently and tactfully. Love, for her, was never an excuse for acquisition.

But, as she had written herself, there are different ways of love. It was something of a miracle that Alida, so young and eager, so overworked and single-hearted, should bother about her at all. Most of the mystery Charlotte created at the Bookshop, through concealment or half-truths, was to preserve for Alida the image of 'Aunty Mew', a priceless Aunty, too, who 'never went on a visit anywhere without coming back with a riotous account of what had taken place'. The two of them began to share one all-important interest, that is, the smaller troubles of life. Wek, for example, had begun to have queer turns. On the other hand old Mrs Monro, Harold's thoroughly disapproving old mother, had been conveying insulting messages to Alida, asking her why she was not using the new 'patriotic' sevenpenny margarine, which Alida thought wasn't fit to grease the boots with. Next, Alida bought for thirty shillings a West Highland terrier which she had seen advertised in *Exchange and Mart*. But how would it behave in the Bookshop, and what would Harold, who was always a cat-lover, say? Red Lion Square and the shop itself were in easy walking distance, and Charlotte, who had been bound for so long by formal engagements, began to 'drop in'. That was quite a new pleasure for her, taking her back to the old *Yellow Book* days. Alida also dropped in at Gordon Street, and yet at times she felt in awe and half-hypnotized by the strangeness of Charlotte Mew. She described Charlotte standing with one tiny foot on the fender, and one hand on the mantelpiece, talking and twisting the ring on her little finger 'in a fascinating manner', or reading a new poem, always with a furious toss of her head at the end, as though to dismiss it.

If Charlotte had given the least hint of her inner nature, Alida unquestionably would have been as bewildered as Mrs Dawson Scott. In 1916 – to illustrate this – she went to supper in Ebury Street with a South African girl whom she had known when they were suffragettes together. They had been on the same pitch in the East End, selling *Votes for Women*, and what with one reminiscence and another they talked so late that

Alida missed the last 19 bus and had to ask if she might stay. During the night the girl walked into her room naked and Alida was 'absolutely terrified', as she wrote to Harold, 'and nearly went off my head . . . I said "go and get a dressing gown" – thinking that once she'd gone I'd lock the door and pretend to be asleep – but she said in a *curious* voice, "No, it's too much fag." ' On this occasion Alida felt like going into a convent with Harold's cat, Pinknose.

There were limits, then, to what Alida, even though she had joined the 'ranks of the emancipated', could possibly be asked to accept. Charlotte knew this as well as Harold did, and both, in their different ways, kept silence. Alida saw clearly enough that Charlotte was 'two people' – split between her strict moral code which made her (or so Alida thought) 'absolutely cut out from her friendship anyone on whom the breath of scandal blew', and an inner self which had written *Fête* and *Madeleine* and understood very well what it was like to struggle 'in the face of a great and overwhelming emotion'. But deeper than this Alida could not be expected to go, and she thought of Aunty Mew's contradictions with a tender, amused affection. She used to quote from *Fame* the phrase 'our tossed beds', and comment that she was sure Charlotte had no idea how a bed got tossed. And yet she had responded at once to the *cri de coeur* of *The Farmer's Bride*.

The Bookshop's idea, when Alida had first written to Charlotte, had been to ask whether she had enough poems to make up a collection, and, rather doubtfully, Charlotte produced seventeen in all. Monro read them, and was prepared to go ahead. But by now it was the winter of 1915, and he was in difficulties of all kinds. The best solution, he believed, would be to bring them out at as a Chapbook – that is, a book bound in rough paper, with a cover design commissioned from one of the Bookshop's artists. Unfortunately, Charlotte was up in arms at once. She wanted her poems brought out, if at all, in a properly bound volume. 'This year', she wrote to him, 'I have been taken up with other things – but if you hadn't asked to see them a few weeks since, I should have done something about a volume next year.' Whatever she meant by this, she was troubled by his offering no money down, only royalties on any copies sold. This suggests that she knew nothing, or very little, about the usual arrangements for publishing poetry. Both Elkin Mathews and Grant Richards expected a contribution from the author of about £15. (Edward Thomas put it at £10, while Ezra Pound (according to his own account) had been asked by Elkin Mathews in 1909, 'Ah, eh, do you care to contribute to the cost of publishing?' and had replied that he thought he had a few shillings on him, if that was any use.) Harold Monro never asked his authors for any payment, only hoped not to lose too much himself. Matters were at a standstill when May Sinclair, still anxious to be of use, wrote (27 December 1915) advising Charlotte, from her thirty years' experience as a writer, to close with the offer, '(1) because it's a chance; (2) the poor chap can't afford to print a regular conventional *book* of poems. And Harold Monro is a benefactor of poets, and so honest and sincere, and cares so awfully for what he *does* care for, that he deserves encouragement. (3) Because the Chapbooks really *are* selling as the regulation books are not.' Monro, May pointed out, had sold 260 copies of Richard Aldington's *Images*, which had been printed as a Chapbook, during one day, and Charlotte had more 'human appeal' than Aldington.

Monro, who might have been pleased by May's letter, if he had ever seen it, had sunk into one of his occasional fits of gloom, which resembled a Scotch mist. The truth was that he didn't feel able to cope with Charlotte, while she, in response, was at her difficult worst. If he had to deal with a woman poet, Monro much preferred, for example, the handsome, forthright Anna Wickham, who could drink level with him and understand, what was more, why he drank himself. He admired Charlotte's poetry and respected her sensitivity, but felt he could have managed better without it. Alida, distressed, tried to explain this away by saying that Charlotte, 'like many people of character and genius, was either greatly liked or greatly disliked. She had her detractors, but there were many who loved and valued her dearly.'

There were difficulties from the start. Monro sent out the poems for an estimate, and closed with a small firm in Clerkenwell. Some of the galley proofs had already been run off when the printer's young son arrived, an embarrassed messenger, to say that their compositor, who was a Methodist, could not possibly set up *Madeleine in Church* because he thought it blasphemous. Why not another compositor? They only employed one. Charlotte was reminded of the editor who had refused *Ken*. It seems not to have occurred to anyone that the little firm might be afraid of legal action, which then lay against the printer as well as the writer and publisher, although *Madeleine* was scarcely, in legal terms, 'so scurrilous and offensive as to pass the limit of decent controversy and to outrage any Christian feeling'. In any case, they regretted that they must give up the commission, and Monro had to go to a large and better known firm, the Westminster Press. Fortunately Gerard Meynell, Alice Meynell's nephew, worked at the press, and through him the whole Meynell family became interested in *The Farmer's Bride*.

In February Monro was able to send Charlotte the galley proofs. The final stages were going to be troublesome, because she insisted on having the very long lines in some of her verses printed without any turn-over, if necessary using the full width of the page. Printers need regular margins, but it was hard to persuade her of this. Monro, however, understood that she was thinking of the text as something to be read aloud – a 'printed score', as he had called it himself, and therefore did his best, settling for an awkward format, almost square, (6½ × 8 inches), which he privately considered very ugly. For the cover, he had been thinking, he said, of a dull green (it was then called Georgian cooking-apple green) and a design by his best-known artist, Lovat Fraser. He did not like to say that it was so difficult to get paper in wartime that he was using some green paper he had bought already. But Charlotte objected to both. She wanted a dark grey cover, and a design by James Guthrie of the Pear Tree Press. Here she may have been well-advised, because Lovat Fraser, though a brilliant decorator, was not an illustrator. The line-drawing which he produced of a thatched cottage with a blank wall and an improbably small window was a very elegant design, but it suggests that he hadn't bothered to read the book.

Monro was used to protesting writers. His position as publisher of the *Georgian Poetry* series put him in the front line, for everyone who was excluded felt personally insulted. The amount of abuse he put up with, even in the long history of poets and their publishers, is quite astonishing. He was accused, for example, of being domineering (one poet referred to him as 'His Lordship'), and of picking and choosing, whereas all should be equal in the republic of literature. Some reminded him that their poems had taken several years to write, and that although his time mightn't be precious, theirs was; or declared that out of 500 verses sent in, one, on the law of averages, must be good. Others lectured him on his religious duties, or reproved him with letting his fellow-creatures starve. Monro, unlike Henry Harland of old, had not much art of persuasion, but he succeeded in getting Charlotte to agree, rather grudgingly, to the cover for her book. At this point he discovered that rising costs and the wartime paper shortage were threatening to shipwreck him altogether. He wrote, therefore, (March 4, 1916) to say that he would have to defer publication for a while.

But Charlotte, even if she had believed (and perhaps still believed) that no-one would want to read her poems, was a writer on the verge of seeing her first book in print, and what was more she had never applied to the publisher – he had made the suggestion himself. She replied stiffly that she knew it wasn't a time to care about personal affairs, but it was just because the future was so uncertain that she wanted *The Farmer's Bride* to come out. She only wished she could pay for publication herself, but, she added confusingly, 'friends who not long ago would have taken a personal interest in it being no longer alive and others – under the present chaotic conditions – wishing me anyhow to get it out', she felt she must hold Mr Monro to his undertaking. Monro, who was kind rather than weak, capitulated, although he pointed out that both his cashier and his traveller would be called up in six weeks' time and because the age limit had just been raised he would soon have to go himself. He agreed to 500 copies, then somehow managed to find enough paper for 1000 – this was a long run for the Bookshop, which often printed 250 for a first edition.

Charlotte thanked him, though her satisfaction, she said, was 'clouded by its being published reluctantly'.

The dedication of her book gives a hint of her feelings about it, which were running much deeper than simply the indignation of a tiresome lady writer. It reads 'To ——. *He asked life of thee; and thou gavest him a long life; even for ever and ever.*' This inscription from Psalm 21 was on her great-grandmother Kendall's grave in Kensal Green Cemetery. The editor of Charlotte's *Collected Poems and Prose*, Val Warner, has suggested, very likely correctly, that 'To ——' means 'To Henry', to the memory of the poor mad dead brother whom she did not care to mention by name. Just at the time, then, when she was making new friends at the Bookshop, Charlotte was turning back more intensely to her family and its past. As to the dedication itself, there was a kind of fascination for all the Mews in the West London graveyard where old Henry Kendall, now buried there, had been cheated over his designs for the mortuary chapel. Edward Herne Kendall, Charlotte's strange uncle, who was now in his seventies, had left Brighton and had come to live in Kensal Town, almost next door to the green expanses of the cemetery; he stayed within a few streets of it, as though obsessed, until his death. Charlotte's blank dedication, then, which must have puzzled Alida, was in memory of someone in Charlotte's life whose name Alida never heard, and whose sad existence was carefully kept from her.

But *The Farmer's Bride*, at least, was out, and in May 1916 it was on the table in the Bookshop kept for new publications, along with Robert Graves's *Over the Brazier* (his first collection, sent from Béthune on his way to the reserve trenches), a special limited edition of eight new poems by Yeats, a Frances Cornford Chapbook (which included 'Oh fat white woman whom nobody loves') and *Georgian Poetry III*, which had been published the previous November. It was twenty-two years since Charlotte had first attracted attention in *The Yellow Book*, and now, once again, she might feel herself in good company.

Her first critic – according to Charlotte herself – was her household help, Jane Elnswick, who had come back to Gordon Street for the duration. Jane attended a Methodist chapel, and was not sure whether to be proud or ashamed of an employer who had wasted so much time in writing verses. Other reviews were scarce. Evelyn Sharp saw to it that there was a piece in *The Nation*, and May Sinclair sprang into action, recommending the book, she said, to every editor she knew, 'but it is very difficult to get poetry reviewed at present – unless it is written from the trenches'. This was true enough. *Georgian Poetry II*, in which Marsh printed the dead Rupert Brooke's *The Soldier*, was another runaway success, selling nineteen thousand copies. It was difficult even to keep two file copies in stock for the shop's records. Alida kept finding that someone had bought them while her back was turned.

But *The Farmer's Bride* moved slowly. By July Monro had to write to Charlotte to say that the little book was 'going dead'. Out of his run of 1000 he had 850 remainders. Charlotte sadly apologized. This, after all, was what she had expected in the first place. She had hoped for more reviews, but she knew hardly any literary people, and even if she had she couldn't have brought herself to ask them to write anything, 'because I am simply not the person, though for your sake I wish I were'. Mrs Dawson Scott had not been far wrong when she said of Charlotte that 'under the curious husk is a peculiarly sweet, humble nature'. Monro, however, never had any of his remainders destroyed, and always kept the type standing as long as possible. He still had faith in *The Farmer's Bride*, he was still the man who said, 'If it is possible to imagine a world without poetry, I for one should not wish to be an inhabitant of it.' Those words might have been his own epitaph, if he hadn't given instructions that after death his ashes should be scattered at the root of a young oak tree. ('This romantic notion', he added, 'should on no account be taken seriously unless it proves practicable.')

Alida, too, refused to consider the slow sales of *The Farmer's Bride* important. Time would show, she believed, that the Bookshop's confidence was justified. In 1916 she herself needed consolation. She knew that among the young men at the front there were some that Harold missed acutely. There was 'Jim', who wrote to say that the larks were singing through the gunfire and that yellow flowers were growing in the trenches, and would Harold send him poetry, any poetry. There was 'Basil', who was killed in action. 'I liked him awfully,' Alida nobly wrote when the news came through. But her heart felt raw. Then in August 1916 Monro, as he had anticipated, got his call-up papers.

THE·POETRY·BOOKSHOP
35·DEVONSHIRE·STREET·
THEOBALDS·ROAD·LONDON·W·C

CHAPTER 16
'J'ai passé par là'

MONRO, who was getting on for forty, was drafted into the
Royal Garrison Artillery and sent to Shoeburyness, where he
did his best to train, but at an early stage was 'threatened' by
the colonel for not attending the educational lectures. At the
end of September he was transferred as a second lieutenant to
an A.A. gunsite at Newton Heath, but could only long to go back
to 'the things I was made for'. He got the impression that the
men hated him, with the exception of one whom he cared for
very much, and that in itself, he knew, might lead to trouble.
These soldiers, after all, were human beings like himself, only it
was against discipline to let them know it. Sitting in a pub,
writing in desperation to Alida – 'Dear child, what shall I do?' –
he relied almost entirely on her strength, feeling that his
fellow-officers were looking at him with half-drunken contempt
through the glass door. Through all these months he was
haunted by an incident in his first training camp, where a
sentry who was said to be 'worried about the war' had hanged
himself. For half an hour the men had simply thought he was
looking over the unfinished perimeter wall. Then they noticed
the colour of his face, a white face and a blue neck. The NCO
who cut him down hadn't been able to forgive him, when there
were so many trees about, for not doing it somewhere outside
the camp.

Monro was aware that his nervous complaints were absurd
while across the Channel slaughter was continuing on two
fronts. But he felt his only source of encouragement – though
that was beyond price – was the thought of Alida opening the
Bookshop every morning.

By now Alida had taught herself book-keeping, hand-printing, proof-reading, copy-editing, lettering and stock-keeping, with the intention of managing single-handed. When the Zeppelins came over, Miss Froude, the lady assistant, retired to a special chair which was kept for her in the cellar. It was a relief when Miss Froude gave notice. After that Alida was too busy to worry much, serving and taking orders all day and delivering them, as soon as the shop closed, on a hand-barrow, which she pushed as far as the carrier's in Goswell Road. The first series of rhyme sheets were coloured by hand, and she sat down to the job, when she could find the time, with a child's paintbox. Here Charlotte Mew, who was always neat-handed, could help. The two of them worked together not only on the rhyme sheets, but the book-covers. The Chapbook editions of F. S. Flint's *Otherworld: Cadences*, Richard Aldington's *Images* and James Elroy Flecker's *The Old Ships* were coloured in with variations of blue, green, red, yellow or grey. Sometimes Charlotte took a parcel back to Gordon Street and coloured them there, sometimes she sat with Alida among the dozing pets. Pinknose, Harold's cat, had lost an eye in an incendiary raid on Milman Street (where Alida now had a couple of rooms) and no longer jumped about the shelves or knocked down the books.

By 1917 there were army huts and a canteen in Russell Square, and the trampling and rumble of convoys through Bloomsbury grew so familiar that when there were a few hours' quiet something seemed to be missing. Charlotte, on her round of semi-official visits, had to sort out field postcards and communications from the War Office in their agonizing variations on wounded and missing, missing believed wounded, missing believed killed. She could understand all the gradations of loss and shock, and underestimated none of them. '*J'ai passé par là*,' she wrote, quite justifiably, to a friend.

In November 1918 she was forty-nine, and Alida sent her a birthday present so generous that Charlotte feared her own standards of living might be getting dangerously high, and she might end by having the brokers' men in. For her part she was worried at Alida's worn appearance, and thought she might be better off in a boarding-house – meanwhile they could always offer her bread and milk at 9 Gordon Street.

Alida, to be sure, was almost at the end of her strength. She had been terrified when Monro told her that he would rather desert and face a military prison or a lunatic asylum than stay with his unit. But in January he had been passed unfit for general service, and in the summer of 1919 he was back in his office. Furious with his own inadequacy, bedevilled by drink, and writing poetry which T. S. Eliot called 'the dourest excruciation', he braced himself, smiling sadly, to take up his business where he had left off.

For *Georgian Poetry IV*, which the Bookshop had published in 1917, Eddie Marsh had taken more advice than for his first two volumes, and he had been persuaded (if he could find one that he approved of) to include a woman poet. Monro, who was then just on the point of leaving for training camp, had strongly recommended *The Farmer's Bride*. Marsh wanted a second opinion and turned to Walter de la Mare, who gave his decision against it. He was doubtful about the farmer, and not at all happy about the poem's metre. De la Mare had a more exact ear (in the sense that a musician has perfect pitch) than perhaps any other English poet. In his verse every pause, as well as every stress, falls into place, like a language we once knew, but have to be reminded of. But in *The Farmer's Bride* (although, as she said, 'Of course I can write smoothly if I choose') Charlotte had followed the bewilderment of the speaker so closely that there were changes of metre once or even twice in a single line. This dismayed de la Mare, and Marsh took his word for it.

Monro had been annoyed, and had asked Marsh what was the point of consulting him if he didn't want his advice? Now, in 1919, the question came up once more, and again Monro spoke up urgently for *The Farmer's Bride*, and again Marsh, with his own brand of mild obstinacy, took no notice. He preferred, it appeared, the work of Fredegond Shove, the wife of a lecturer in economics at King's. The Bookshop was in arms at once. Alida denounced Mrs Shove's 'Cambridgeness', her arid rooms and hard furniture. But Charlotte was perhaps fortunate. In the new post-war climate *Georgian Poetry* was beginning to seem old-fashioned, so that, although the new volume still sold in its thousands, it was becoming less of a privilege to appear in it.

The Farmer's Bride itself was selling a little better and Monro took the opportunity to write to Macmillan, New York, about an American edition. 'During the past three months', as he put it, 'there has been an enormous demand for Miss Mew's work, and we feel that you will find a good market.' Macmillan replied that they didn't want a book that had been out for several years, they would prefer something entirely new. Monro, knowing how difficult it was to get Charlotte to produce anything, suggested a new edition with some additional poems. Whether there were any of these in existence or not he did not know.

At about the same time Alida had been seized with a new idea. She had been introduced to a man who seemed to her a little ridiculous but very important, and able to do great things. He was Sydney Cockerell, the director of the Fitzwilliam Museum in Cambridge, who had been brought to one of the Bookshop's poetry readings. They must send him a copy of *The Farmer's Bride*, it must go by the very next post. It was as the result of this notion of Alida's that Charlotte entered upon yet another new relationship, one she could hardly have expected. She acquired an elderly admirer.

CHAPTER 17

Sydney

ALTHOUGH she made her friends' husbands somewhat uneasy, Charlotte usually aroused a protective instinct in men. Her letters mention 'shaggy young gentlemen' who helped her with her luggage, and kindly older ones who showed her the way, or gave her advice. Sydney Cockerell was in fact only two years older than Charlotte, but she impressed him from the first as someone who must be looked after.

Cockerell was one of the six children of a Brighton coal merchant who died when he was quite young. This meant a hard start, but, as he told his biographer, Wilfrid Blunt, 'I was protected by poverty from marriage until I was forty.' During that time he was able to develop his two ruling passions – the arts (or rather the classification and collecting of them), and the cultivating of great men. When he became Director of the Fitzwilliam in 1908 he identified the Museum completely with himself, and heroic indeed were his efforts to tap bequests, endowments, and death-bed legacies which would enrich it in every department. He calculated that during his lifetime he had made a quarter of a million pounds for the Fitzwilliam, and about a dozen enemies. Perhaps he had rather more than that. There were some who considered him a tiresome and even sinister busybody. But his acquisitions were there for everyone to see, and his reverence for Ruskin, Morris and Hardy was genuine. He was sure of the greatness of great men. It was only that they were often incapable of managing their affairs as well as he could himself, hence he hovered around them. Genuine, however, was his kindness and his interest in the minute personal concerns of other people, some of whom were not important at all. All he asked, he said, was that they should

Sydney Cockerell. Photographed in 1917,
the year before he met Charlotte Mew.

have 'morals of some kind, however unconventional'.

Cambridge was Cockerell's natural habitat, from which he spun his tireless web. Every day was exactly accounted for, and, from 1886 onwards, recorded in the tiny, exquisite handwriting of his diaries. For future generations, who might be lazier than himself, he summarized every page of these diaries in the top margin. 'I learned', he told Blunt, 'to answer every letter by return of post; and I learned that if two jobs had to be done, the duller one must be done first.' But in truth, nothing that had to be done was dull for Cockerell. Anything properly arranged and completed gave him satisfaction. In the Georgian world of art and letters he had many rival arrangers, collectors, and fixers – Edmund Gosse, for example, Edward Garnett, and, of course, Eddie Marsh. But in the long term, none fixed so well as the Director of the Fitzwilliam.

Although Cockerell, according to his own account, never kissed a woman until he was twenty-eight, and even then only when he was kissed first, he understood very well how women were to be pleased. Thoughtful attentions, letters enclosing small presents, compliments, little outings to London theatres and exhibitions, all made a woman feel singled out, although she might be disconcerted when the punctual Sydney looked at his watch and darted off to catch the 2.34 or the 4.40 back to Cambridge. Kate Cockerell, the most unselfish of wives, understood his need for innocent and ponderous flirtations. In 1916 her long-standing ill-health had been diagnosed as multiple sclerosis. Almost housebound in Cambridge, with nothing to look forward to except increasing uselessness and pain, she had to give up her own work as an illuminator and designer, and worried only about the three children and about Sydney's well-being. Knowing that she herself was not much of an organizer, she tried to make up her mind, in a perfectly rational and cheerful way, as to which of the youngish or middle-aged ladies whom he liked to take out would be best suited to look after him when she herself was gone.

In the July of 1918 a copy of *The Farmer's Bride* arrived in Cockerell's vast daily post, with a stiff little note from Charlotte, hardly a recommendation. No worry, however, about his reading it; he always read everything, and he fell in love immediately with *The Farmer's Bride*. To Charlotte Mew's poetry, the simplest reactions were always the best, and Sydney's were very simple. In spite of his weight of specialist knowledge, he still laughed out loud at a comedy, and, if he was reading a poem on the tram or in the Underground, often gave way to tears, 'blubbering', as he put it, 'before all and sundry'. With all his fussiness, he too could hear the *cri de coeur* in Charlotte Mew's poems.

He wrote to thank her, and Charlotte diffidently told him that the whole secret had been in Miss Klementaski's reading. He replied that it hadn't – the melody was in the lines themselves. But, a schoolmaster at heart (he even corrected his own wife's letters to himself), he ventured to put forward a few improvements. In the title poem, he thought that 'down' and 'brown' ought not, 'by the strictest standards', to rhyme together twice, and he was particularly worried by what could possibly be meant by 'the brown of her'. 'I suppose her sunburnt arms and neck?' he suggested doubtfully.

Charlotte replied that she was grateful for his practical interest, but she was not only unwilling to, but quite incapable of altering a line. (This, incidentally, was not true – she often revised, and had accepted an alteration from Harold Monro.) Sydney retreated at once. 'Of course you are wholly right. When I had posted my letter I realized my impertinence.' With that he began his courtship of Charlotte Mew.

In the summer of 1918 he already had a lady friend *en titre* and several others whom he admired, including Alida herself and a charming artist, Dorothy Hawksley, who often came in for supper and a game of chess. Charlotte Mew, he saw, would need a different approach. When he was asked to tea at Anne's studio he offered to wash up, something which he had probably never done in the whole of his life. Both the sisters refused to let him try, but they were touched. The next step was to ask Charlotte to Cambridge for the week-end to see his treasures, but to this there was unexpected resistance. She flatly declined to stay 'in Cambridge or any other strange house with strange people, for the good of my soul and body'. She and Anne were 'happy enough', she said, 'if you could believe it, behind our prison bars'. This last phrase partly explains the trouble – the Mews, by the end of the war, were reduced to living in the basement rooms of 9 Gordon Street, and the whole of the rest of the Quiet House was let off. 'Our dungeon', as Charlotte called it, was too cramped for any visitors except Alida, and it was quite impossible now to conceal the presence of the lodgers. She was too proud – it was the old trouble – to accept a Saturday to Monday invitation without making any proper return.

Cockerell, as Alida had hoped, busied himself with sending *The Farmer's Bride* to everyone he could think of, while he waited for Charlotte to relent. He always insisted on replies, and his friends found that, on the whole, it was easier to make them at once. Wilfred Scawen Blunt, the celebrated lover, horseman and traveller, thought, as might be expected, that it was a great mistake for a woman to write from the point of view of a man. He found the situations in Charlotte's poems puzzling and questioned their 'sexual sincerity'. Siegfried Sassoon was captivated at once and remained her faithful reader always. A. E. Housman replied (9 September 1918) with his usual glacial severity. He liked the little book, although he complained that, like most female poets, Miss Mew put in ornament which did not suit the speaker. The 'short piece', *A Quoi Bon Dire*, was, he thought, the best.

> Seventeen years ago you said
> Something that sounded like Good-bye;
> And everybody thinks that you are dead
>   But I.
>
> So I, as I grow stiff and cold,
> To this and that say good-bye too;
> And everybody sees that I am old
>   But you.
>
> And one fine morning in a sunny lane
> Some boy and girl will meet and kiss and swear
> That nobody can love their way again,
>   While over there
> You will have smiled, I shall have tossed your hair.

Housman seems to have forgiven the shaky grammar of the first verse for the sake of what he so well understood himself, the outlawed emotion confined into an elegant form, and the strange dislocation of time, where the only true contact is between the living and the dead. Cockerell did not know Housman, who was then the Kennedy Professor, well enough to press him further. But he sent another copy of the book to

Thomas Hardy, and this was one of the greatest kindnesses he ever did Charlotte.

In 1916 one of the tasks of the second Mrs Hardy was to read aloud in the evenings at their Dorchester home, Max Gate, to the old great man whom she so carefully tended. It was difficult to know what he would and wouldn't like. He couldn't, for instance, bear *Wuthering Heights*, he disapproved of May Sinclair's novels, but he took to *The Farmer's Bride*, and Florence Hardy was able to write to Charlotte, telling her that the little book was on her husband's study table, and that he was quite engrossed. Hardy was too old to be anxious to see many new people, but he did express a wish, if possible, to meet Miss Mew.

This was equivalent to a royal command, and Charlotte must have been anxious about her clothes. Her only piece of finery was a scarlet Chinese embroidered scarf and Anne's pearl brooch, which she was always willing to lend. But Florence wrote to say that there would be no need for evening dress, as Hardy thought that changing for dinner in winter made him catch cold. The date of the visit was put off, first when Florence had neuritis, then when the cook at Max Gate was discovered to be a secret drinker. Finally the 4th of December 1918 was fixed upon.

Max Gate has been described by Florence's sympathetic biographers, Robert Gittings and Jo Manton, as ugly, damp, and comfortless, with a tiny spare room and no lighting but oil-lamps. The garden (according to another account) was darkly green and overshadowed, 'with a distinct flavour of churchyard'. But it was no gloomier, with its crowded pictures and furniture, than 9 Gordon Street, and probably very much like it. The 'dog to the household', Wessex, was a menace to most visitors, but Charlotte emerged unbitten. The visit to her was what she whole-heartedly called it: 'a great honour'.

Florence, at first, seems to have been surprised and perhaps disappointed. Charlotte, who was ten years older than herself, struck her as a 'pathetic little creature', plain and frail, who chattered throughout the whole two days. 'We have never had anyone here who talked so much.' Hardy had been kind, but 'she was not his type of woman at all' – although this may have been a relief to Florence, who had to bear patiently with the crazes, 'the throbbings of noontide', which sometimes overcame him even in the evening of life.

If Charlotte talked too much, it was certainly from nervousness at meeting the man who for so many years had been her 'King of Wessex'. There was, as it happened, a great deal in common between Hardy and her own father. Both had been country boys, trained as jobbing architects, coming up to London and marrying 'above them'. But such things were not mentioned or discussed during the week-end at Max Gate. Charlotte and Thomas Hardy met as poet to poet. It was Hardy who persuaded her to stay for two nights. He read some of his own poems to her, and she read him something which pleased him very much, *Saturday Market*. It would be interesting to know, in this dialect poem, what he thought of her Island accent, as true to childhood as his own.

Florence soon changed her mind about Charlotte. Out of the little book of poems, it was romantic and dramatic *Madeleine in Church* which had appealed to her, and the thought of Madeleine's 'white geraniums in the dusk' made her decide to plant some herself in the Max Gate greenhouse. These dreams and intimations (as Gittings has shown) were connected in Florence's mind with her own earlier ambitions to be a writer, an independent 'scribbling woman'. And Charlotte, after all, was a poet who had attracted notice, and lived in London, where the conscientious Florence every now and then allowed herself a day out. The usual invitation to tea in Anne's studio seemed an exciting step into an almost Bohemian world, and it was a great disappointment to Florence when she was unable to come, because Hardy had required her to go and see a niece of his first wife's who was in a lunatic asylum. Later, however, she managed it, although Charlotte warned her that the Hogarth Studios were by no means easy to find, and 'people have been known to arrive in a state of suppressed or unsuppressed rage,

Thomas and Florence Hardy in their garden at Max Gate.

having wandered round Bloomsbury, in their own words, "for hours"'. But this did not make it any less romantic. Florence brought with her a sister, who was a professional nurse, carefully explaining that 'she is not in the least literary . . . and her life has been exceedingly narrow'. She herself, she implied, understood these things, and she was delighted to be among Anne's canvases and half-finished work, while Charlotte herself was modelling some little plasticine figures. Florence knew that the Mews had an old invalid mother, and this aroused her ready sympathy, for she had one herself, but, apart from this anxiety, what an enviably free life the two sisters seemed to lead! She had almost given up her own dreams of being a writer, though she ventured to question one or two passages in Charlotte's poems which she hadn't quite understood. 'But how all this must irritate you!' she added.

Hardy himself always sent Charlotte a message of 'kindest regards'. He was firm in his opinion that she was 'far and away the best living woman poet, who will be read when others are forgotten'.

Sydney Cockerell was delighted with the success of his introduction. But surely there must be more poems for him to read, and to send to other people? He liked to keep things moving. Charlotte replied that poems couldn't be turned out when wanted, like puddings. But Siegfried Sassoon, who happened to be in Cambridge, brought Cockerell the first number of Monro's new shilling magazine, *The Monthly Chapbook*. On the last page was Charlotte's *Sea Love*, certainly a new poem, which delighted both of them (and delighted Hardy too when it arrived at Max Gate). Sydney's accumulative instincts, as usual, had been right. It was unkind of her, her told her, to keep her work under lock and key. This courtly tone (which made Charlotte write to him sometimes as 'Dere Sydnie') was, he had decided, the right one. By now he felt it was not enough for Charlotte to 'sup' with him before spending an evening at Alida's flat. She ought to come to the theatre or the cinema. Charlotte replied that she could not. She was struggling with the three great miseries of daily life, the kitchen range (which kept going out), the boiler (which threatened to blow up), and 'flu. 'Flu had laid low both Anne and old Anna Maria. The basement of 9 Gordon Street must have been dismal indeed at the beginning of the 1920s, and it is difficult to imagine how Charlotte could have written *Sea Love* there. When her two invalids had recovered, she still refused Sydney's invitation.

> Why so touchy? [he wrote to her (2 February 1920)] When I am merely seeking a means of providing you with three hours of exquisite artistic sensation and happiness.
> Why so diffuse? When 'No, and be damned to you' would have said the same thing in six monosyllables.
> Why so proud? I stood for two hours this morning in a queue of people, who were buying tickets for themselves and for friends at a distance.

Charlotte gave in. After all, it is something to be queued for, at the age of fifty, by the distinguished director of a museum, who, even if he is an over-zealous old fuss-pot, is a true admirer. She felt this, and felt the novelty of being escorted to Les Gobelins, Sydney's favourite restaurant just off Regent Street (it had waitresses, and imitation tapestry on the walls), and of being asked whether she preferred this table or that, and what she would like to eat and drink. They were modest outings, of course. Charlotte only took an occasional glass of wine. In fact, she sent Sydney (still, and for the next two years, 'Mr Cocker-ell') a Breton poem which she had come across when she was 'grubbing about' in the North Room of the British Museum.

> Femme qui boit du vin
> Fille qui parle latin
> Soleil qui se lève trop matin
> Dieu sait quelle sera leur triste fin.

To Sydney, who wrote, as his biographer puts it, 'millions of words and never a coarse one', this little verse would have seemed almost daring. And as a regular visitor to France who could never learn to speak the language, he liked to hear her talking and reading French. He and Charlotte agreed that they would both be French in their next reincarnation. She carefully saved up for him, too, the kind of story he liked her to tell, just on the edge of the macabre: for example, a hearse driver runs over a man in the street and kills him. A conductor from a passing bus sees the corpse and calls out: 'Greedy!'

CHAPTER 18
The Shade-Catchers

SYDNEY COCKERELL'S CHARLOTTE, as one might expect, turned out to be a Miss Lotti, but with a sharp and witty edge – however, still recognizably Miss Lotti, grateful for a treat, deferential to his knowledge of the world. She didn't at all mind being fitted in, as all his acquaintances had to be, between numerous important errands. Once up in London, he always had auctions and exhibitions to attend, or an Armenian manuscript to glance at, or an interview with someone who might be of use, or an official visit, or a valuation. On one occasion he appeared with a little bronze, worth £6000, in his black bag which 'might be wanted for the museum'. Everything was written up in the diaries which, Charlotte and Anne decided, contained no secrets whatever. They called him 'the blameless Pepys'. Cockerell, if he had known this, might have been a little dashed (though he recovered quickly). He saw himself more as a knight errant, coming to the rescue with unguessed-at treats. From time to time he was careful to include Anne, whom he found bright and charming, sometimes Florence Hardy and Dorothy Hawksley as well. He was happy surrounded by ladies, indeed his capacity for happiness was great, and was one of the most attractive things about him.

Charlotte spent the Christmas of 1919 with Elsie O'Keefe, who had come back after four wartime years in Canada, where James had been acting as British financial adviser. They had settled into a house in Richmond, but their children were too old by now for the Christmas pantomime. Fortunately the Cockerells' little daughter was almost of an age for *Peter Pan*, and it was arranged that, when the time came, no-one would be allowed to take her to it but Charlotte.

'And what of Alida the charming?' asked Sydney, who had been too busy of late to go to the poetry readings, but had heard rumours of 'a Bookshop wedding'. In fact, Harold Monro's divorce had been made absolute in 1916, and now in peacetime his friends (particularly, for some reason, those whose own domestic affairs had run into difficulties) were pressing him to marry Alida. 'Dear Alida, with all my heart I wish you happiness, and if it [is] not fatally bad for you, your heart's desire,' wrote Charlotte in an affectionate, though ambiguous note (20 March 1920). The marriage took place at Clerkenwell Register Office, and immediately afterwards Monro disappeared. Alida had to go down alone to the cottage in Sussex which they were supposed to share (she had bought the crockery for it and the kitchen things). She told her friend, the poet and story-teller Pamela Travers, that when Harold eventually arrived and got into bed he said, 'Come here, boy.' But Alida added, what indeed everyone knew was true, that Harold and she were everything to each other. When they went together to a restaurant, she said, no-one could ever believe they were a married couple, because they had so much to say to each other.

Cockerell knew nothing of all this, and Charlotte told him as little as she could, though she was not at all surprised when the following spring Alida went to the South of France by herself. Sydney, however, was amazed that a newly married woman should behave in this way. 'He evidently sees you as much painted,' Charlotte told her, 'with a bright green parasol – flinging gold about in the casino.'

It was in 1920 that Cockerell at last persuaded Charlotte to come down to Cambridge for a week-end visit – 'packing a toothbrush', he called it, to indicate (as Florence had) that no grand clothes would be needed. 3 Shaftesbury Road was a hospitable place where Sydney impressed his visitors, but innocently. His study, heavily curtained with Morris fabric, was the heart of the house. His books were massed there, and in the drawers there were smaller things, including a strand of Lizzie Rossetti's hair in a locket, to be shown to the favoured. Always he produced examples of his wife Kate's beautiful illumination, which her crippled hands could no longer manage. This process of showing, and then letting somebody touch and even hold, while watching their nervous pleasure and awe, was a satisfaction to Sydney. Ruskin, after all, had recommended that there should be open museums, where people could pick up the exhibits. And Cockerell, who in London could look something of an old woman as he fussed over his appointments, recovered all his dignity in Cambridge. There he was unmistakably what his biographer called him, 'the friend of Ruskin and Morris'. His study fire was lit early in the morning, while the rest of the household shivered. (This was a Victorian custom which lingered well into the 1920s. 'Women are doomed to cold and hunger for at least two hours every morning,' Alida said, 'until they can get some fires lighted and water boiled.') Once, when Charlotte got up too late to say good-bye to Sydney before he caught his London train, she went into the study, and 'my black heart', she said, 'was truly touched to find – fire burning – pen – ink-pot and slabs of paper laid out'. She sat down, she went on, to write a letter or so herself in the warmth, but if there was a shade of irony in this, perhaps on Kate's account, she could be quite certain that Sydney would never notice it.

On Sundays, whenever Charlotte came, he was surprised to see her 'sally forth to Mass'. She certainly didn't do this at Max Gate, where Florence would have been upset by anything that looked like Romanism. But although Sydney had no faith himself, and was bored by religious discussions, he had a kind of yearning interest, as towards something he had failed to get for his collection, in Catholic ritual and doctrine. His most prized correspondent was a scholarly Abbess, Dame Laurentia McLachlan of Stanbrook, and it was a puzzle to him that Charlotte, though respectful, seemed not quite willing to benefit from her counsel. When the question of Dame Laurentia came up, Charlotte used to insist that she was a 'poor infidel' and could only admire from a distance. Her mass-going was probably partly nostalgia for Brittany (after the war she could never afford to go to France again), and partly, perhaps, to flutter Sydney a little.

If Charlotte was going to talk about her own conviction of

sin, guilt, suffering and mercy, it was more likely to be with Kate. The friendship of Kate Cockerell was, to her, the most unexpected benefit of her visits to Shaftesbury Road. In the face of someone so transparently good, and so ill – the treatments were almost as bad as the pain, and quite ineffective – Charlotte dropped her defences. Kate could not express herself at all in written words. All she cared about was beauty in music and painting and the heart's affections, and although she had been the only female student, in her day, in the Academy Schools, she now felt quite useless, with nothing at all to offer anyone. Like Anne, she never complained. She simply wished that she was not too shy and clumsy to give dinner parties. To her, Charlotte Mew 'was one of the few people I have ever known with whom I could be quite intimate without the fear of being laughed at'. Shyness can only be cured by someone more shy. Charlotte was touched, but surprised, having always considered herself, as she said, not a tonic but an irritant. Other visitors to the house remember her as 'pale and withdrawn', or droll, witty, and profound, but with poor Kate Cockerell she did not need to be either.

Charlotte, by now, had eleven new poems to make up the promised new edition of *The Farmer's Bride*, which appeared in March 1921. The American edition came out as *Saturday Market*, which Macmillan selected as a better-selling title. It was a modest undertaking, Monro sending 250 copies in sheets for £14.11s.0d., the best he could do 'in the present difficult conditions'. But it caught the attention of that good friend of English poetry, Louis Untermeyer, who had already been carried away by *Madeleine* when Siegfried Sassoon read it to him the year before. 'May the Lord bless you and keep you et cetera,' he wrote effusively from West 100th St, New York. *The Farmer's Bride* itself attracted much more notice on its second time out. Edith Sitwell reviewed it favourably in the *Daily Herald* (4 April 1922). My own father, who had come back from three years in the trenches to his old job in the *Punch* office, was immediately told by his editor that he must do a series of parodies on well-known poets of the day, and that one of them must be Charlotte Mew. *The Sphere* wrote for a photograph, but 'your poor Auntie', she told Alida, 'hasn't one'. *Poems For To-Day* wanted biographical details, but Charlotte, it seemed, hadn't any of those either. Virginia Woolf wrote to R. C. Trevelyan that she had got a copy of Charlotte Mew's book and 'I think her very good and interesting and unlike anyone else.' Virginia Woolf would not, I think, have claimed to be a judge of poetry, but of originality she certainly was – also of that 'plan of the soul' which she was to put hesitantly forward in *A Room of One's Own*. 'Perhaps a mind that is purely masculine cannot create, any more than a mind that is purely feminine.'

Besides *Saturday Market* and *Sea Love* there was in the new volume a small, unobtrusive poem, at the very opposite pole from the impersonations and dramatic monologues, as quiet as a passing remark on something just seen in the street.

> I think they were about as high
> As haycocks are. They went running by
> Catching bits of shade in the sunny street:
> 'I've got one,' cried sister to brother,
>   'I've got two.' 'Now I've got another.'
> But scudding away on their little bare feet,
> They left the shade in the sunny street.

The Shade-Catchers has seven four-stress lines, with a different rhythm for every line, but then, of course, something different happens in every line. It was probably one of the 'little technical experiments' which she mentions once or twice in her letters. It is not a Georgian poem, no Georgian poet would leave the reader undecided between the value of hayfields and streets (the children belong to both) or, for that matter, between sun and shade (it is shadow that the children are collecting), or between the various meanings of the last line. And, although *The Shade-Catchers* records a passing moment, it is not an Imagist poem either, if Pound's definition of 'the precise instant when a thing outward and objective transforms itself, or darts into a thing inward and subjective' is to be accepted. Charlotte Mew is a story-teller here as usual, and as usual 'not like anyone else'.

It was a favourite poem of Alida's, a kind of password between herself and Charlotte, recalling the London summers of the 1920s – the last, too, of Charlotte's poems about living children and their world of games which she observed with such respect. She had nearly entered that world in Dieppe when the fishermen's children let her chalk the pavement for *pelote*. More often, she watched on the sidelines and marvelled. There had been a good wartime game, she told Alida, in the poor streets near Paddington Station. One little boy, selected as a German prisoner, was crammed into a sack and dragged and bumped over the uneven pavements by the rest of them. The boys were in competition. Every one of them desperately wanted to be the prisoner.

CHAPTER 19

Delancey Street

WEK WAS POORLY. For some time now he had been suffering
from a muscular weakness, which made it difficult for him to
hold on to his perch. He had probably been affected by the
damp of the Gordon Street basement, which had also ruined
some of Charlotte's books. According to Alida, Charlotte
'would frequent the parrot house of the Zoo at any moment of
the day, and sometimes at night if she could knock up the parrot
man, to get help for him'. But even the assistant keeper could
not arrest old age, and by 1921 he had to give it as his opinion
that the bird ought to be destroyed. May Sinclair had been
faced with the same problem in 1914, when her black cat,
Tommy, was sinking. Having asked the vet for the exact lethal
dose, she had administered it herself, holding Tommy on her
lap until he ceased to move. It was one more example of May's
strength of mind.

Anne and Charlotte felt quite unable to undertake anything
of the sort, and, since the tough old bird disliked men so much, it
was impossible to call in the vet. Among their friends only Alida
was young, strong and practical enough to help them, and Wek
had no objection to her. Alida, then, was 'summoned' (as she
put it) to Gordon Street, where she found that the two sisters
had already been to the chemist for chloroform and a sponge.
They also had a cardboard box ready, of the right size for a
parrot's coffin. In a room at the back of the basement, in
complete darkness except for one candle, she followed her
instructions, put the anaesthetic in Wek's cage and covered it
with a blanket. Then 'the dreary procession of three' sat down
next door to count the correct number of minutes prescribed by
the chemist. This dependence on 'what the man had said' was
Miss Lotti-like in the extreme. He turned out to be wrong,

Mr Alden, assistant keeper of the parrot house at the London Zoo
in the 1920s and 30s.

however. When Alida went back and put her hand into the cage
Wek gave her a sharp nip, and, dreading to prolong her
situation, she wrung his neck.

Wek had been at Doughty Street and even, when Anna
Maria was still a girl, at Brunswick Square. His cantankerous
nature had seemed proof against time. Now the childhood of
two generations was buried with him in the cardboard box in
the dark back garden. Sydney Cockerell showed a rare tact in
offering childlike consolations. He gave Charlotte a spray of
white heather and stood her supper with vanilla ice-cream,
then 'having a little time to spare before my train went with her
to a cinema near the Tottenham Court Road tube and saw
Charlie Chaplin in a war piece *Shoulder Arms*. We had neither of
us (strangely enough) seen him before and we were delighted.
He is a very remarkable artist and is now in London, and
without doubt the most popular hero in the whole world.' (One
can feel Cockerell hesitating here, but Chaplin would never be,

in his sense of the word, 'a great man'. He was not likely to have anything to contribute to the Fitzwilliam.)

Charlotte seems to have had no holiday in 1921 except for a few days during October at a hotel in Salisbury. She had once spent half-an-hour there in the Cathedral close between trains, and remembered the rooks, and she came down to hear them cawing again. In this kind of mood she might, on an impulse, go anywhere. In her letters to Florence Hardy she speaks of walking by herself, undaunted by anyone she met on the roads, and getting 'a rough tea' for threepence. She did not so much want to see new places as to visit cities where, for however short a time, she had once been happy.

The end of the year, in spite of the mild success of the new *Farmer's Bride*, was overshadowed by worries about 9 Gordon Street. The lease would be up in 1922, but the Mews had, of course, always known that. They seem to have hoped, though without any encouragement from the Bedford Estate, that they might be allowed to stay on at the same rent, keeping the lodgers. The Estate, on the contrary, now required them to leave and to pay all the inside dilapidations on the damp and neglected house.

Walter Barnes Mew was no longer in practice, and Charlotte employed another firm of solicitors, Layton's. In spite of her usual deep suspicion of any man with whom she had business transactions, she managed to get this firm to write a very good letter for her. Hugh Layton told the Estate that his client, Mrs Mew, was 'about ninety' (she was actually eighty-four) and constantly under a doctor's care. Her trust property brought in about £300 p.a., but of that £130 had to go to support Freda, who was described simply as 'very delicate'. Of the other two daughters, one 'does some light work which brings in a very trifling income'. Searching round for any kind of evidence that they had improved the property, Layton recalled the £100 spent on the drains about ten years before. Finally he spoke of the shock to his client, at her age, of moving house, and felt sure the Estate would want to spare her any additional anxiety – i.e. the worry over the bill for dilapidations might kill old Mrs Mew and in that case they would be little better than murderers.

Perhaps anxious to get rid of their impoverished lease-holders without any fuss, the Estate agreed to release them from liability.

It was not a good time to look for a new place. London was full of demobilized young men, hoping to marry or to find room for the families they had already. And Charlotte and Anne, only half-recovered from 'flu, were not too well either. They seem (probably in order to cut down the medical bills) to have done a certain amount of self-doctoring. Certainly their *Culpeper's Herbal*, that great standby (particularly for female ailments), had fallen almost to pieces, and was too shabby to be lent to Florence Hardy, who also wanted to consult it.

On the 17th of December Cockerell called on the Mews and 'heard a sad story about their having to turn out of their house in March. They have a great struggle against poverty, adversity and ill-health.' A proof of his genuine concern, which Charlotte and Anne must have felt, is that they gave way at last to the luxury of confiding in him. 'I have told practically no-one about our affairs,' Charlotte told Sydney, 'and don't mean to untie the hens!' Over the New Year she went down to Cambridge and, as a particular treat, Sydney showed her the Brontë letters in the Fitzwilliam, and let her hold one of them in her hand.

But by the end of February Charlotte had found nothing suitable, and was seriously thinking of selling the furniture and moving into a hotel. In addition to her own furniture, Anna Maria had inherited all Aunt Mary Kendall's 'household articles', and although a certain amount must have been discreetly parted with over the years there was still some nice china left, a set of Adam chairs, the Chippendale looking-glasses, and so on. It would be a desperate step, and Ma might well 'take notice' and ask where the things had gone. Still, at all costs, and even if it meant a hotel, they must stay within the familiar Bloomsbury and Regent's Park area where they had lived almost the whole of their lives.

Charlotte patrolled the house agents, as she had once done for May Sinclair. Only in March, the cold, wet March of 1922, did she find somewhere that might do, the upper two floors of 86 Delancey Street, between Camden Town and Regent's Park.

There were, she said, two rooms, two attics and a dark kitchen, fewer rooms than in the dungeon at Gordon Street, but it could pass as a 'good address', and it had the advantage of being high up and airy. Looking down from the windows, you could get a glimpse of children playing and sometimes a Punch and Judy in the street below. Opposite there was a convent with green-painted shutters which reminded Charlotte a little of France. 'But so long as you can come it's no matter where,' she wrote to Sydney.

Delancey Street is farther to the north of London than Bloomsbury, and gradually the Mews began to see more of friends in Hampstead. This was particularly true of Anne, who had a good friend, Katherine Righton, an artist at West Hill Studios. Katherine was a figure-painter; so too were Henry and Margaret Jarman, who had a studio in the same block. Anne herself was not exhibiting anything at the moment, only going round other people's shows with her usual good humour, making Charlotte think that 'whatever the others are, Anne, poor Angel, must be the most long-suffering of the lot'. It was probably Anne's idea that Henry Jarman, who exhibited at the Academy from 1899 to 1938 and was a very reliable, pains-taking artist, should do a portrait of Charlotte, to be hung in the Fitzwilliam. But Charlotte, with the fierceness of a primitive who fears that his likeness may be stolen, refused. She did not want to sit. This didn't disconcert either the Jarmans or Katherine Righton, who loved her for Anne's sake.

Meanwhile the routine of the Bookshop had been severely upset by the Monros' strange marriage. In February, March and April the readings had to be suspended, 'owing to the unavoidable absence of those responsible for their organiz-ation'. By this was meant Alida's trip to France and Harold's withdrawal to a clinic for alcoholics. *The Chapbook* had to be suspended for a time and even after that appeared irregularly, although some of its most interesting numbers (Gordon Craig's essay, for example, on the political value of marionettes) and some of its most beautiful cover designs date from 1921–2. There was no shortage of contributors either. They besieged the shop, and Monro was obliged to print an announcement that on no account could he read manuscripts brought round by hand. But conditions were hardly right for idealists to run a business. Its early success had given rise to competitors. In Devonshire Street itself a Peasant Shop had opened which offered, besides books, hand thrown pottery, plaited felt rugs and slippers, shepherd smocks, dalmatics, 'Thibald' jerkins, handmade jewellery and figurines of the Ballets Russes – all the software, in fact, of the Higher and Simpler Life, while Monro continued to stock only poetry and drama and books about them. Furthermore the Peasant Shop unkindly put it about that the Bookshop stayed open until 6.30 because its daytime sales were so small, whereas the late hour was really to help office workers for whom (in Wilfrid Gibson's words) poetry would be 'like sparkling water running over grass'.

Charlotte was not needed any more to help out with her water paints – the rhyme sheets were colour printed after the first series and the price raised to fourpence each – but her letters show that she went often to the Bookshop, and it seems likely that she lent a hand there in some capacity. She had to take a bus now from Delancey Street, but, as it turned out, she was glad to have left Gordon Street. In 1922 speculators had begun to clear the south side of Euston Square Gardens, just at the top of the street, to replace it with more pavements and more houses. 'They are cutting down the great plane trees at the end of the garden,' she wrote in *The Trees Are Down*, feeling her heart go with them. 'Half my life it has beat with these.' Better, after all, to look down out of the Delancey Street windows, where you could get at least a glimpse of the green tree-tops of Regent's Park.

CHAPTER 20

The Loss of a Mother

OLD MRS MEW never went up and down the steep stairs at Delancey Street without help. But on 8 December 1922, what Charlotte and Anne most dreaded happened, in spite of all their vigilance. Ma fell, and broke her femur. A nurse had to be called in for some of the day duties, and the two sisters took on the night watch between them. Poor old Anna Maria was no more than a dried husk, a sliver, a tiny bag of bones, clinging on to life through her two sane daughters who fought to keep her from slipping away. The doctor could only say that her condition was 'dangerous'.

Charlotte, whether it was her turn of duty or not, slept very little and wrote her letters, she said, between one and two in the morning. During some of the time snatched for herself she wrote what was her last poem sent out for publication (although a number of others, which cannot be dated, remained in manuscript). These three verses, *Fin de Fête*, appeared in *The Sphere* for 17 February 1923.

Sweetheart, for such a day
    One mustn't grudge the score;
Here, then, it's all to pay,
    It's Good-night at the door.

Good-night and good dreams to you –
    Do you remember the picture-book thieves
  Who left two children sleeping in a wood the long night through
  And how the birds came down and covered them with leaves?

So you and I should have slept, – But now,
    Oh, what a lonely head!
With just the shadow of a waving bough
    In the moonlight over your bed.

The speaker in *Fin de Fête* accepts frustration (even if the sweetheart grudges it). He is not mad or even in danger of madness, still there is the characteristic lapse back into the language of childhood. The lovers have to pay with loneliness for what in any case seems to be innocent, with a fairy-tale's innocence. The two babes in the wood in the story, however, had their enemies, otherwise the birds would never have had to hide them. But *Fin de Fête* has none of the bitterness of *Saturday Market*. There is no resentment against whoever it is who has prevented what should have been. The whole of Charlotte Mew's upbringing and her whole emotional experience had made it plain to her that there is a 'score' for human happiness and that we have no right to avoid payment.

Sydney Cockerell made one of his rare miscalculations when he offered to take Charlotte's mind off things by getting up a lunch party, the kind of thing he liked to call 'a little gathering of understanding folk'. She refused. 'Sympathy is not the forcible administration of one's own patent remedy,' she told him, 'but a consideration for – even if one cannot understand it – the other person's point of view.' Then she added, relenting a little, 'I know very well that your intent is kindness, but *quand même*.' On 12 May 1923 Ma died in hospital, of bronchial pneumonia.

'My dear Mrs Hardy,' Charlotte wrote to Florence on mourning paper, edged with black, 'my mother has been with me all my life and as yet I don't know how much of my own has gone with her. But for her it is release.' Florence, of all her friends, old and new, probably understood these feelings best, being a natural looker-after and guardian, with an old and delicate mother of her own. Charlotte could neither eat nor sleep. She described the death, which the doctor had understandably called 'inevitable', as 'a stupefying blow – and I feel like a weed dug up and thrown over a wall'. The simile is striking, comprising as it does the death, the move from the old house, and the feeling of worthlessness which, in the very depth of her being, she believed must be punished and rooted out. But the saddest part of the situation was that to most of their acquaintance Anna Maria's death seemed an absolute bles-

Charlotte Mew in 1923.

sing. The two talented daughters had done all that they possibly could for their old parent; now at last they were free. Edith Sitwell, who had met Charlotte at the Bookshop in 1919, saw her as a grey and tragic woman 'sucked dry of blood (though not of spirit) by an arachnoid mother'. And even Alida, whose own mother had died that February, had always thought of Ma as a kind of joke, 'treated very much as if she were a naughty child'. Secrecy brings its own penalties, and it would have been necessary to have stood by Henry's graveside and visited Freda at Whitelands to know what Anne and Charlotte felt when they buried Anna Maria.

Now, in the hours suddenly left empty after night and day nursing, they had to think how to manage next. The Kendalls had always intended that Charlotte and Anne, the family's last hopes, should be looked after. But between the Kendall women, their solicitors, and the easy-going Fred, this forethought had come to very little. With Anna Maria's death, all three shares of the grandmother's trust fund had reverted to the mysterious Edward Herne Kendall, and were being administered for him. This money in time would come to the descendants, Charlotte, Anne and Freda, but at the moment he was still living, a solitary old man, near Kensal Green Cemetery. As to Anna Maria's own inheritance, most of that had been converted into the annuity of £300 p.a., which expired with her. What was left was divided between her three daughters, but not equally, because Freda must of course have her maintenance made up to the sum (they now decided) of £100 a year. Of their own, Charlotte and Anne still had a small income from the Brighton house properties left to them by Aunt Mary Kendall. They might possibly have £150 a year between them altogether, after Freda was properly cared for, and the rent of 86 Delancey Street (probably because they had had to take it in a hurry) was high. Charlotte had lamented to Alida that, in order that Ma should not feel their 'lowered social position', two-thirds of their income would have to go on rent. This may have been an exaggeration, but the rent was probably over £100 a year. Finally, Anna Maria's remaining effects were valued at £272.12s.8d. These sums must have been very discouraging.

There are various estimates as to how little a writer could manage on at the beginning of the 1920s. The short-story writer H. E. Bates thought that £250 was easily enough, provided you lived in the country. Robert Graves and his first wife were managing on £150, including his disability pension, but his mother-in-law had bought a cottage for them. T. S. Eliot, when a fund was being raised by his friends to rescue him from his job in a bank, said it would have to be not less than £500 a year. Alida's salary from the Bookshop, after the war, was £156. In London she was still living in one room, and going down to the basement to put a penny in the gas for hot water, but Harold paid for the country cottage, the housekeeping, and for a number of other expenses.

To look at the problem from another viewpoint, what could Charlotte and Anne not do without? They needed tea and cigarettes (on which they were said to live), a little coal in winter, their subscription to Mudie's Library (though Charlotte had a reader's ticket for the British Museum), and third-class railway fares; all their loyal old friends pressed them to come and stay, this being the most acceptable, perhaps the only, way of relieving poverty without giving offence. They needed postage stamps, writing paper, something for buying Christmas presents, painter's materials for Anne. No new clothes – Florence Hardy had thought Charlotte 'shabby' when she first came to Max Gate, and shabby she remained, though her boots and umbrella were not of the kind which would ever wear out. The studio might seem an obvious extravagance, but Charlotte knew this must never be given up. It was a proof that Anne, even if she wasn't doing much at the moment, was still an artist, and would soon be working again. But besides the studio, where there was only a cold-water tap on the landing, they needed a roof over their heads.

The old rule, on which the Mews had been brought up, was one-tenth of your income on charity, one-eighth on rent. By these standards, and indeed by any standards, Delancey Street was ludicrously more than they could afford, and it seems puzzling that they did not surrender the lease at once. But that would have meant the nightmare of moving house twice in one year, and of losing the 'good address' which, whatever their lamentations, meant almost as much to them as it had to Ma. Of course they would have to go soon, and of course in no circumstances must they think of selling the Brighton property. To break into their small capital, the capital which was always felt to stand between the unmarried woman and the workhouse, would have been a sacrilege. The truth was that they could not think what to do. They were worn out, both of them. Anne went to Hampstead, Charlotte first to the Olivers, and then to Cambridge. On the 21st of July Sydney recorded: 'Charlotte Mew for the weekend. After tea I took her to the Botanic Garden and we sat on the grass looking at the waterlilies.'

'Wednesday 25th of July 1923. Dull, much rain . . . to Downing Street, to the Prime Minister's secretary, E. P. Gower, about a Civil List pension for Charlotte Mew. Had a very satisfactory interview with him.' It was one of Sydney's happiest ideas, a little arrangement to fix up which should please everyone, including himself.

Cockerell knew the Prime Minister, Stanley Baldwin, who was the nephew of his old friend, the painter Edward Burne-Jones. But these matters were never entirely straightforward, (otherwise they would not have appealed to Sydney). The position had been well put, twenty years earlier, by W. B. Yeats. 'The difficulty in these cases is that they are, I think, always given for a combination of worth and need . . . . Tennyson's pension, for instance, was given when the alternative was probably his doing some kind of pot-boiling – Pensions like this are an exception, the majority are probably given because of real want.' So far, so good – the Mews, even when they could bring themselves to leave Delancey Street, would be in real want. But there were, as Cockerell knew well, other possible difficulties. Richard Jefferies had refused to take money from the Royal Literary Fund because he believed the fund was maintained by 'dukes and duchesses'. A Civil List pension had been arranged for the always penniless poet Lascelles Abercrombie in 1914, but there had been a terrible outcry because he wasn't doing war-work; he had to be persuaded into a munitions factory. Then there were the writer's sponsors – three were needed, and their voices must carry authority. Cockerell had started by having a word with one of his rivals in the art of fixing, Edmund Gosse. Gosse, as Librarian of the House of Lords and a 'man of letters', of the kind which no longer exists, would have counted very high, but he refused. He said, without explaining what he meant, that he had some reservations as to the quality of Charlotte Mew's work. Recovering from the check, Sydney had approached three poets, Thomas Hardy, John Masefield and Walter de la Mare. Masefield, always kind and always anxious to do the right thing, undertook to write the application. Hardy could be relied upon, and de la Mare also agreed; either he had changed his opinion of *The Farmer's Bride*, or else he concentrated on the question of 'real want'. He himself had been delivered, in 1908, from his job as a book-keeper with Anglo-American Standard Oil by a Civil List pension of £100. Indeed, his success as a poet had fulfilled, in real life, the romantic dreams of the thirty-bob-a-weeker.

Knowing Charlotte's circumstances as well as he did, Sydney suggested asking for £75 p.a., which would increase the sisters' income by about a third. He himself would not appear in the matter at all, although everyone would know that it was his doing. What pleased him particularly was the magical or Dickensian aspect of the whole transaction, the unlooked-for surprise, for Charlotte had not asked him for anything or dreamed that anything could be done. Of course, while the application was still being arranged he could say nothing, but four days after he had been to the Prime Minister's Office he felt himself at liberty to call round at the studio and break the joyous news. The reaction was all that he could have wished. Charlotte couldn't believe that Baldwin would take the suggestion seriously; she hadn't herself at first – then when she had seen Masefield's letter she had felt as though she had fallen into deep water and couldn't get out, without being ungracious to people greater and better than herself. In a curious phrase, she said it made her feel 'a sort of suicide'.

Some persuasion was still necessary. Charlotte was seized with a kind of scrupulous doubt – she did not believe she was going to write any more poetry. The impulse, she thought, had died at last. Would it be right, in that case, to accept a poet's pension? Sydney reassured her. He helped her, too, with her letters of acknowledgement, telling her exactly what to say to each of her sponsors, and to the Prime Minister's secretary, and how to address the envelopes. And Charlotte accepted all this humbly. She had never pretended to be able to spell, and she did not want to let him down.

As Christmas drew near, Sydney proposed a scheme which had long been close to his heart. He wanted – and evidently this was a good time – to introduce Charlotte to Walter de la Mare. The two poets must be his guests one lunch time. He attached great importance to this little party, and one would have thought the best arrangement would have been to confine it to the three of them, but at the last moment he seems to have lost his head and booked a table at the Gobelins for six, inviting three more ladies, Anne Mew, Alida, and Florence Hardy. For Florence it must have been a great treat, since Hardy had been ill and did not like her to go up to London often, if at all, but the party was now somewhat unbalanced. Sydney was probably guarding against Charlotte's diffidence or even ferocity in the face of anyone new. What he did not know, though of course Alida and Charlotte did, was that de la Mare had not thought *The Farmer's Bride* good enough for *Georgian Poetry*.

Probably (it would have been like her) it was because of this embarrassment that Charlotte was suddenly at her best. Sydney, who was something of an anxious impresario with his two celebrities, was much relieved, and had never seen her 'more sparkling and at ease'. De la Mare (as he explained in a letter of thanks) had thought Charlotte Mew would be quite different. Whatever he might have expected from the wild confessionals of *Madeleine* and *In Nunhead Cemetery*, it could hardly have been this tiny, neat, ironically glancing figure, who looked for all the world like the heroine of his own *Memoirs of a Midget*. She told stories, he said, which afterwards he could remember perfectly, but couldn't repeat without losing the essence of them. All this is the more remarkable because de la Mare himself habitually talked without stopping and gently disputed every point (he once argued for two days over whether marmalade could properly be called a kind of jam). But on this occasion he listened, as he listened to music. 'She just knows humanity,' he told Cockerell, 'one of the rarest things in the world.'

At the end of December the formal notification of the pension came through, and even the Mews themselves were not more delighted than Sydney.

CHAPTER 21

The Loss of a Sister

1924 AND 1925 were two of the happiest years, certainly the last happy ones, in Charlotte Mew's life. Although the sales of poetry had dropped considerably since the end of the war, the new edition of *The Farmer's Bride* continued, in a modest way, to do well, and her reputation spread. There is a photograph of Charlotte with Robert Bridges, the Poet Laureate, at his Boar's Hill house near Oxford. Siegfried Sassoon brought Louis Untermeyer, over from New York, to the studio; he also recommended *The Farmer's Bride* to that legendary patroness, Lady Ottoline Morrell, who resolved to collect the new poetess into her circle. Past her great days by this time, Lady Ottoline was preparing to leave Garsington for London, and to inaugurate a new salon where women would be invited as well as men. Like a splendid bird of prey with plumage a little bedraggled, she called once, twice, at the Hogarth Studios without finding anyone at home. Eventually she got her invitation to tea, and talked at length. Afterwards Charlotte wrote to her and sent her a quotation from Conrad, 'the passing wind and the stirring leaf hear also', but resolutely refused to appear in any salon whatsoever. As to Conrad himself, he too had been drawn in by the tireless Sydney. On Christmas Day 1923 the two of them had lunch together, and travelled up to London by train. Not having read any of Conrad's novels, Sydney tried *The Farmer's Bride* on him, and Conrad (admittedly he could hardly have done otherwise) replied, with continental politeness, that he greatly admired Miss Mew.

She was still cautious, guarding herself against photographers, and suspicious of anthologists, perhaps unduly so. Poor Harold Monro was disconcerted when she refused to allow anything of hers into Macmillan's *Golden Treasury of Modern Lyrics*. After all, he reminded her, she had given permission, or seemed to, when he came to tea at the studio, and Anne had been there and had been delighted at the idea of one of her sister's poems 'in a standard work'. This is the authentic Anne, gently conciliating, proud of Charlotte's success, hoping to make her difficult life easier.

Charlotte, however, had no objection when Alida broadcast *Sea Love* from the BBC's Savoy Hill studio – radio was one of the new wonders, she said, for which no doubt we shall all be much better and wiser. Altogether she regarded the 1920s as a source of dry amusement, but largely on account of their music and their art. It cannot be said that she was politically minded. She never even registered for the vote, and probably the only reference she ever made to the country's problems was in a letter to Sassoon, when she quoted from Robert Louis Stevenson's *Child's Garden of Verses*:

> If I could find a higher tree
> How much, much farther I could see

and suggested that this might be good advice for politicians. This does not mean that she did not understand what some of these problems were. She never forgot the afternoon in 1913 when she had broken into an old people's home and found an old woman upstairs, alone, and too weak to make herself tea or to write a postcard. She knew the face of sickness and poverty, just as she knew that she herself was, by nature, one of society's outsiders. But she could not see where the solution lay, and when Sassoon told her that perhaps civilization itself depended upon poetry, she could only tell him that if that were really true, poetry, like politics, would have to shift its load up higher.

The Civil List pension brought her an advantage, which can only be truly appreciated by those who have been greatly troubled, and greatly helped. Now that her daily life was a little easier, she was able to exercise her old art of stimulating or consoling (no matter which) any of her friends who needed her. Kate Cockerell always did. 'Dear Charlotte – Do come and stay with us,' she wrote in her eager, untidy scrawl, very unlike

Sydney's neat hand, 'it is such a Chance.' Florence was also in deep distress, this time over Hardy's infatuation with a young amateur actress who was appearing in a local production of *Tess of the D'Urbervilles*. This tiresome obsession over-shadowed the Max Gate household, and Charlotte offered poor Florence her own remedies for 'nerves'; best to try and make something with your hands, or to design something, or to look at the trees and the sky and remember 'that they are not for any of us for ever – [that] pulls one up'. Certainly these were not very original suggestions, but originality was not what Florence wanted – she needed to feel understood, and by a poet. When the Hardy Players brought their production to London, Charlotte went with her to the chaotic rehearsals, and when in 1924 Florence had to be admitted to a nursing-home in Fitzroy Square, Charlotte visited her there. It was an operation to remove a swollen gland from the neck. On one occasion Charlotte called at the same time as Virginia Woolf. They confronted each other at Florence's bedside, but unfortunately both of them were too shy to speak.

In May 1925, when Florence was facing the 'exhausting birthday week' which she always feared would be too much for Hardy, she particularly wrote to thank Charlotte for her thoughtfulness. Every other visitor to Max Gate had the idea that 'others may tire him, but not me', and only the day before, when a very talkative lady had called, Hardy had left the room abruptly and had been found collapsed on a sofa. Sydney Cockerell had become a great offender. As Florence acidly put it, 'I think it is a pity he pursues people so ardently, as it seems to be wearing him out.' Charlotte knew that this was not so, and that Sydney drew new energy from the chase. But she herself was quite content to wait till the autumn to go down again to Max Gate. Part of the very hot summer of 1925 she spent with Alida in one of her long series of country cottages, this particular one near Rye, in Sussex. All of them had earth closets and well-water, and had to be adapted to the needs of six dogs and a cat. Harold Monro, meanwhile, was often abroad, seeking cures for what Alida called 'the enemy' though she also felt that the continent, where wine was sixpence a bottle, was 'not the place to fight such a battle'. Monro had been deeply depressed by the patriotic glitter of the 1924 Wembley Empire Exhibition; in one of his satiric dream poems he envisaged an exhibition of the future, where the last Georgian Nature Poet would be on show, dressed in tweed and sipping beer, in a specially designed case. The Bookshop, he knew, was near bankruptcy, and Alida had pathetically asked him whether she would have to sell her dogs. Responsible as he was for her future, Monro did not dare to risk much more of his money in the business. He saw himself and Alida as two helpless creatures, with nothing left but determination to come out of the other side of the tunnel.

Charlotte had told Sydney that she would write no more poems, but this had been when she was still recovering from the shock of her mother's death, and in what Edith Oliver called 'one of her fits of the blues'. Alida certainly hoped for another collection. The Bookshop must publish what it believed in, even if, to meet the printing costs, she had to let her own bedroom or, worse still, 'open a criticism bureau'. It was probably at this time that Charlotte showed her some of the other things she had written and put away, or published but not reprinted in *The Farmer's Bride*. She also gave to Sydney the present he wanted most of all – indeed he told her that he 'prized' and 'hugged' it – the manuscript of a poem. She often wrote out verses that people particularly liked, so that they could have a copy of their own, but this was a different matter – it was an original draft of *Requiescat*. Looking at it made Sydney feel, he said, a fraud or an impostor, someone who could only give advice, but could create nothing himself. In his opinion *Requiescat* (which was not included in *The Farmer's Bride*) should be reprinted. He never, of course, had any suspicion of the perverse element in Charlotte which might suppress this poem simply because Ella had liked it.

For Christmas 1925 Lady Ottoline sent a copy of Emily Brontë's poems, a well-chosen present, although Charlotte had one already. She marvelled at how many friends her own small book seemed to have brought her. Just at the time when Alida was seized with a sudden fear she was reaching 'the dangerous age', Charlotte, for her part, emerged for a short while into a kind of humorous serenity. It can be felt in a letter she wrote to Dorothy Hawksley in April 1926, agreeing that Shakespeare's plays, which they both loved 'can't possibly have been written by a literary person'. But she refused to dispute about Queen Elizabeth's virginity. 'If we deny that, we'll soon be hearing that Victoria wasn't a widow.' She was on the easiest possible terms with Dorothy, a talented artist and a kind, practical woman whom Kate Cockerell had decided must be the one, when everything was over, to look after Sydney. Charlotte, who had done her best to resist for years both painters and photographers, agreed to sit to Dorothy, who made in 1926 the sensitive pen-and-wash drawing which is now in the National Portrait Gallery. In this, Charlotte looks melancholy, but not as though life had no compensations.

In May 1926 the General Strike made any kind of visiting difficult. Alida (though in sympathy with the miners) flew to extremes, thinking it might be 'the end of everything' and it would be best if as many of her friends as possible moved down to her cottage, where they could live on vegetables and home produce till the crisis was past. Meanwhile she had to look for new premises for the Bookshop, since the Devonshire Street lease was almost up. With so much in hand she was beginning to find housework intolerable. Polygamy, she had told Charlotte, would be a better solution, with extra wives to share the work. But there would always be an odd one out whom the husband preferred, Charlotte told her, and if that one tried to share the profits there'd be a strike.

It is hard to say exactly when Charlotte began, not to worry, but to worry seriously about Anne. Ever since Ma died, Anne had not liked being left alone at night, but this could have been no more than the dependence of someone who was always very much the younger sister. In the December of 1925 she had felt too ill to come with Sydney and Charlotte to Noel Coward's *Hay Fever*, but after that she had made a good recovery, and had begun to paint again. In the spring of 1926 she had submitted three pictures to the Academy for the Easter show, but they were rejected, and the sisters had made up their minds not to go to Varnishing Day, until they remembered that Dorothy, who was on some Academy committee or other, might be there. In the summer they were both reading *Gentlemen Prefer Blondes*, which they decided to recommend to Sydney. Then, in the autumn, Anne began to feel pain which the doctor could not account for, and Charlotte felt a pang of fear, which took the form of sudden decision. To everyone brought up as a Victorian, a 'change of air' was the great remedy. 86 Delancey Street, which had always been a ridiculous extravagance, must be given up, and Anne must be taken away out of London to the country to breathe fresh air and escape the winter fogs. Charlotte decided on Chichester, near the sea and the downs, and began to write off for suitable rooms. One advantage might be visits from Alida. She had rented yet another cottage, this time at Sidlesham, just outside Chichester, and would be able to drive over in her 'chariot', a 1924 Jowett which she had won in a newspaper competition ('Please be excited and glad about it!' she had begged Harold). All that Anne asked for was somewhere quiet.

The move was so sudden that Sydney, who had been on a cruise round the Aegean, had known nothing about it, and had to be told by Alida. Unfortunately, she took the opportunity to tell him at the same time about the Bookshop's difficulties (the bank account was down to £27). In alarm Sydney replied that he could do nothing and on no account would he 'induce people to enter into any business investments whatsoever in the Bookshop'. 'I did not know Charlotte had gone away,' he added. 'I do not know where she has gone.' Here was the other, less agreeable side of Cockerell. He did not like to be asked for anything directly, and he was only happy when he was in charge himself.

Charlotte terminated the lease at Delancey Street, put the furniture into store, and booked two rooms until the spring at St George's House, opposite Chichester Cathedral. Exactly what they would do when they came back she didn't know, but by October she and Anne were settled in to a life of extreme quiet, watching the starlings on the roof opposite as they drank their evening cocoa. From the coast they could look over the calm autumn sea towards the Isle of Wight. Anne grew no better.

By November Charlotte had to admit that neither the quiet nor the sea air were doing any good. There was nowhere else to go now but the studio, the last refuge. They had never before contemplated living there, or even spending the night, there was no hot water and anything they wanted to eat had to be brought up from the cook-shop in Fitzroy Street. Obviously it was no place for an invalid, but Charlotte, knowing that there were heavy medical bills ahead of them, did not dare to look round for another flat. Just before Christmas they saw a specialist, who seems to have told them only that something was 'seriously wrong' with Anne, and that she was not strong enough for treatment. Anne by now had grown very thin, and as pale as wax.

It was Maggie Browne's 'turn' in 1926 to invite the Mews for Christmas. As soon as they got to 'Anglefield' Professor Browne decisively told them that Anne must have proper treatment. After the holiday he arranged for her to go at his own expense to a nursing-home in Nottingham Place. Such are the surprises which the dullest friends, the ones always taken for granted, can produce. The professor's name was not to be mentioned, and Charlotte referred to him in her letters simply as 'the Good Samaritan'. In the New Year Anne consulted another specialist, who diagnosed cancer of the liver. It was too late to operate, and he gave Anne three months to live.

Anne, who had been too nervous to spend a night in the house alone, and had quailed at the death of a parrot, faced this sentence with absolute cheerfulness and calm. 'The brutal finality or fatal silence of doctors doesn't move her,' Charlotte said. 'She simply says "I am all right" and talks of coming out in three weeks' time.' Sydney Cockerell, calling round on the 10th of January, found her dressed and sitting by the fire. 'Assuming the doctors to be right in saying that Anne had but three months to live, I urged that she should be allowed to do as she pleased about going out, whatever the risk.' On his advice, Anne was removed at the beginning of February from Professor

Browne's responsibility and taken to the Etoile in Charlotte Street, which had rooms to let above the restaurant, and was only a few doors away from the studio. Sydney liked to have his advice taken, and perhaps he was right in this instance, for it was almost like bringing Anne home. The Etoile itself was at that time a medium-priced Italian restaurant, favoured by publishers and their readers and writers of the unassuming sort. There was a cheerful noise, a sound of singing and a smell of cooking, and Charlotte stayed with Anne all day and only went away at night to sleep in the studio. A local GP, Dr Horatio Cowan, was called in. By April, however, Anne was so much worse that the hotel management were anxious for her to leave. Charlotte, distraught, begged Dr Cowan to let her nurse her sister in the studio, or, once again, to try 'a change of air'. These things were impossible and another nursing-home had to be found, this time in Priory Road, West Hampstead, which was near to Katherine Righton and the Jarmans, but a long trip for Charlotte. Sometimes, however, they let her sleep in Anne's room. She came every day with new novels to read aloud and amuse them both, starting with David Garnett's *Go She Must*. If that failed, she described to Anne what the tortoise in the garden next door was doing, hour by hour.

Terminal illness is a great simplifier of daily life, everything being reduced to the same point of hope against hope. Anne's mind was at rest. She had made a will, a very short one, leaving everything she possessed to Charlotte. Her Christian faith had never faltered. Visitors came, and she seemed untroubled by what was virtually the ordeal of dying in public. Among them was one of the Mew cousins, Ethel Louisa, now an elderly teacher on the verge of retirement. Ethel had known the sisters for more than fifty years, and during that time, as far as she remembered, they had never been parted for more than a few weeks. It worried her to remember that 'a long time ago' Charlotte had spoken of taking her own life. She took the opportunity of saying something in private about this, and was relieved when Charlotte said that now 'she would not do it'. On the 7th of May Alida wrote to Harold Monro:

Last night Charlotte Mew came round and said that though Anne could not speak she was always writing down that she wanted to see me and so I had to go. I have never seen anyone so near death before and because of her illness (some wasting liver disease) she has no flesh on her at all hardly and looks like a skeleton. She could just speak and I talked of our flight to Paris and the robbery practised by the French porters, which interested her.

Queer how, looking towards the gas fire, and talking of the spring warmth we shall soon be feeling, she should have murmured 'I shan't want a fire soon.' As I talked to her and she shut her eyes I felt they were sealed on her face and would never open, but they did. Aunty Mew says that Dr says any moment she may go down to earthly mould. Poor little Mew, it is more tragic than I can tell you – Her rough little harsh voice and wilful ways hiding enormous depth of feeling – now she will be entirely alone and her relation with Anne has been one of complete love, and I imagine the love of sisters (or brothers) more marvellous than any other as there can be no fleshly implications or sexual complexities, Alas –

But Charlotte knew that, however completely loving, she was guilty. In the summer of 1926, before she had decided that she must take Anne away, she had begun – in spite of what she had told Cockerell – to write a story. The setting is Brittany – the Brittany before 1914. The subject is two sisters living in the same house. Aglaë, the older one, stays at home and makes lace for a living. Germaine goes out to work, marries a fisherman (Aglaë can hear them together through the thin bedroom walls) and bears a child, Odette. Odette loves her Aunt Aglaë (who can play children's games so well) 'with an odd passion', more, it turns out, than she loves her mother. The young husband is killed in an accident – 'not yet thirty, and already under the earth behind the high iron gates at the top of the long hill'. Germaine soon picks up a lover, and reproaches Aglaë, who disapproves of him, with being no more than a *vieille fille*, a born spinster. And Germaine repeats Marguérite Gauthier's cry: '*Je veux vivre!*' Aglaë has nothing to answer. True enough, she has only been kissed once, *au fin de fête*, by a drunk. But it was the drunk's kiss which had made her realize that, all the time, she had wanted her sister's husband.

After this the story begins to peter out, rambling along in a hopeless confusion of French and English. At one point Odette's pet rat has to be poisoned, and buried in a cardboard box in consecrated ground. At another, Aglaë thinks passionately of Christ crucified 'who had spoken gently to the woman taken in adultery and the Magdalen'. All the broken things in Charlotte's life are assembled in this unfinished story as though by their own volition, and look more broken than ever. Even if the injuries to Anne existed only in her imagination, they were destroying her now. In the last few pages of the manuscript Aglaë is left alone with her sister's new man, and realizes with deep repulsion that he wants to make love to her. 'She thought . . . "I belong to myself from my head to my feet, for he is not one of us, we are clean, but his hands are all stained."' Then (after a missing page) the same man is claiming sympathy for his sister, who has never been allowed to marry because she has tuberculosis. The last phase has been reached, and she is dying. She looks calm enough, but her one dream has been of a happy marriage. Now she is condemned for ever.

In the spring of 1926 Charlotte almost lived at 43 Priory Road, deaf to the outside world. To Lady Ottoline, who still persevered with her invitations, she wrote a flat refusal, 'as my sister is dangerously ill in a Nursing Home and I spend all my time with her and consequently have none for seeing anyone else'. To Sydney's postcard, 'I could come and take you out if that would help at all – My love to you,' she gave a gentler answer, but she would not see him. By now it was bright early summer, but Anne was too weak to look out of the windows. 'If there's a mercy it can't be long,' Charlotte told Alida. After a terrible twenty-four hours, during which Charlotte never left her, Anne died at midnight on the 18th of June 1927.

'Dear Sydney,' Charlotte wrote, 'Yes – it was over at midnight on Saturday – and now she can never be old, or not properly taken care of, or alone.' Nor, she might have added, would Anne ever have to be 'wonderfully cheerful' again in the grip of intense pain, or answer brightly to enquiries, or be pitied as someone whose gift for painting had come, after all, to so

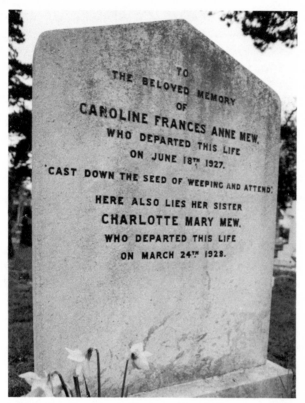

Anne and Charlotte's grave in Fortune Green Cemetery, Hampstead.
'I desire my remains to be buried in the same grave
as my late sister . . . .'

little. Only very few people were asked to the funeral at Fortune
Green Cemetery, but many more came, and people who had
scarcely known Anne sent handfuls of flowers.

Edith Oliver was there to offer help, as she had been at the
Gower Street School, as she had been when Charlotte ran off to
Ella D'Arcy. Professor Oliver had retired from Kew, and the
family was living at 2 The Grove, Isleworth, but in the same
sober Quakerish surroundings, with the same agreeable drawings by Arthur Hughes on the walls. If ever Charlotte was to
find peace, it would be here. Lady Ottoline, still determined to
capture the eccentric poet, motored down to the quiet suburb

and left flowers and messages. Eventually she sent a letter, 'but as it hasn't been answered,' Charlotte wrote, 'I hoped you would understand as everyone else has been good enough to do without my saying so that I am only seeing and writing to old friends. I came here to some – for quiet.' Lady Ottoline had come up against a celebrity who did not care about celebrity, and she graciously admitted defeat.

The last of Charlotte's visits that year was to Cambridge. In September Sydney was off again, this time on a tour of the classical sites of Greece, and the household, though Kate would never have admitted it, seemed to give a sigh of relief. She had invited Charlotte for two whole weeks (it would in fact be thirteen days, Sydney had corrected her). This was a precious time. It was not that Kate's health was any better, only that she felt free, and it was not that Charlotte had recovered from Anne's death, only that she knew that at Shaftesbury Road she was needed and wanted. On the 8th of October Sydney came back, and after two days' furious activity making up his work at the Museum he saw Charlotte off on the 3.52 train to London.

The studio was as she had left it. Anne's painting things were there, a screen she had decorated, a little head of a baby in plaster which they had taken with them through all their changes in fortune, the medicines, the old letters, Charlotte's trunks, but, on top of that, all the clothes and bits of furniture they had decided not to store. It was not only a place of unbearable memories but a muddle, wretched to live in, impossible to ask anyone to.

Fortunately a stray cat was waiting for Charlotte outside the Studios. Indeed, it seemed to be expecting her. Otherwise she could hardly have brought herself to go in. But she told Kate Cockerell that she couldn't bother to turn the place out. 'It doesn't seem worth while for oneself.' She apologized for her wild handwriting, also for the way she was expressing herself, which seemed to have something quite wrong with it, *'mais il faut écouter le coeur* when there's nothing else to listen to'.

CHAPTER 22

Fin de Fête

🎴

1928 WAS A YEAR of stress for Alida Monro, Florence Hardy and Sydney Cockerell. During the snowy December of 1927, Hardy had fallen ill and showed signs of being tired of life, while Cockerell (to Florence's growing irritation) spent more and more time at Max Gate. He was in attendance, waiting to take charge. When Hardy died, on the 11th of January 1928, Sydney, as literary executor, had his hands full. He had taken it upon himself to arrange the funeral and a fitting great man's memorial, there was a mass of urgent business of all kinds, and he had asked Florence to read aloud to him, chapter by chapter, the manuscript of Hardy's memoirs. This occupied most evenings, and yet, when he was going through the desk drawers and found a piece of paper on which Hardy had copied out *Fin de Fête*, he took the trouble to send it to Charlotte at once, knowing what it would mean to her.

Alida, for her part, was almost worn out by the business of moving the Bookshop from Devonshire Street (where the lease had finally run out) to Great Russell Street. The new premises were smaller and had to be shared with another publisher, Kegan Paul, and Alida despaired of recreating the old magic. The readings continued, but had to be held, at first, in the room set aside for Harold's bedroom and office. When he went away (as he sometimes did) taking the key with him, she had to cancel the reading and explain things as best she could to the audience.

For Harold Monro himself, as he noted in his diary, this 'period of horror' began slowly. Conrad Aiken, in *Ushant*, recalls T. S. Eliot coming out of this same room and giving a warning that Monro was 'not altogether himself'. And Aiken 'found the unhappy man seated at a table, his head in his hands, all but speechless, or his speech reduced to four-letter words . . . incapable of serving the cold collation which had been laid out on the sideboard, he rolled his head in his hands . . . and cursed his existence, but above all cursed the utterly meaningless caprices and bad jokes and filthy connivings of a destiny that would compel one to fall in love, for instance, with a dishonest little tailor's assistant, who was utterly incapable of fidelity; and thus to destroy all that one had believed in, or been faithful to, in one's life, all that was good'. Yet even in these dark straits Monro sent his authors their accounts for the New Year.

At the beginning of 1928, then, Charlotte would hardly have expected to see much of Alida or Sydney. She had spent Christmas with Katherine Righton in West Hampstead, wanting, no doubt, to be close to those who had been close to Anne.

In the New Year she went back to Hogarth Studios. Since Anne's death she had dressed entirely in black, and, instead of her usual little hard felt, put on very straight, she wore a large black hat. In appearance she had become one of the eccentric little old ladies of the *quartier*, emerging only to go to the corner shop for cigarettes. But a close look would show how much she had changed since Dorothy Hawksley's drawing of 1926. 'Her wind-blown grey hair, her startled grey eyes, her thin white face, belonged to a reluctant visitor from another world, frightened at what she had undergone in this one.'

Now, when it scarcely mattered to her any longer, she found herself no longer poor. On the 31st of January her uncle, Edward Herne Kendall, aged 84, died of myocardial degeneration at his lodgings in the Harrow Road. Charlotte, as the last survivor (except Freda), became the sole inheritor of Grandmother Kendall's trust fund, which amounted to about £8000.

The trust's lawyers, James & James of Holborn Circus, must have been notified that the old man was sinking. It was probably at their suggestion (since Charlotte would soon have something considerable to dispose of) that on the 3rd of January she made her will. There were a number of small legacies and gifts; Kate Cockerell was to have any piece of china or silver she liked; Anne's gold watch proved too difficult to bequeath and the problem of who was to have it was left to her friends. £2,200 was set aside for Freda's maintenance, and the rest of the estate was divided between Florence Ellen Mew, Ethel Louisa Mew and Katherine Righton. Charlotte asked that when she died she should be buried in the same grave as Anne. On the headstone there was to be an inscription: 'Cast down the seed of weeping, and attend.' The line is from the *Purgatorio*, Canto XXXI, where Beatrice reproaches Dante for his sins, and might be translated 'this is no time for tears, consider what you have done'. It must be the most chilling inscription in all the rambling acres of Fortune Green Cemetery.

It also points clearly enough to Charlotte's state of mind. If she looked, by this time, like 'a reluctant visitor from another world', it was from a purgatory of her own, the circle of self-punishers. In the will she had also given instructions that her main artery was to be severed, to ensure death, before she was placed in her coffin, and now she began to torment herself because she had not done the same thing for her sister, who might, in consequence, have been buried alive. Then it began to seem to her that Anne had not really died of cancer, but had been infected by the little black specks which could be seen everywhere in the studio. After a while Charlotte became terrified that she too was contaminated by the black specks, and would contract the same illness.

She went to Dr Horatio Cowan, whose consulting-room was just round the corner in Fitzroy Square, and who had attended Anne. He had the black specks analysed. They were soot.

Charlotte, in a sense, must have known this perfectly well. In the 1920s London was still a place where everything in the street, and everything indoors that was left undusted for a few hours, left black marks at a touch. 'Laundry is the curse of civilization', she had once said. But unluckily the new language of hygiene – contamination, impurity, resistance, fight against germs – recalled the old nursery evangelical language of sin. The room itself was sinful. As best she could, Charlotte wanted to wash her soul white.

In this compulsive fear of dirt and acute sense of her own

unworthiness, Charlotte was in danger of passing from the neurotic to the psychotic. She not only felt a survivor's guilt, she saw it on her own window-sill. Help was needed, as it had often been before, in 'getting my nerves under control'. The doctor had nothing more to offer and sent her to a 'mental specialist', simply to find out whether or not, on the evidence, she could be certified. The specialist said that she could not.

Dr Cowan then tried to persuade her to enter an asylum – the house of 'darkly stained or clouded glass' – as a voluntary patient. Charlotte refused, but on the 15th of February he got her to go to a nursing-home which he recommended, 37 Beaumont Street, near Baker Street Station.

In Priory Road Anne had had at least a view over a garden and could see the trees. In Beaumont Street Charlotte had a miserably furnished back room, with windows looking out on a blank wall, and only an occasional glimpse of a sparrow or a pigeon. The matron was called Miss Lutch. There is something inexplicable in the choice of this place.

Although there is no record of Charlotte receiving any form of treatment, she seems to have made a determined effort to return to normal. On the 20th of February she wrote two letters. One was an acknowledgement to Harold Monro. The other was to Evelyn Millard, who had sent a book of religious poetry, *The Power of Silence*. 'I quite understand how it is you value it and that it has helped you,' Charlotte wrote, '. . . but faith is given us like every other good gift and if we haven't got it we can but pray for it. One faith I have and that is in the wonderful everlasting kindness of my friends who have borne so much and done so much for me – and where that comes from I cannot doubt.'

On the 24th Sydney snatched a day in London. He was obliged to catch the 4.30 back to Dorchester, but before that he would have liked to take Charlotte, as so often before, to some kind of entertainment, something that everyone was going to see – not the Matisse exhibition, for he could not believe there was anything to be said for pictures so hideous, but perhaps Queen Mary's doll's house, with its library of tiny books specially written by England's most respected authors. He found Charlotte unwilling to go out. She was 'in a state of great depression, with nothing and nobody to live for' and he could not cajole her.

Kate Cockerell, he had told her, seemed a little better, and Charlotte wrote that night to congratulate her and to hope that she would get out into the fresh air.

> Yes one can bear hard things under the open sky but for weeks now I have seen little of it except through a window. You do not know how much or with what affection I have thought of you. What you gave me at Cambridge that fortnight can't be told this side of silence – for myself I won't say much. I just tried my best to keep going and broke down – it was so lonely – I try still but it is lonelier here – You understand – and a little I hope – how I think of you.
>
> Dear Kate – my love –
Yours Charlotte.

This letter makes one wonder what Charlotte, who (as she gratefully acknowledged) always had the homes of her friends open to her, was doing at Miss Lutch's establishment. The only explanation seems to be that she had set herself to be as independent as possible and to find her own way back to what she had called 'the great broken world'.

On March 12th Alida came, and was appalled by the dreariness of the room. There was a visit, too, from Cousin Ethel. For the next ten days no-one seems to have called except the doctor, who thought his patient was progressing favourably. During this time Charlotte apparently lost some battle, or perhaps, as she had suggested at the end of *The Quiet House*, she had gone to meet herself at last.

March 22nd was Henry Mew's birthday, the day on which she and Anne had often gone together to his grave in Nunhead Cemetery. On the 23rd, Alida came to Beaumont Street again. Charlotte went across to a wretched-looking chest of drawers and took out the copy which Hardy had made for himself of *Fin de Fête*. She gave it to Alida, telling her that she would like her to have it. This sounds unmistakably like a form of farewell, but Alida was too distracted and hard-driven to recognize it.

Charlotte was not so much obsessed with death as too familiar with it. Of her own death she had written, 'I mean to go through that gate without fear.' She had not expected, however, to face it alone.

> One day the friends who stand about my bed
> Will slowly turn from it to speak of me
> Indulgently, as of the newly dead . . .

On March 24th, just before one o'clock, she told Miss Lutch that she was going out for fifteen minutes. She did go, but only far enough to buy a bottle of Lysol. Lysol is a solution of creosote which at that time was on sale everywhere as a household disinfectant. It has a violent corrosive action, and was the cheapest poison available. Back in her room, she poured half the bottle into a glass, drank it and lay down on her bed.

Although it was a Saturday, Dr Cowan seems to have paid a routine visit that afternoon to Beaumont Street. When he arrived, Miss Lutch took him to Charlotte's room, where they found her in great pain, foaming at the mouth and talking to herself. The doctor administered olive oil, but it was useless. He made (in his own words at the inquest) 'every endeavour to pull the deceased round, but all efforts were unavailing'. For a short while she recovered consciousness, and said, 'Don't keep me, let me go.' This was her last attempt to speak to anyone, this side of silence.

Charlotte Mew's candlesticks.

Notes and References

ABBREVIATIONS

AM   Alida Monro
CADS   Mrs Catherine Amy Dawson Scott
FH   Florence Hardy
HM   Harold Monro
MS   May Sinclair
SCC   Sydney Cockerell
CMCP   *Charlotte Mew: Collected Poems and Prose*, edited by Val
       Warner, London and Manchester 1982.
Davidow   *Charlotte Mew: Biography and Criticism* (unpublished
       Ph.D.thesis, Brown University, 1960.)
Memoir   Alida Monro's *Charlotte Mew: a Memoir*, the preface to
       Collected Poems of Charlotte Mew, London 1953.
NYPLB   Bulletin of the New York Public Library.
Berg   Berg Collection of the New York Public Library.
Buffalo   The Lockwood Library, University of Buffalo.
Texas   Humanities Research Center, The University of Texas at
       Austin.
MW   Collection of Mrs Marjorie Watts.

CHAPTER I

p 9   'George and James went first . . .' Their home and business
      address was 26 Surrey Square, Old Kent Road.

p 10 'the great builder Thomas Cubitt . . .' Cubitt was in charge of
      the work at Osborne 1844–6. The stucco façade, with other
      details, was criticized because Cubitt was only a tradesman,
      and not an architect.

p 10 'Manning and Mew . . .' Michael Prendergast Manning
      became an associate of the RIBA in 1866, and retired in 1902.
      His office was at 6 Mitre Court.

p 10 'The New School of Design at Sheffield.' Later the College of
      Art, Arundel Street. The drawing was exhibited in 1856.

p 10 'his grand old father . . .' Henry Kendall, 1776–1875.
      Charlotte Mew did not much care for her great-grandfather's
      work, and used to deplore his convent for the Kilburn Sisters
      in Brondesbury.

p 12 'Sir John Paul . . .' John Samuel Paul, 1849–1912.

p 12 'Kendall's *Modern Architecture.*' (1846) In his *Designs for Schools and Schoolhouses* (1847) Kendall claimed to be able to build an 'artistic and tasty village school' for £300, cheaper still if the casements had wrought iron frames and the gargoyles and parapets were made in cement. He was, however, a serious student of historical styles and of the fitness of the materials used to the locality.

p 13 'When Kendall drew up his will . . .' on 13 May 1863 Kendall bequeathed the residue of his estate to his wife and Fred Mew jointly, on condition that the survivor should convert it into Government or real securities in England. Mrs Kendall was to get the income during her lifetime, and after her death the capital was to be divided between the surviving children.

p 14 'Mrs Lewis Cubitt . . .' Thomas Cubitt (1788–1855) and William Cubitt (1791–1863) split up their joint business in 1827. During the 1830s William worked with his brother Lewis. All the Cubitt undertakings were successful.

p 14 '30 Doughty Street.' Not 10 Doughty Street, as has often been stated. At the time of writing this house has been taken over by Camden Borough Council for restoration.

p 17 'Oh! King who hast the key . . .' *Exspecto Resurrectionem* (CMCP p. 28)

p 18 'To us as children . . .' *An Old Servant* (CMCP p. 401)

p 18 'flung into the festooned disorder . . .' *An Old Servant* (CMCP p. 403)

p 20 'an essay of 1901 . . .' *Miss Bolt: A Study* (CMCP p. 338) appeared in *Temple Bar* April 1901. A T/S in the British Library (Add MSS 57754) shows that Charlotte made alterations to disguise the real names and addresses. It includes several passages cut by *Temple Bar*'s editor.

p 20 'Give a thing, and take a thing . . .' Not in the published article.

p 22 'Past the white points of the Needles . . .' *The Hay-Market* (CMCP p. 408)

p 23 'Tide be runnin' . . .' *Sea Love* (CMCP p. 34) first appeared in *The Chapbook* no 1, July 1919.

p 23 'But on Sundays . . .' Most of these details are from *The Country Sunday* (CMCP p. 370). Charlotte has altered some details – for example, the lace factory at Broadlands House, Barton, becomes a 'rope factory'.

p 23 'St Paul's, Barton . . .' A 'Norman Style' church built in 1845, less than a mile to the S.W. of Newfairlee Farm.

p 24 '*Line Upon Line, or a Second Series of the Earliest Religious Instruction the Infant Mind is Capable of Receiving, with verses illustrative of the subject, by the Author of The Peep of Day*, London 1837.

p 24 'In early years . . .' *An Old Servant* (CMCP p. 405)

p 24 'Saturday Markets . . .' These were held at Whitsun and on three successive Saturdays before Michaelmas.

p 25 'I remember one evening . . .' *The Trees Are Down* (CMCP p. 48)

p 25 'the picture of the Shining City . . .' The detailed history of this picture is given in an article by F. W. Leakey, *Baudelaire et Kendall, Revue de Littérature Comparée*, 1956 no 1, pp. 53–63.

CHAPTER 2

p 27 'Miss Bolt had warned . . .' in another cancelled passage from Charlotte's *Miss Bolt* (see note for p. 20). The only exceptions to the rule 'what you're made, that you will be' were, it seems, female impersonators.

p 27 'sheets of pathetically laboured manuscripts . . .' *An Old Servant* (CMCP p. 402)

p 27 '*The Changeling.*' This poem (CMCP p. 13) first appeared in *The Englishwoman*, 17 Feb 1913, although the style seems earlier.

p 27 'children of her acquaintance . . .' (Information from Mrs Marjorie Watts.)

p 28 'the headmistress, Miss Lucy Harrison . . .' Most of the following details about her are from *A Lover of Books: The Life and Literary Papers of Lucy Harrison* by Amy Greener, London 1916.

p 30 '*Social Geography for Teachers and Infants*' by Lucy Harrison, London 1903. The passage quoted is on p. 93. In an earlier lesson (p. 12) the children are asked: '*Why do we wear clothing?* 1. For warmth. 2. To keep us from injury. 3. For ornament. 4. Because it is right.'

p 35 '*Catarina to Camoens*' from Elizabeth Barrett Browning's *Poems 1844*.

p 36 '*Left Behind*' (CMCP p. 57) was first published from the manuscript by Muriel Davidow, 1960.

p 36 'restless ghosts . . .' *Ces Plaisirs*, Paris 1932, reissued Paris, 1941, as *Les Purs et les Impurs*, par Colette.

CHAPTER 3

p 37 'It is a legend in my family . . .' CM/CADS 1 March 1914. (MW)

p 38 'Old Kendall had died . . .' on 4 Jan 1875. He left effects valued at less than £100.

p 38 'greatly assisted . . .' *The Builder* vol 48 pp. 883–4.

p 39 ' "Sir," wrote an unsuccessful competitor . . .' *Hampstead & Highgate Express*, 6 May 1876.

p 40 'that though the work . . .' *Hampstead & Highgate Express*, 8 June 1877.

p 41 'The Capital and Counties Bank . . .' in Clare Street, Bristol. The bank is illustrated in *The Builder,* 12 Dec 1885.

p 44 'Freda lived for another sixty years . . .' She died on 1 March 1958, leaving effects valued at £1960.9s.6d.

CHAPTER 4

p 45 '*On the Asylum Road* and *Ken* . . .' (CMCP p. 19 and 15)

p 47 'the first editor to see *Ken* . . .' (CM/HM 9 Feb 1916), quoted in *Memoir* p. xvii.

p 47 'for a coffin . . .' *The Narrow Door* (CMCP p. 3)

p 48 'the horse-trough is always there . . .' *The Hay-Market* (CMCP p. 408)

p 48 'If there were fifty heavens . . .' *Madeleine in Church* (CMCP p. 25)

p 48 '*The Architectural Association* . . .' founded in 1847 to encourage original ideas and to help young architects to pass the RIBA exams.

p 48 'a dignified but pathetic letter . . .' *The Builder,* 6 Feb 1897, p. 128.

p 49 'Anything that appears foggy . . .' Fred Mew/Walter Barnes Mew, 4 Jan 1893, F. B. Adams Collection, quoted in Davidow.

p 49 'the Royal Female School of Art . . .' Founded in 1842, the School acquired premises at 43 Queen Square, Bloomsbury, and remained there until 1908 when it amalgamated with the Central School of Art. Fees were 15 guineas for 2 terms, half fees for artisans.

p 50 'Please you, excuse me . . .' A very early poem (CMCP p. 54), first printed after Charlotte's death in *The Rambling Sailor,* 1929.

p 50 'a blade of grass which dare not grow too high . . .' *A Country Book* (CMCP p. 411)

p 53 '*The Outlook* . . .' *The Outlook* changed its name to *The New Review* in 1898, so Charlotte presumably sent in her article earlier than this.

p 53 'It set my own heart beating . . .' *A Country Book* (CMCP p. 411). This is an apparently unpublished essay on Richard Jefferies' *Field and Hedgerow*, perhaps inspired by Edward Thomas's *Life and Work of Richard Jefferies*, 1909.

p 54 'Elsie Millard . . .' Elsie exhibited landscapes and miniature portraits between 1893 and 1916 at the Royal Academy, the Royal Hibernian Academy, and the Society of Women Artists.

p 54 'a strange group of Goodman relatives . . .' *An Old Servant* (CMCP p. 405)

p 55 '*A Wedding Day* . . .' This unpublished T/S was printed for the first time in CMCP (p. 216). The T/S is dated 1895.

p 55 'yet another magazine . . .' The preliminary announcement of *The Yellow Book* came out at the beginning of March 1894.

CHAPTER 5

p 57 'John Lane . . .' (1854–1925)

p 57 'Henry Harland . . .' (1861–1905)

p 59 'St James's, Spanish Place . . .' The architect was George Goldie (1828–87). Charlotte, as the story implies, did not approve of his work.

p 61 'hurrying-through-mean-streets stories . . .' In vol 2 of *The Yellow Book*, where *Passed* appeared, Harland also printed Frederic Greenwood's *The Gospel of Content*. Here the air is 'thick with darkness and drizzling rain' and the narrator hurries through the 'squalid streets of King's Cross' to the rescue of a Russian nobleman who has been reduced to selling dolls' hats made out of his starving children's clothes.

p 62 'Victoria Crosse . . .' Her real name was Vivien Corey, and her *Keynote* (no 5 in Lane's series) was *The Woman Who Didn't*, written in reply to Grant Allen's best-selling *The Woman Who Did*.

p 62 'He wanted the story toned down . . .' These details are from Henry Harland and CM letters in the F. B. Adams Collection, printed in Davidow.

p 63 'the down-and-out Frederick Rolfe . . .' Rolfe ('Baron Corvo') left Aberdeen in February 1894 and lived in London in a state of semi-starvation until the middle of 1895.

CHAPTER 6

p 67 'It sounds like a regional play . . .' It was broadcast in dramatized form on BBC Western Region, 12 Nov 1953.

p 67 'Newlyn lights . . .' CM/Mrs Hill 24 July 1913. (Buffalo.)

p 71 'the run was cut short . . .' The play was withdrawn on 9 May.

CHAPTER 7

p 72 'Charlotte, taking charge . . .' Her letters are in the F. B. Adams Collection and are printed in Davidow.

p 74 'Mrs Clement Parsons . . .' She was the sister-in-law of Alfred Parsons, the flower painter. In 1901 she published *The Child At Home*.

p 74 '*The Governess in Fiction*' (CMCP p. 335) appeared in *The Academy* on 12 August 1899. It was identified as Charlotte's work by Mary Davidow.

p 75 'Her fears began . . .' Professor A. G. Tansley/S. C. Cockerell 27 June 1944. (Berg.)

p 75 '*In Nunhead Cemetery*' (CMCP p. 8). The last eight verses, which show the 'gradual lapse into insanity', were omitted in the *Collected Poems* published by Duckworth in 1953.

p 76 'The essence, never the solution . . .' Alida Monro's note on Charlotte Mew in *The Chapbook* for June 1920 (*A Bibliography of Contemporary Poetry with Notes on Some Contemporary Poets by a recorder.*)

p 76 'Kipling's young chemist's assistant . . .' in *Wireless* (*Traffics and Discoveries*, 1908)

p 77 'she danced the can-can . . .' This story is told by Michael Holroyd in *Unreceived Opinions* p. 156 (New York 1967).

p 79 'Ellen Mary . . .' Ellen Mew, who took the name of Sister Mary Magdalen, was interviewed by Mary Davidow.

p 79 'He was alive to me . . .' *Madeleine in Church* (CMCP p. 28)

p 80 'She could seem so gay . . .' *Memoir* p. xiv.

p 81 'Mary Kendall . . .' In April 1904 *Temple Bar* printed an article describing the writer's visit in Paris in 1901 to the Princess Mathilde Bonaparte 'while staying with an aunt . . . who for years had been one of [her] most intimate friends'. The article is signed C.M., and Mary Davidow believed that it was by Charlotte, and that the aunt was Mary Kendall. This is almost certainly a mistake. Charlotte never signed herself C.M. (though sometimes C.M.M.), and the 'aunt' is said in the article to live in Paris, whereas Mary Kendall lived at 29 Sillwood Road, Brighton. Apart from this, she was gravely ill in 1901. CMCP gives the article in an appendix, p. 439.

CHAPTER 8

p 82 'I do care for money . . .' This and the following quotations are taken from Ella D'Arcy's letters to John Lane 1894–7, in the William Andrews Clark Memorial Library, University of California.

p 82 'a brutal portrait of me by Wilson Steer . . .' This portrait had been exhibited in Brussels in 1893 and Lane had in fact printed it in *The Yellow Book* for July 1894 as '*Portrait of a Lady.*' Cf. Bruce Laughton, *Philip Wilson Steer, 1860–1942* (Oxford 1971). Catalogue no. 110.

p 83 'This new wife . . .' Annie Eichberg King. In 1924 she recommended André Maurois' life of Shelley, *Ariel*, which Ella translated for John Lane. *Ariel* was reissued in 1925, 1935 and 1950, but Ella seems not to have benefited from its success.

p 83 'My dear, I scarcely know where to begin . . .' CM/Edith Oliver [undated] April 1902. (Buffalo)

p 87 '*Rooms* . . .' (CMCP p. 38)

p 87 'I remember rooms . . .' (CMCP p. 38). The T/S in BL Add MSS 57754 gives 'wearing out of the heart' instead of 'slowing down'.

p 87 'No record . . .' Ella died in London, 5 Sept 1937, of 'senile dementia'. Katherine Lyon Mix, the author of *A Study in Yellow* (Kansas City, 1960) writes to me: 'I first met Ella when she came to London from Paris in 1930. I was rather shocked at her appearance for she had dyed her hair a dreadful red orange . . . . Yet she was a bright and witty talker, with sharp comments about life.' By the 1930s Ella had become embittered, and, as always, was chronically short of money. (Ella D'Arcy's letters to Mrs Mix are in the library of Penn State College.)

CHAPTER 9

p 88 '*The Quiet House* . . .' (CMCP p. 17)

p 88 'to me the most subjective of the lot . . .' CM/Mrs Hill 4 Jan

1917. Buffalo. Mrs Hill was related by marriage to the Hill family, for whom Fred Mew had built Ivy Lodge, Hampstead, where Belsize Lane meets Haverstock Hill.

p 90 'Gordon Street was, in fact . . .' CM/Edith Oliver 27 June 1911. 'The noise of Gordon Street seems 10,000 miles away.' (Buffalo.)

p 91 'Jane Elnswick . . .' the name is given in Alida Monro's draft for her memoir of Charlotte Mew, BL Add MSS 57755.

p 91 'The Federation's handbooks . . .' The Report for 1914–15 advises a six-months' training course for leaders, but there is no evidence that Charlotte did any training at all.

p 92 'a good imitation . . .' In *A Fatal Fidelity* (CMCP p. 201) Charlotte even tried to write in the style of W. W. Jacobs, whom she met at a tea-party early in 1914.

p 92 'The heroine of his *New Grub Street* . . .' in Chapters 5 and 7.

p 94 'the last sentence of *Wuthering Heights* . . .' In fact Mr Lockwood 'wondered how anyone could imagine unquiet slumbers for the sleepers in that quiet earth'.

p 95 'Anglefield . . .' This house has now been converted into flats.

p 96 '*Requiescat*' (CMCP p. 51)

p 96 'Looking through some of Ella's old letters . . .' CM/CADS 12 May 1914. (MW.)

p 97 'more typical tourist's letters . . .' CM/Edith Oliver June 1909. (Buffalo.)

p 98 '*Péri en mer* . . .' (CMCP p. 61)

p 99 'she read his *The Old Sceptic* . . .' CM/Edith Oliver 27 June 1911. (Buffalo.)

p 99 'Religion is like music . . .' *Men and Trees 11*, (CMCP p. 396)

p 99 'This time they went to Boulogne . . .' CM/Edith Oliver 27 June 1911. (Buffalo.)

CHAPTER 10

p 101 '*The Farmer's Bride* . . .' (CMCP p. 1)

p 103 'The change in metre . . .' This has been compared with the change of metre in Hardy's *The Voice*, but *The Voice* is one of the *Poems of 1912–13*, and was first published in *Satires of Circumstance* (1914).

p 104 'The quality of emotion . . .' CM/Mrs Hill, 4 January 1917. (Buffalo.)

p 104 'Charlotte once saw a woman . . .' *The Hay-Market* (CMCP, pp. 409–10)

p 105 'my idea of a rough countryman . . .' CM/SCC 10 July 1918. (Berg.)

p 105 'an Imp with brains . . .' Mrs Dawson Scott's diary for early 1913. These diaries were not strictly kept by the day.

CHAPTER 11

p 106 'She was entirely deluded . . .' Herman Ould, *Shuttle* (London 1947) p. 322.

p 106 'her first published work . . .' *Sappho* appeared in 1889.

p 108 'give a reading . . .' All details about these readings are from Mrs Dawson Scott's diaries for 1913. (MW.)

p 108 'Evelyn Underhill . . .' (1875–1941) was a lecturer on the philosophy of religion. Her book of poems, *Immanence*, was published in 1912, and her study, *Practical Mysticism*, in 1914.

p 110 *'Fame . . .'* (CMCP p. 2)

p 111 'a first-class devil . . .' CM/CADS 26 Dec 1913. (MW.)

p 111 'you made me feel rather a vampire . . .' CM/CADS 10 March 1914. (MW.)

p 111 'I read next to no poetry . . .' CM/CADS 3 Feb 1913. (MW.)

p 112 'We only have about half-an-hour . . .' Mrs Dawson Scott's diaries for September 1913. (MW.)

p 112 'sleeping stuff . . .' CM/Mrs Hill 12 March 1913. (Buffalo.)

p 112 'Frederic Whelen . . .' Whelen/CM 25 April 1914. BL Add MSS 57755. Whelen was presenting his own successful 'grotesque play', *The Lethal Hotel.*

p 113 'I have a studio At Home . . .' CM/Mrs Hill 12 March 1913. (Buffalo.)

p 113 'described in an article . . .' *Men and Trees 1* (CMCP p. 388)

p 113 'a delightful girl of 14 . . .' CM/Mrs Hill 12 March 1914. (Buffalo.)

p 115 'She is tiny . . .' Mrs Dawson Scott's diaries, early 1913. (MW.)

p 115 'May Sinclair . . .' (1863–1946). The only complete account of her life is *Miss May Sinclair: Novelist. A Biographical and Critical Introduction* by Theophilus E. M. Boll (Farleigh Dickinson University 1973).

CHAPTER 12

p 117 'She came to dinner sometimes . . .' I. A. R. Wylie, *My Life With George* (New York 1940) p. 178. I. A. R. Wylie also mentions that there was an escape route for suffragettes across May's back garden and out through her front door.

p 119 'her *Defence of Idealism* . . .' published in August 1917.

p 120 'and as the radiant and vehement life . . .' *The Combined Maze* (London 1913) pp. 23–5.

p 122 'My dear Miss Mew . . .' 4 July 1913. (Berg.)

p 123 'Pound suggested . . .' *The English Review*, under the editorship of Ford Madox Ford, was the first magazine to publish Pound in England (June 1909). In 1912 he began to collect contributors for Harriet Monroe's *Poetry*, warning them that his standards were 'the stiffest in Europe'.

p 123 'All verse gains by being spoken . . .' CM/CADS 26 June 1913. (MW.)

p 124 'in this form I am only a beginner . . .' CM/Mrs Hill 24 July 1914. (Buffalo.)

p 124 '*Madeleine in Church* . . .' (CMCP p. 22)

p 124 'a favourite part of Evelyn Millard . . .' She first appeared in it at the Adelphi in 1894, with George Alexander.

p 126 'Charlotte acknowledged this . . .' CM/CADS 26 Dec 1913. (MW.)

CHAPTER 13

p 127 'Privately May told Sappho . . .' MS/CADS 18 Feb 1914. (MW.)

p 127 'Only, May warned . . .' MS/CM 8 May 1914. (Berg.)

p 127 'I simply hate telling . . .' CM/CADS 12 March 1914. (MW.)

p 129 'And all my days . . .' MS/CM 8 May 1914. (Berg.)

p 129 'It makes all the difference to me to be in the right place . . .' CM/Edith Oliver 8 April 1914. (Berg.)

p 131 'Not by way of an answer . . .' MS/CM 14 May 1914. (Berg.)

p 131 'finish, finish your courtisan . . .' MS/CM 13 June 1914. (Berg.)

p 131 'if Christ had seemed to notice her . . .' This was an idea which haunted Charlotte. She refers more than once to 'an old Spanish priest' who had told her: 'You are always thinking of the Saviour' – 'If He was only here – if we could

only see Him'. '– Oh, ye of little faith!' CM/Evelyn Millard
20 Feb 1928. (Buffalo.)

p 131 'as the Russians are doing . . .' CM/CADS 26 June 1914.
(MW.) Chekhov's *Russian Stories*, translated by Marian Fell,
were published by Duckworth in 1914.

p 131 '*Chance* . . .' from the first (1914) edition.

p 132 '*Qu'avez-vous fait?* . . .' this poem is undated. The MS is on
paper headed 9 Gordon Street. (Davidow.)

p 133 'Rebecca West sent . . .' Dr Boll published this letter in
NYPLB Vol 74 Sept 1970 pp. 445–53 (*The Mystery of Charlotte
Mew and May Sinclair: An Inquiry*). In NYPLB vol 75 March
1971 pp. 295–300 Mary Davidow replied to Dr Boll, pointing
out that Margaret Chick had told her personally that
Charlotte Mew was 'the soul of probity', and that her
brother, Sam Chick, had once wanted to 'keep company' with
Charlotte. She also felt that the time and place (soon after
May's move to 1 Blenheim Road) was improbable. 'Here
were two women of fifty and forty-four. Suddenly the younger
one, seized by a wild fit of passion, gives chase to the older
woman, who makes a dash for the bedroom, of all places, and
amid moving-crates and cartons and displaced furnishings,
leaps the bed five times.'

p 134 'My mother told me . . .' Marjorie Watts: *Memories of Charlotte
Mew*, PEN Broadsheet no 13, Autumn 1982 p. 13.

p 134 'Margaret Radclyffe Hall . . .' Her *The Well of Loneliness*
(1928) defended the natural and social rights of lesbians, and,
at the same time, her own relationship with Una Troubridge.

p 134 'Blindest of all things . . .' *Ne Me Tangito* (CMCP p. 43)

p 134 'I don't think there's anything quite so deadly . . .'
CM/CADS 12 March 1914. (MW.)

p 136 'people are only disappointing . . .' CM/CADS 24 June 1917.
(MW.)

p 137 '*A Journal of Impressions of Belgium*' was published by
Hutchinson in 1915. 'I began to feel . . .' p. 324.

p 137 '*The Pinprick*'. This story appeared in *Harpers* Feb 1915. Cf.
also May Sinclair's *The Divine Fire* (1904) p. 217: 'People in
trouble don't change to other people – they change to
themselves.'

p 138 '*Ne Me Tangito*' (CMCP p. 43)

p 139 '*Saturday Market*' (CMCP p. 33)

p 139 'in Saturday Market nobody cares . . .' Cf. *Men and Trees 11*
(CMCP p. 399). 'We must not speak in the market-place of
what happens to us in the forest,' says Hawthorne – I think it
was in *The Scarlet Letter*. Who was Hawthorne? There are no
scarlet letters. Everything happens in the market-place.
Where else? But the market-place is not real: the real things
are happening in the forest still.'

p 140 'Poets shouldn't be ridiculed . . .' MS/CM 9 June 1915.
(Berg.)

p 140 'In her book . . .' *The Life and Eager Death of Emily Brontë*
(London 1936)

CHAPTER 14

p 142 'The Poetry Bookshop . . .' For a detailed history of the
Bookshop, see Joy Grant: *Harold Monro and the Poetry Bookshop*
(London 1967).

p 143 'They have underneath the shop . . .' quoted in H. S. Ede: *A
Life of Gaudier-Brzěska* (London 1930) p. 131.

p 144 'I don't know men . . .' Harold Monro: *Strange Meetings* (1917).

p 145 'a source of free drinks . . .' according to F. S. Flint's
Biographical Sketch in Monro's *Collected Poems* (London 1933).

p 146 'The grand old man, to whom all looked up . . .' For instance,
An Anthology of Modern Verse, chosen by A. Methuen, which
went through 25 editions between 1921 and 1929, is dedicated
to Thomas Hardy, 'Greatest of the Moderns'. This anthology
includes T. S. Eliot's *La Figlia che Piange* and T. E. Brown's
My Garden ('A garden is a lovesome thing, God wot.')

p 146 '*Georgian Poetry 1911–12* . . .' Half the profits went to the
Bookshop, and half were divided between the contributors.

p 147 'a Hampstead-Polish-refugee family . . .' The Klementaski
grandfather came from Poland in the 1860s. He was a
Catholic, but married a Jewish wife in Holland en route.

p 147 'She and Harold Monro . . .' The following account is mainly
from the correspondence between Alida and Harold Monro
in the British Library (BL Add MSS 57748–52).

p 150 'Are you Charlotte Mew? . . .' *Memoir* p. vii.

CHAPTER 15

p 151 'comparing it later to the wind . . .' CM/SCC 6 July 1918.
(Berg.)

p 152 'two cousins . . .' Ethel Louisa and Florence Ellen were sisters, the daughters of Richard Mew of Newfairlee Farm.

p 152 'She was shown Henry Kendall's picture . . .' F. W. Leakey: *Baudelaire et Kendall* (see note on p. 25) p. 62. Alida said that she could remember 'an airy lightness in the picture, but couldn't put more to it'.

p 153 'one young girl cared for her . . .' Sylvia, the daughter of Mrs Clement Parsons.

p 154 'a South African girl . . .' AM/HM 9 Dec 1916. (BL Add MSS 57748).

p 155 Pamela Travers told me this story, but added that Alida only saw what she wanted to see.

p 155 'this year . . .' CM/HM 14 Dec 1915. (Buffalo.)

p 156 '(1) because it's a chance . . .' MS/CM Berg 27 Dec 1915. (Berg.)

p 157 'his best-known artist . . .' Claud Lovat Fraser (1890–1921) a self-taught artist, was already famous for his book designs and decorations when he joined up in 1914. In 1916 he was invalided home, and *The Farmer's Bride* was one of his first commissions when he started work again.

p 158 'James Guthrie . . .' the genial printer, painter and designer, who illustrated a most successful edition of Monro's *Trees* (1916).

p 158 'friends who not long ago . . .' CM/HM 12 March 1916. (Buffalo.)

p 158 'enough paper for 1000 . . .' 1000 is the correct number, although Alida gives 500 in her *Memoir*.

p 159 'the book was dedicated . . .' Possibly, however, this dedication was to Lucy Harrison, who died 13 April 1915.

p 160 'it is very difficult to get poetry reviewed . . .' MS/CM 10 Feb 1916. (Berg.)

p 160 'because I am simply not the person . . .' CM/HM 29 July 1916. (F. B. Adams Coll., quoted by Davidow.)

CHAPTER 16

p 163 'The first series of rhyme sheets . . .' see Appendix p. 234.

p 163 'Pinknose, Harold's cat . . .' Alida's dog was also shell-shocked in a Zeppelin raid, and when Alida took up professional breeding she chose the kennel-name Firebrave.

p 163 '*J'ai passé par là* . . .' CM/Mrs Hill 4 Jan 1917. (Buffalo.)

p 165 'During the past three months . . .' HM/Macmillan New York. (BL Add MSS 57755.)

p 165 'an American edition . . .' It eventually appeared under the title *Saturday Market*. This was the 1921 edition of *The Farmer's Bride*, which contained eleven additional poems.

CHAPTER 17

p 166 'Sydney Cockerell . . .' later Sir Sydney (1867–1962). For the details of his life I have depended on *Cockerell* (London 1964), the biography by his literary executor, Wilfrid Blunt.

p 168 'a stiff little note . . .' CM/SCC 3 July 1918. (Berg.)

p 169 'an alteration from Harold Monro . . .' At Monro's suggestion Charlotte changed 'lush grasses' in verse 4 of *The Changeling* to 'shy grasses'.

p 169 'a charming artist, Dorothy Hawksley . . .' Dorothy Webster Hawksley (1884–1971) exhibited at the Royal Academy and the St John's Wood School of Art between 1909 and 1940.

p 169 'in Cambridge or any other strange house . . .' CM/SCC 1 Sept 1919, printed in *Friends of a Lifetime: Letters to Sydney Cockerell*, edited by Viola Meynell (London 1940), p. 317.

p 171 'Hardy was too old . . .' SCC/CM 18 Sept 1918 describes Cockerell's delicate negotiations for the visit to Max Gate. (Texas.)

p 171 'Florence's sympathetic biographers . . .' Robert Gittings and Jo Manton, *The Second Mrs Hardy* (London 1979).

p 172 'a pathetic little creature . . .' FH/SCC 6 Dec 1916. *Friends of a Lifetime*, p. 300.

p 172 'decide to plant some herself . . .' FH/CM 2 Oct 1921. (Berg.)

p 172 'in a state of suppressed rage . . .' CM/FH 23 Jan 1921. (Berg.)

p 175 'Why so touchy? . . .' SCC/CM 2 Feb 1920. (Berg.)

p 175 'for the next two years, Mr Cockerell . . .' On 5 April 1923 he wrote to her: 'My dear Charlotte – Yes, of course, if I may be Sydney. I have long since ceased to think of you as Miss Mew.' (Berg.)

CHAPTER 18

p 176 'a little bronze . . .' CM/AM 24 Feb 1924. (Buffalo.)

p 176 'the blameless Pepys . . .' CM/FH 5 Oct 1921. (Berg.)

p 177 'And what of Alida the charming? . . .' SCC/CM 8 May 1919. (Berg.)

p 177 'He evidently sees you as much painted . . .' CM/AM 24 Feb 1921. (Buffalo.)

p 179 'one of the few people I have ever known . . .' *Cockerell*, p. 168.

p 179 'My own father . . .' E. V. Knox ('Evoe'). His parody of Charlotte Mew appeared in *Punch* 4 Aug 1921.

p 180 'I think her very good . . .' V. Woolf/R. C. Trevelyan, 25 Jan 1920. *Letters of Virgina Woolf* ed. Nigel Nicholson, vol. 2, (London 1976), p. 419.

p 180 *The Shade-Catchers* (CMCP p. 31). This poem bears out John Freeman's critical article in *The Bookman*, June 1929 p. 145–6. 'She could put a constraint upon her deepest feeling, but none upon her form . . . the nearer her verse keeps to the normal stanza, the more delicate its movement.'

CHAPTER 19

p 184 'The Estate, on the contrary . . .' The letters between Layton and the Bedford Estate are quoted in Davidow from the F. B. Adams Coll.

p 185 'and don't mean to untie the hens . . .' CM/SCC 18 Dec 1921. (Berg.)

p 186 'But so long as you can come . . .' CM/SCC 9 May 1922. (Berg.)

p 187 '*The Trees Are Down* . . .' This poem (CMCP p. 48) appeared in *The Chapbook* for January 1923.

CHAPTER 20

p 188 '*Fin de Fête* . . .' (CMCP p. 40.)

p 189 'Sympathy is not . . .' CM/SCC 26 April 1923. (Berg.)

p 191 'treated very much as if she were a naughty child . . .' *Memoir* p. ix.

p 193 'The difficulty in these cases . . .' W. B. Yeats/Percy Withers, 7 Jan 1912. Withers Coll., Somerville College, Oxford.

p 195 'a sort of suicide . . .' CM/SCC 29 July 1923, *Friends of a Lifetime*.

p 195 'De la Mare, as he explained . . .' His letter is in *The Best of Friends; Further Letters to Sydney Cockerell*, ed. Viola Meynell, (London 1956), p. 33.

CHAPTER 21

p 197 'the sales of poetry had dropped . . .' see Harold Monro: *The Publisher Speaks*, in *The Chapbook* March 1923. Sales of Rupert Brooke had gone down by 70%, Walter de la Mare by 20%, only D. H. Lawrence remained steady.

p 197 'a photograph of Charlotte Mew with Robert Bridges . . .' This is in the F. B. Adams Coll.

p 197 'sent her a quotation . . .' CM/Ottoline Morrell 8 Sept 1925. (Texas.)

p 197 'As to Conrad himself . . .' SCC/CM 25 Dec 1923. (Berg.)

p 198 'when Alida broadcast *Sea Love* . . .' The programme eventually went out on 24 Aug 1926, and Charlotte received half a guinea.

p 198 'she had broken into an old people's home . . .' CM/CADS 28 March 1913. (MW.) The home was called The Hawthornes.

p 198 'Dear Charlotte – Do come and stay with us . . .' Kate Cockerell/CM 28 May 1924. (Berg.)

p 199 'remedies for "nerves" . . .' CM/FM 31 Dec 1924. (Berg.)

p 199 'On one occasion . . .' 17 Oct 1924. 'I ought to dash in [i.e. into the diary] Mrs Hardy in a nursing home, having had her tumour cut out; with Miss Charlotte Mew.' *The Diaries of Virginia Woolf* ed: Anne Oliver Bell, vol. 2, p. 319.

p 199 'I think it is a pity . . .' FH/CM 2 Oct 1921. Quoted in Davidow.

p 200 'in one of his satiric dream poems . . .' *Dream Exhibition of a Final World* in *The Earth for Sale* (London 1928).

p 200 'he "prized" and "hugged" it . . .' SCC/CM 12 March 1925. (Berg.)

p 201 'It can be felt in a letter . . .' CM/Dorothy Hawksley 28 April 1926. Quoted in Davidow.

p 201 'painters and photographers . . .' Charlotte had refused to be photographed by Hoppé in 1923 because her mother was ill, and because she said she had already been photographed three times that year. (Information from Mrs Marjorie Watts.)

p 201 'Polygamy, she had told Charlotte . . .' CM/AM 7 March 1921. (Buffalo.)

p 202 'In alarm Sydney replied . . .' SCC/AM 27 Oct 1926. BL Add MSS 57756.

p 203 'The brutal finality . . .' CM/SCC 5 Jan 1927. (Berg.)

p 204 'She had made a will . . .' at 86 Delancey Street on 14 Dec 1922, that is, shortly after Mrs Mew's fall. It was witnessed by the ever-helpful Professor Browne.

p 204 '*Aglaë* . . .' This unfinished short story was first printed from the MS in the Poetry Collection, Lockwood Library, University of Buffalo, in CMCP (p. 307).

p 206 'as my sister is dangerously ill . . .' CM/Ottoline Morrell 12 June 1927. (Texas.)

p 206 'Sydney's postcard . . .' SCC/CM 27 April 1927. (Berg.)

p 206 'it was over at midnight on Saturday . . .' SCC/CM 27 April 1927. (Berg.)

p 208 'but as it hasn't been answered . . .' CM/Ottoline Morrell 4 Aug 1927. (Texas.)

p 208 'a little head of a baby in plaster . . .' After Charlotte's death this went to Dorothy Hawksley, who had specially asked Sydney Cockerell if she might have it as a souvenir.

p 208 '*mais il faut écouter le coeur* . . .' CM/Kate Cockerell 27 Oct 1927. (Berg.)

CHAPTER 22

p 209 'Hardy had copied out *Fin de Fête* . . .' according to Alida, on the back of a British Museum Reading Room slip.

p 210 'the period of horror . . .' It should be said that Harold Monro's diaries from 1923–6 show that he continued gallantly with his lecturing and reading engagements up and down the country.

p 210 'Conrad Aiken, in *Ushant* . . .' *Ushant*, Aiken's memoirs of his first visit to England (New York 1952), p. 258–9.

p 210 'Her wind-blown grey hair . . .' See the entry on Charlotte Mew in S. Kunitz & H. Haycraft: *Twentieth Century Authors* (New York 1942).

p 210 'Edward Herne Kendall . . .' He died at 285 Harrow Road, and was registered as 'formerly an Architect's assistant'.

p 211 'she made her will . . .' Charlotte left personal estate valued at £8,608.

p 211 'small legacies . . .' Edith Oliver, Elsie O'Keefe and Katherine Righton were all mentioned, but not Maggie Browne.

p 211 'Cast down the seed of weeping . . .' *Purgatorio* xxxi v. 45 '*pon giù il seme del piangere, ed ascolta.*'

p 211 'Laundry is the curse of civilization . . .' CM/AM 7 March 1921. (Buffalo.)

p 212 'I quite understand how it is . . .' CM/Evelyn Millard 20 Feb 1928. (Buffalo.)

p 213 'Yes, one can bear hard things . . .' CM/Kate Cockerell 24 Feb 1928. (Berg.)

p 214 'this side of silence . . .' On 24 March 1928 Cockerell wrote in his diary: 'A tragic end to the tragic life of a very rare being. After dinner wrote a little memoir of her for *The Times*.' (His tribute was printed in *The Times* on Thursday, 29 March.) Alida told him that she intended to write something herself, but kept thinking of Charlotte tossing her head at the very idea, and 'smiling that wicked little smile'. Meanwhile, Alida was distressed by reports of the inquest in the local press, which referred to 'Charlotte Mew, said to be a writer' and 'Charlotte New, a writer of verse'. Florence Hardy wrote to Siegfried Sassoon (28 March 1928): 'To-day I hear that poor, tragic little Charlotte Mew is dead. . . . Had I been in London I would have gone to see her – but I do not expect that would have made any difference. I believe she had several friends looking after her, but this was the only escape from her misery.'* She added that Walter de la Mare also wished that he had called on Charlotte. Humbert Wolfe wrote to de la Mare: 'How I wish I'd taken a little pains to see her.' (30 April 1929 BL Add MSS 57756).

The grave of Anne and Charlotte Mew is in Fortune Green Cemetery, London N.W.6, Section M11, No. 28829. In her will Charlotte asked for an almond tree, or some other small tree, to be planted, but, if this was ever done, the tree has not survived. There are some daffodils, however, which flower every spring on the grave, planted by well-wishers.

---

* A copy of this letter was kindly sent me by Dr Robert Gittings.

APPENDIX

A Note on the Poetry Bookshop Rhyme sheets

SERIES I. 23 × 8ins. Nos. 2, 4, and presumably 1 (I have not seen an example) are headed THE RHYME SHEET from free lettering by Charles Winzer. Only Nos. 1 to 7 are hand-coloured by Alida Monro (then Klementaski) and Charlotte Mew.

1. *Oh, What Shall the Man?* decorated by Charles Winzer. (Out of print by 1916 and not replaced). 1d plain 2d coloured.

2. *The Cow* by Roden Noel, *A Widow's Weeds* by Walter de la Mare, *The Shepherd* by William Blake, decorated by Charles Winzer. Listed as *For Children.* 1d plain 2d coloured.

3. *Poems by William Blake*, decorated with head and tail pieces from Blake's illustrations to Virgil. 1d plain. Replaced by *Poems by Wordsworth* decorated by Albert Rutherston. 1d plain 2d coloured.

4. *Overheard on a Saltmarsh* and *Wind in the Dusk* by Harold Monro, decorated by Charles Winzer. 2d coloured.

5. *Arabia* by Walter de la Mare, decorated by Charles Winzer. 2d coloured.

6. *Beautiful Meals* by T. Sturge Moore, who also did the decorations. 1d plain 2d coloured.

7. *A Christmas Legend* by Frank Sidgwick, decorated by Ethel Pye. 1d plain 2d coloured.

Select Bibliography

Conrad Aiken: *Ushant: An Essay* (New York 1952.)

Wilfrid Blunt: *Cockerell* (London 1964.)

Boll, Theophilus E. M.: *Miss May Sinclair, Novelist* (New Jersey 1973.)
> *The Mystery of Charlotte Mew and May Sinclair: An Inquiry* (NYPLB LXXLV Sept 1970, pp. 445–53.)

D'Arcy, Ella. Interview in *The Bookman* (*American Bookman*) December 1895, p. 260.

Davidow, Mary C.: *Charlotte Mew: Biography and Criticism.* (Brown University Ph.D. thesis, 1960.)
> *The Charlotte Mew–May Sinclair Relationship: a Reply* (NYPLB LXXV March 1971, pp. 295–300.)

Del Re, Arundel: *Georgian Reminiscences* (Studies in English Literature, University of Tokyo, 1932 and 1934.)

Eliot, T. S.: Critical Note to *Collected Poems of H. M. Monro* (London 1933.)

Flint, F. S.: Biographical Sketch in *Collected Poems of H. M. Monro* (London 1933.)

Freeman, John: *Charlotte Mew* (*The Bookman*, vol. LXXVI, June 1929, pp. 145–6.)

Gittings, Robert, and Manton, Jo: *The Second Mrs Hardy* (Oxford 1979.)

Holroyd, Michael: 'Said to be a Writer', in *Unreceived Opinions* (New York 1974) pp. 153–60.

Jepson, Edgar: *Memoirs of an Edwardian and Neo-Georgian* (London 1938.)

Kendall, Henry: *Modern Architecture* (London 1846.)
> *Designs for Schools and Schoolhouses* (London 1847.)

Long, W. H.: *A Dictionary of Isle of Wight Dialect* (Newport 1886.)

Meynell, Viola, ed.: *Friends of a Lifetime: Letters to S. C. Cockerell* (London 1940.)
> *The Best of Friends: Further Letters to S. C. Cockerell* (London 1956.)

Millard, Evelyn: *Shakespeare for Recitation* (London 1894.)

Mix, Katherine Lyon: *A Study in Yellow* (Kansas and London 1960.)

Monro, Alida: *Charlotte Mew – A Memoir* (preface to *Collected Poems of Charlotte Mew*, London 1953.)

    Charlotte Mew. (A critical note on her poetry in *The Chapbook*, June 1920.)

    The Poetry Bookshop (a BBC Third Programme talk, 21 February 1955. The script of this talk seems unfortunately to have been lost.)

Monro, Harold: *Collected Poems* (London 1933.)

Moore, Virginia: *Charlotte Mew* (in *Letters and Comment, Yale Review* Dec. 1932, pp. 429–30.)

    The Life and Eager Death of Emily Brontë (London 1936.)

Nelson, James Gordon: *The Early Nineties: a View from the Bodley Head* (Harvard 1971.)

Nelson, T. ed., *The Isle of Wight: its Towns, Antiquities and Places of Interest* (Newport 1884.)

Ould, Hermann: *Shuttle* (London 1947.)

Rogers, Timothy: *Georgian Poetry 1911–22: The Critical Heritage* (London 1977.)

Rolfe, Frederick: *Nicholas Crabbe: or the One and the Many* (London 1958.)

Ross, Robert H.: *The Georgian Revolt* (London 1967.)

Sharp, Evelyn: *Unfinished Adventure: Selected Reminiscences from an Englishwoman's Life* (London 1933.)

    'Nineties Evenings'. (*Manchester Guardian*, 19 Jan 1924, p. 7.)

Sinclair, May: *The Combined Maze* (London 1913.)

    A Journal of Impressions of Belgium (London 1915.)

    The Pinprick (*Harper's Magazine* Feb 1915, p. 392.)

Swinnerton, Frank: *Charlotte Mew* (*The Georgian Literary Scene 1910–1935* (London 1935) p. 251.)

Syrett, Netta: *The Sheltering Tree* (London 1939.)

Watts, Marjorie: *Memories of Charlotte Mew* (PEN Broadsheet no. 13 Autumn 1982, pp. 12–13.)

    P.E.N. The Early Years 1921–26 (London 1971.)

Wylie, I. A. R.: *My Life With George* (New York 1940.)

Index

INDEX

33 + 13   EDITH
102 - 6
138 - 6   NOLI

33 + 13 EDITH
102 - 6
138 - 6 NOLI